All You Need
to Know About
Disability
is on
STAR TREK

Also by Ilana S. Lehmann, Ph.D.

Dear Student: Inside the Twisted Mind of An Exasperated Professor
(Summer 2014)

The Completely Useless Dictionary of Higher Education
(Fall 2014)

All You Need
to Know About
Disability
is on
STAR TREK

Ilana S. Lehmann, PhD., C.R.C.

Mind Meld Media

Cover design by 4 Monkeys.
Edited by Susan Frager

Library of Congress Control Number: 2014912203

Lehmann, Ilana S., 1961 -
    All You Need To Know About Disability Is On Star Trek   / Ilana S. Lehmann – 1st edition
    Included index.
    ISBN 978-0-9904540-0-7

This book is intended for educational purposes only. It was not prepared, approved, licensed or endorsed by any entity involved in creating or producing the Star Trek television series or movies.

TABLE OF CONTENTS

Preface

Writing this book has been more fun than a Klingon drinking song. This is actually quite a statement, considering this is a book about disability written by an academic. And, while there is nothing funny about disabilities, there are plenty of funny things that can be said about *Star Trek*. While teaching at a public university on the East coast, I used to tell my classes that once I got tenured I would write this book.

When it became clear getting tenure would entail an uphill fight, I decided to withdraw from the process, move out of state, and lick my wounds. The timetable turned out to be about the same. I had published articles in scholarly journals. I had even won an award for outstanding research from the American Rehabilitation Counseling Association in 2009. I had written two book chapters for textbooks. Now it was time to write my first book. Until I came across a title, I simply referred to my book as "Star Trek and Disability," which is why my Facebook page bears that name. The final title, "All You Need to Know About Disability is on Star Trek" is cheeky, like me. Doing the research for this book, watching every episode of every series and all the movies again, was the most enjoyable research I've ever completed.

The original series episode "Is There in Truth No Beauty?" was memorable for me on two levels. First, there is a powerful woman in the story. Second, the woman is blind. I had a friend who was blind, and before I saw this episode, I had felt sorry for her. I learned that the last thing I should do is *pity* someone just because they're different. I think that show is probably how I ended up becoming not only a rehabilitation counselor, but also a professor of rehabilitation counseling.

When I began writing this book, I joined a writers' critique group in Vancouver, Washington. So many of the text books I had assigned to my classes were, at best, dry. And that's being kind; most were just plain boring. Disability can be an interesting subject if discussed in terms of *individual differences* rather than the traditional *limitations* labels. So, I decided to write this book as a devious means of getting people to understand why I think *Star Trek* has a lot to say about the future for people with disabilities. Members of my critique group encouraged me to abandon my professorial voice and write about disability in a more engaging manner.

Being snarky was easy; I've always had a sarcastic sense of humor and adore puns. Some of my favorite episodes of *Star Trek* are the ones where they don't take themselves too seriously. At the same time, I also love the episodes that deal with social justice, prejudice, and cool technology like the holodeck.

By the time I had been writing for six months, my biggest challenge was limiting each chapter. Many chapters could have become books in themselves. I may develop them into books in the future. There is so much that can be said about these issues that it was difficult to limit myself to a reasonable length.

It is my good fortune that my friend and this book's editor, Susan Frager, is both a published author and a *Star Trek* fan. Susan even flew out to Seattle when I did my first panel at Emerald City Comic Con in 2014. Much to my surprise and delight, I talked about "Genetic Engineering: Star Trek versus Reality" to a packed room.

You might say I'm an educator at heart. While I hope you find my writing entertaining, my purpose in writing the book is to make disability more understandable to others. And to move us away from an *us and them* concept to an *all of us* concept. This is not an official guide or in any way associated with those who hold the copyrights to the *Star Trek* franchise. Like many academics before me, I have found that because *Star Trek* is so widely known, it provides a common language, a common experience, which can illustrate my points in a kind of science fiction shorthand. The dialogue I use in the book is from transcripts of the shows and movies. The descriptions of actor movements are my own.

I wrote this book primarily for *Star Trek* fans with disabilities. Families and friends of these fans will also enjoy this book because I provide a bridge between the experience of life with a disability and the *Star Trek* universe. I've rebelled against those who advised me to write this book for *everyone* interested in disabilities. If you don't like *Star Trek*, it's highly unlikely you're going to find this book enjoyable. At the same time, if you like *Star Trek*, you're going to enjoy this book tremendously and hopefully learn something of interest to you about disability issues. And you, my friend and fellow *Star Trek* fan, are my audience. This one is for you, for us.

ALL YOU NEED
TO KNOW
ABOUT DISABILITY
IS ON STAR TREK

Style and Abbreviations

For your convenience, I have developed the following format to allow you to easily find the movies and episodes I discuss in this book.

Movies appear with the year they were released.

Episode titles appear in quotation marks followed by (in parenthesis) Year first aired, Series identifier; Season number: Episode number.

Series Identifiers:

      TOS: The original series of Star Trek
      TAS: Star Trek: The Animated Series
      TNG: Star Trek: The Next Generation
      DS9: Star Trek: Deep Space Nine
      VOY: Star Trek: Voyager
      ENT: Star Trek: Enterprise

The season and episode numbers will correspond to most online video collections.

Chapter 1
"Dammit Jim, I'm a Doctor Not a Dictionary"

I'm a doctor, not a bricklayer. – "The Devil in the Dark"

I'm a doctor, not an engineer. – "Mirror, Mirror"

I'm a doctor, not a mechanic. – "The Doomsday Machine"

I'm a doctor, not an escalator! – "Friday's Child"

I'm a doctor, not a coal miner. – "The Empath"

I'm a surgeon, not a psychiatrist. – "The City on the Edge of Forever"

Definitions of Disability

Dr. Leonard "Bones" McCoy often defined himself by describing his limitations–or what he was not. Some limitations are disabilities, others are not. Being tall isn't a disability unless you want to be a racing jockey, and being short is only a disability if you want to be a professional basketball player. So what is *disability*? In this chapter I explore definitions from the *World Health Organization* and the Americans with Disabilities Act. I also illustrate the medical, social, and moral models of disability. For the purpose of illustrating these various models, I apply current definitions of disability to episodes of *Star Trek*, even though some of the episodes were written decades before the definitions were developed. To begin, I'll relate the definition of disability from the *World Health Organization* to an episode from the first *Star Trek* series, written in 1968 "Is There In Truth No Beauty?" (1968, TOS; 3:5). (Since we capitalize Vulcans and other aliens, I will also capitalize Humans.)

Dr. Miranda Jones is the Federation liaison to Medusan ambassador Kollos. Medusans are an alien species so hideous that when Humans look at them, they become violently insane. Dr. Jones has been assigned to use her innate telepathic abilities to communicate with Kollos. Larry Marvick, her assistant, is helplessly in love with Dr. Jones. Unfortunately, when he professes his love and Dr. Jones rejects him, Marvick attempts to kill Kollos out of intense jealousy. During the murder attempt, Maverick sees Kollos and goes insane. He seizes control of the USS Enterprise, ultimately leaving the ship adrift in uncharted space. Jones insists that she, not Mr. Spock, should mind-link with Kollos and pilot the starship back to their original position, but Dr. McCoy intervenes.

> McCOY: Now wait a minute. I realize that you can do almost anything a sighted person can do, but you can't pilot a starship.
> KIRK: What?
> [Spock waves his hand directly in front of Dr. Jones' face but she doesn't react because she cannot see his hand.]
> SPOCK: Fascinating.
> McCOY: I'm sorry, Miranda, but you must be realistic. You are blind, and there are some things you simply cannot do.

While the episode doesn't explain how McCoy knew Jones was blind, it's likely that as the ship's doctor, McCoy was given her medical file. It's apparent from this scene that McCoy had kept her blindness confidential up until the point where her proposed actions put the ship at risk. This raises an unanswered question: how was Dr. Jones able to *see* the IDIC medal on Mr. Spock's uniform at dinner, but not well enough to pilot the USS Enterprise?

The 2002 *International Classification of Functioning, Disability and Health* (ICF), published by the World Health Organization, present a "biopsychosocial model of disability." Even though the model was written more than thirty years after "Is There In Truth No Beauty?" aired, I believe the episode provides an excellent opportunity to illustrate the ICF definition.

The ICF defines a disability in terms of the interactions among *health condition, impairment, activity limitation,* and *participation restriction.* A *health condition* includes both physical and psychological components of well-being. *Impairment* refers to differences in the ability of the person when compared to their peers. An *activity limitation* is measured based on an individual's ability to complete a task the majority of people are able to perform. Finally, a *participation restriction* refers to the person's capacity to experience inclusion.

To apply these terms to Dr. Jones, I would argue that although she is blind, her blindness is not a *health condition* because it doesn't interfere with her well-being or the other three levels of functioning. Her blindness isn't an *impairment*, but rather an asset in her role as the liaison for the ambassador. Her vision is different from others because she sees by virtue of her sensory net, a beautiful bejeweled mesh that she wears over her dress. *(Yes, assistive technology will be a fashion statement in the future, as well as promote inclusion for people with disabilities.)* She has no *participation restrictions* because as long as she uses her assistive technology, no one other than Dr. McCoy can even discern she's blind. Unless she's caught without her net.

Total blindness is the most severe form of vision impairment, but with her futuristic assistive technology, Dr. Jones is no more disabled than I am because of my dependence on reading glasses. Blindness doesn't impair her ability to function in her position as the intermediary between Kollos and the Federation, but rather is a unique qualification for working with the Medusan.

[Spock touches the decorated over-dress she always wears.]

SPOCK: Evidently a highly sophisticated sensor web. My compliments to you— and to your dressmaker.

KIRK: Yes, of course. It's the only reasonable explanation. You can't see and Kollos can't hurt you.

SPOCK: An elegant solution. But I fail to understand why you apparently try to conceal your blindness, Dr. Jones.

KIRK: I think I understand. You said it. Pity is the worst of all.

JONES: Pity, which I hate. Do you think you can gather more information with your eyes than I can with my sensors? I could play tennis with you, Captain Kirk. I might even beat you. I am standing exactly one meter, four centimeters from the door. Can you judge distance that accurately? I can even tell you how fast your heart is beating.

According to the ICF, the interaction between the person and the environment defines the existence and severity of a disability. It's only when Dr. Jones asserts she can take the Enterprise back into charted space that her blindness becomes an *activity limitation*. In order to steer the Enterprise, Dr. Jones must be able to see—not just sense. However, Dr. Jones considers herself disabled because her telepathic ability provides her with the knowledge that others pity her when they learn of her blindness.

Stigma is a participation restriction if it causes someone to avoid social relationships. In many ways, Dr. Jones' telepathy is a greater disability than her blindness. It's her ability to sense the pity of others that actually jeopardizes her health in terms of her psychological well-being. In short, according to the biopsychosocial model of the ICF, Dr. Jones isn't disabled in her normal role as the liaison between Kollos and the United Federation of Planets. However, at the time "Is There In Truth No Beauty?" aired, our society hadn't yet adopted this model. In 1968, a common response to disability was pity. Dr. Jones' telepathic ability meant that she'd sense pity from others regarding her blindness, overshadowing any respect for her achievements. If Dr. Jones weren't telepathic, she'd likely experience no participation restrictions because she would be capable of experiencing complete inclusion, unaware that anyone pitied her.

The Social Model of Disability

Before the biopsychosocial model of the ICF, disability was previously defined by the *social model*. In the social model of disability, individuals are considered disabled due to a complex interaction between their abilities, the social environment (think stereotypes and stigma), and the physical barriers to inclusion (think stairs). Just as in the biopsychosocial model, the *source* of the disability isn't solely attributed to the person, but a failure of the society to allow for the person to participate fully. The social model of disability can be illustrated with the episode "Melora" (1993, DS9; 2:6).

Ensign Melora Pazlar is a cartographer (with one of the prettiest hairstyles ever seen on *Star Trek*) who comes to Deep Space Nine to chart an area of the Gamma Quadrant. She's the first Elaysian to join Starfleet. Because her home planet is low in gravity, she doesn't have enough fully developed muscle tone for activity at Earth gravity levels, and must therefore use an exoskeleton, a cane, and a motorized wheelchair to perform her work. Deep Space Nine was built by Cardassians and is full of structural barriers that make the station only partially accessible to her. (Apparently they never passed a *Cardassians with Disabilities Act*.) In anticipation of her arrival, modifications have been made to as many areas on the station as possible.

Pazlar is sensitive to how others view her abilities in so-called normal gravity. When she arrives for a meeting with Commander Benjamin Sisko about her upcoming trip to the Gamma Quadrant, she's angry to discover that Commander Sisko, Lieutenant Dax, and Dr. Bashir are already discussing her mission without including her.

SISKO: Welcome, Ensign. I'm Commander Benjamin Sisko.

PAZLAR: Am I late?

SISKO: Not at all.

PAZLAR: It looked as though the meeting had already begun.

SISKO: Dax and Bashir were just telling me about your request to pilot a runabout alone.

PAZLAR: Wouldn't it have been more appropriate to include me in that conversation?

[In order to enter Sisko's office, Pazlar must get out of the motorized wheelchair, use her assist bands, and lean on her cane to climb the stairs.]

SISKO: I was getting a briefing by my senior officers, Ensign. We discuss personnel matters all the time.

PAZLAR: I'm sorry if I seem overly sensitive, but I'm used to being shut out of the Melora problem. The truth is—there is no Melora problem until people create one. This may sound ungrateful, because Dr. Bashir has been wonderfully helpful in the preparations for my arrival, but frankly, I wonder why a medical opinion is necessary in this discussion.

Sisko assures Pazlar that his concerns are not about her physical abilities, but her unfamiliarity with piloting a shuttle through the wormhole, something she hasn't done before. He orders her to allow Dax to accompany her on the mission.

Later, while trying to retrieve an extra piece of equipment, Pazlar trips on the lip of the door to a cargo bay and falls on the controls of her exoskeleton, making her limbs flail. She's unable to extricate herself. Dax rescues her and takes her to sickbay.

PAZLAR: It was so—Flopping back and forth like a broken toy. I didn't want anyone to find me like that but I couldn't get up by myself.

BASHIR: Why didn't you wait for Dax before you went into an area that was un-modified with ramps?

PAZLAR: I didn't need Dax. If I'd just paid attention—

BASHIR: Melora, no one on this station is completely independent. In space we all depend on one another to some degree.

PAZLAR: I just want you all to know that you can depend on me.

BASHIR: You've proven that. Now, what do the rest of us have to do to convince you?

PAZLAR: Of what?

BASHIR: That you can depend on us.

After Pazlar and Dax return from the Gamma Quadrant, Bashir shows Pazlar his work on a medical treatment that would end her need for assistive technology in Earth gravity, but at the cost of never being able to live on her home planet again. Dax illustrates the dilemma by comparing Pazlar's decision to that of the Little Mermaid in the classic fairy tale. The Little Mermaid trades her fins to walk on land and marry the prince with whom she has fallen in love, but she can never return to the sea. Likewise, the budding romance between Bashir and Pazlar motivates her to trade the mobility she enjoys on her home planet for unimpaired movement in Earth gravity. Although Pazlar initially begins the treatments, she decides to stop them after a near-death experience at the hands of a kidnapper. It's her ability to function in low gravity that allows her to disarm the kidnapper and save herself, Dax, and Quark in the process. She decides to stay the way she is, thus fully accepting herself.

PAZLAR: Julian, I'm not going ahead with the treatments.

BASHIR: Well, you can always try it again someday, if you change your mind.

PAZLAR: I don't think I will. I like being independent—but to give up everything that I am to walk on land, well, I might be more independent, but I wouldn't be Elaysian anymore. I'm not sure what I'd be. Besides, maybe independence isn't all it's cracked up to be. I kind of like how it feels to depend on someone for a change. And I'm glad you got me to unlock the doors to my quarters so I could finally let someone into my life.

Unlike the medical model of disability, which I'll discuss next, the social model doesn't consider a disability to reside in the person, but rather how the person is treated. Pazlar isn't disabled on her own planet in the low-gravity environment, where there are neither physical barriers nor paternalistic attitudes of so-called concern. However, on Deep Space Nine, she must use a motorized wheelchair, and is unable to access the entire space station due to the raised entryways. Although Sisko denies that his order to take Dax with her into the Gamma Quadrant is due to Pazlar's physical limitations, there are no other episodes where Dr. Bashir is consulted about science missions involving other Starfleet officers—no matter how junior.

The Medical Model of Disability

The definition of disability according to the medical model is that of pathology. In other words, any difference from the typical or normal is considered to be, by definition, abnormal. Accordingly, any person who functions differently would be considered disabled, even if that difference actually created a superhuman ability. Although people with special abilities are rarer in our present world than on *Star Trek*, there are currently recognized *disorders* that might actually be considered desirable. For example, *synesthesia* is a rare neurological disorder where stimulation of one sensory pathway, such as sound, is also experienced by the person in a secondary sensory pathway, such as color. People with this form of synesthesia can literally *see* sounds. People with *hyperthymesia* have perfect autobiographical memories, meaning they can recall the vast majority of their personal experiences with almost photographic perfection. Both of these conditions have been shown to be the result of anomalies in the brain.

In the episode "Plato's Stepchildren" (1968, TOS; 3:10) the crew of the Enterprise responds to a distress call from a planet where all the inhabitants, except one, possess psychokinetic powers. Alexander, a *little person* (the correct term for a person with dwarfism),is the only Platonian without psychokinetic powers. However, he considers his size to be his greatest disability.

ALEXANDER: I thought you were talking about my size, because they make fun of me for my size. But, to answer your question, I'm the only one without it. I was brought here as the court buffoon. That's why I'm everybody's slave and I have to be ten places at once, and I never do anything right.

SPOCK: How does one obtain the power?

ALEXANDER: As far as I know it just comes to you sometime after you're born. They say I'm a throwback, and I am, and so are you. I'm sorry. I shouldn't have said that.

KIRK: Don't worry about it. We're happy without it.

ALEXANDER: You know I believe you are. Listen, where you come from, are there a lot of people without the power and my size?

KIRK: Alexander, where I come from, size, shape, or color makes no difference, and nobody has the power.

The medical model defines disability as something being wrong with the person. Both Alexander's size and his lack of psychokinetic ability are therefore disabilities, because these conditions cause him to be different from the rest of the Platonians. Sadly, the other Platonians have no qualms about abusing Alexander or anyone else without their powers. The Platonians start to torment Kirk and Spock in an effort to blackmail McCoy to agree to stay on the planet as their doctor. Alexander realizes the Platonians' cruel behavior has more to do with their meanness than his size.

ALEXANDER: …They were treating you the same way they treat me. Just like me. Only you fight them. All the time, I thought it was me—my mind that couldn't move a pebble. They even told me I was lucky they bothered to keep me around at all, and I believed them. The arms and legs of everybody's whim. Look down, don't meet their eyes. Smile. Smile. These great people, they were gods to me. But you showed me what they really are. And now I know, don't you see. It's not me, it's not my size. It's them! It's them! It's them!

While there's no discussion in the episode about reversing Alexander's dwarfism, Kirk offers him the opportunity to acquire the psychokinetic power through medical treatment. Alexander declines. In the end, Alexander chooses to transport back to the Enterprise and be transported to a planet where his size and lack of psychokinetic powers aren't considered disabilities. (Incidentally, "Plato's Stepchildren" is most famous for the first interracial kiss on television between Captain James T. Kirk and Lieutenant Uhura. The book *Beyond Uhura: Star Trek and Other Memories* by Nichelle Nichols provides an excellent discussion of the scene's historical significance and repercussions.)

Americans with Disabilities Act

The legal definition of disability is far more political than most people would imagine. In the United States, the Americans with Disabilities Act (1990), which was based on the medical model, is the legal basis for determining whether an individual is considered disabled. There are three components to the definition of disability under the ADA. The first two components are the easiest to identify.

First, a person must have a condition that limits them in at least one "major life activity." Major life activities include obvious things like seeing, hearing, and walking. However, major life activities may also include less apparent things such as working, learning, or interacting with others.

Second, there needs to be a record of the limiting nature of the condition. It may be a medical, school, employment, or other type of record. Somewhere in the course of an individual's life, there needs to be a document that recorded a limitation. Just as in the medical model of disability, the ADA definition of a disabling condition is dependent on a record of a person's impairment. The ADA was drafted to protect people with disabilities against discrimination and mandates construction of environmental accommodations that allow for their participation in the workforce and society in general.

Tam Elbrun in "Tin Man" (1990, TNG; 3:20), meets both the first and second components of the ADA definition. Elbrun is introduced as a former patient of Counselor Deanna Troi, who she treated while studying psychology at a university on Betazed.

Elbrun's past includes a history of mental instability and a botched diplomatic mission that resulted in the deaths of forty-seven Starfleet officers. The record and nature of his disability is plainly depicted.

CRUSHER: Well, according to his medical records and psych profile, he's very high on the ESP scale. A sort of prodigy.
PICARD: A prodigy? In what sense?

TROI: Well, in most Betazoids our telepathic gifts develop at adolescence.

PICARD: You mean you're not born reading minds?

TROI: No. Except for some reason that no one understands, occasionally a Betazoid child is born different.

PICARD: How different?

CRUSHER: Born with his telepathic abilities switched on.

TROI: Most Betazoids born like that never lead a normal life.

CRUSHER: The noise of other people's thoughts and feelings must be over-whelming, incomprehensible, especially to a child.

TROI: And painful. Early diagnosis and special training did help Tam adjust, but he has some problems.

PICARD: You mentioned a hospitalization.

TROI: For stress. Repeatedly—throughout his life.

CRUSHER: I always wonder what holds one person together through that kind of struggle, while another goes under.

PICARD: Yes, well, he's evidently done more than hold together. He's the indispensable man, the Federation's finest specialist in communication with unknown life forms.

CRUSHER: The more unusual a life form is, the better he likes it. His personnel file shows that he's gravitated toward assignments that isolate him from other humanoids.

In addition to Elbrun's record of hospitalizations for stress, there's a personnel file documenting the difficulties Elbrun has with interpersonal relationships. Elbrun is thus considered to have a condition which limits him in at least one major life activity—interacting with others. While on the USS Enterprise, Elbrun chooses to work closely with Data because he can't sense Data's thoughts, which is a relief in comparison to working with others.

The sympathy expressed by Dr. Crusher could lead to discrimination based on how she views Elbrun's ability to handle stress while performing his job. There's a fine line in cases such as these between compassion and prejudice.

The third and last part of the ADA definition recognizes that at times people are perceived as having a disability when, in fact, they have no *impairment*. This is one of the most debated aspects of the ADA because the presence of an impairment or limitation isn't necessary for someone to be considered protected under the law. *Star Trek* provides an excellent illustration of this third part of the ADA definition of disability in "The Outcast" (1992, TNG; 5:17).

The main character, Soren, a member of an androgynous species called the J'naii, falls in love with Commander William Riker while working to rescue other J'naii trapped in null space. According to Soren, the very idea of gender isn't only considered primitive, but also offensive in her culture. Contrary to the prevailing dogma on her planet, however, Soren considers herself female. At a hearing on the J'naii home world, Soren explains there's nothing wrong with how she feels.

> SOREN: I am tired of lies. I am female. I was born that way. I have had those feelings, those longings, all of my life. It is not unnatural. I am not sick because I feel this way. I do not need to be helped. I do not need to be cured. What I need, and what all of those who are like me need, is your understanding and your compassion. We have not injured you in any way. And yet, we are scorned and attacked; and all because we are different. What we do is no different from what you do. We talk and laugh. We complain about work and we wonder about growing old. We talk about our families, and we worry about the future. And we cry with each other when things seem hopeless. All of the loving things that you do with each other, that is what we do. And for that we are called misfits and deviants and criminals. What right do you have to punish us? What right do you have to change us? What makes you think you can dictate how people love each other?

She clearly is "regarded as disabled" and if there's any doubt that the J'naii considers gender a disability, it's made plain by the fact that the answer to her deviance is treatment. Noor, the presiding judge at Soren's hearing, explains to Riker:

> NOOR: We are concerned about our citizens. We take our obligations to them seriously. Soren is sick, and sick people want to get well.
> RIKER: Did it occur to you that she might like to stay the way she is?

NOOR: You don't understand. We have a very high success rate in treating deviants like this. And without exception, they become happier people after their treatment, and grateful that we care enough to cure them. You see, Commander, on this world, everyone wants to be normal.

The last scene of the episode makes it clear that Soren's belief in being female was a disability, because after she receives the "psychotectic" treatment, she no longer considers herself female.

"The Outcast" depicts a thinly disguised analogy to the history of homosexuality in the United States. In 1973, the American Psychiatric Association removed homosexuality as a disorder from its "Diagnostic and Statistical Manual" (DSM)–the document which outlines, categorizes, and describes psychiatric illnesses. Furthermore:

> In December of 1998, the Board of Trustees issued a position statement that the American Psychiatric Association opposes any psychiatric treatment, such as "reparative" or conversion therapy, which is based upon the assumption that homosexuality per se is a mental disorder or based upon the a priori assumption that a patient should change his/her sexual homosexual [sic] orientation. In doing so, the APA joined many other professional organizations that either oppose or are critical of "reparative" therapies, including the American Academy of Pediatrics, the American Medical Association, the American Psychological Association, The American Counseling Association, and the National Association of Social Workers. (APA, 2000)

I consider "The Outcast" as an outstanding example of how *Star Trek* was often ahead of its time. "The Outcast" first aired on March 6, 1992, only two years after the passage of the Americans with Disabilities Act. However, it took the American Psychiatric Association another six years to publish their position statement against reparative therapy.

The *Americans with Disabilities Act* contains the provision that if someone is regarded as disabled, they're legally protected under the Act. The ADA recognizes that sometimes society treats a person *as if* they're disabled when they're not; what may currently be considered a disability may be regarded as simply an individual difference in the future.

While working as a rehabilitation counselor in the 1990s, I worked with a woman whose face and neck were badly scarred in a house fire. The burns on her face had no effect on her skills as a laser technologist. However, she was often treated *as if* she was disabled during job interviews—to the point where sometimes people interviewing her spoke louder and slower than normal because they assumed she had other impairments. This special treatment meant that she was protected from job discrimination under the ADA. Even though sexual orientation is not a disability, Soren would have been protected from discrimination under the ADA, because others in her society treated as if her gender identity were a disability.

The Moral Model of Disability

Significantly older than the models I've previously described, the *moral model* refers to the belief that people are somehow morally responsible for their disabilities. Although the origins of this model are founded in religions, which are hundreds, if not thousands, of years old, there are still modern examples. Pa'nar syndrome from *Star Trek: Enterprise* is a reference to AIDS and an excellent example of the moral model. In "Fusion" (2002, ENT; 1:17) T'Pol, the Vulcan science officer and subcommander, mind-melds with Tolaris, one of the *V'tosh ka'tur* ("Vulcans without logic.") T'Pol becomes angry when Tolaris refuses to stop the mind-meld at her request. The fact that she experiences anger is likewise disturbing to her as she, like other Vulcans, keeps her emotions repressed. The mind-meld infects her with a fatal disease called Pa'nar syndrome.

Many stardates later, in "Stigma" (2003, ENT; 2:14), Dr. Phlox tells T'Pol that her Pa'nar syndrome is no longer responding to his treatment. Dr. Phlox has difficulty obtaining research findings from Vulcan scientists regarding Pa'nar syndrome. The Vulcan Dr. Oratt explains:

> ORATT: We're hesitant to discuss Pa'nar syndrome, Doctor. This illness is unique to a subculture, a small percentage of our population. Their behavior is neither tolerated nor sanctioned.

Throughout the episode, the stigma surrounding Pa'nar syndrome is illustrated in the dialogue. The moral judgment is particularly conspicuous in this exchange between Captain Archer of the *USS Enterprise* and Dr. Stromm, one of the Vulcan physicians:

Throughout the episode, the stigma surrounding Pa'nar syndrome is illustrated in the dialogue. The moral judgment is particularly conspicuous in this exchange between Captain Archer of the *USS Enterprise* and Dr. Stromm, one of the Vulcan physicians:

STROMM: Pa'nar syndrome is a disease that's unique to an undesirable segment of our population. Thankfully, there are very few of them.
ARCHER: And because you find them undesirable they're not entitled to medical care?
STROMM: We don't condone the intimate acts that these people engage in. They defy everything our society stands for.
ARCHER: Intimate acts? You're talking about mind-melds.
STROMM: We take great pride in our ability to contain emotions. Sharing them is offensive—

Fortunately, one of the younger physicians, Dr. Yuris, provides T'Pol with the research Dr. Phlox was seeking. Dr. Yuris confesses to T'Pol that he's a member of the minority able to mind-meld. However, after promising T'Pol not to divulge how she contracted Pa'nar syndrome, Dr. Yuris later breaks his promise in order to defend her at the medical hearing. As a result, the reasoning behind T'Pol's silence is also revealed.

YURIS: The mind-meld was performed against her will.
ORATT: Can you verify this?
T'POL: Why? So you can perpetuate your double standard? Condemn the infected when they meld by choice and sympathize with them when they don't?

Throughout history, there have been sexually transmitted diseases. The arguments about Pa'nar syndrome openly demonstrate how our society often reacts not only with a lack of compassion, but also with contempt for those infected. Many people believe that when AIDS was primarily a disease among homosexuals, our government provided limited research funding for treatments. Funding only increased after the disease spread to the heterosexual population and other methods of transmission such as blood transfusions were discovered. Unfortunately, there are still many people who openly proclaim that AIDS is a punishment for immoral behavior. Research funds are determined by many factors and barely related to the percentage of the population at risk for the medical condition.

In the last season of *Star Trek: Enterprise*, T'Pol is cured of Pa'nar syndrome by mind melding with T'Pau in the episode "Kir'Shara" (2004, ENT, 4:10). In this quick exchange between T'Pau and T'Pol, the conspiracy of those in power is revealed:

> T'PAU: Pa'nar syndrome. Do you still suffer from it?
>
> T'POL: There's no cure.
>
> T'PAU: Another lie perpetrated by the High Command. Pa'nar has been known since Surak's time. It's caused by melders who have been improperly trained. One with great experience can correct the neurological imbalance.

Although certainly unfortunate, I believe it's more understandable when intolerance is the result of a strong religious conviction than when it emanates from the scientific community as it did among the Vulcan physicians in the episode "Stigma." Physicians are generally held to higher standards of behavior: the Hippocratic Oath, principles of medical ethics, and legally defined standards of professional practice. One of the characteristics of these behavioral codes is that physicians *have a duty* to treat their patients without regard to their own personal beliefs. In fact, physicians are not only required to care for patients who are stigmatized by others, but they're required to work actively toward reducing erroneous prejudicial beliefs held by the general public. This will be further discussed in the chapter on medical ethics.

The rules governing physician behavior are important to people with disabilities because of the historical disparity in healthcare between those with and without disabilities. *Star Trek* is one of the few examples where those inequalities have been largely eliminated. At the same time, the future as portrayed on *Star Trek* is not entirely ideal.

Chapter 2
"Boldly Going Beyond The Prime Directive"

The Prime Directive and the Hippocratic Oath

The Prime Directive, the decree which binds Starfleet officers against interfering with the natural progress of alien civilizations, is a moral compass on *Star Trek*. In addition to the Prime Directive, physicians are governed by the Hippocratic Oath and the principles of biomedical ethics. Therefore, Starfleet physicians on *Star Trek* are in the unenviable position of having multiple rules for their behavior.

Just as in this century, physicians on *Star Trek* have an important role in the lives of people with disabilities. Keep in mind the medical model of disability considers the source of the impairment to be the person's medical diagnosis. Therefore, the power of physicians to determine the type or amount of treatment an individual receives may be in conflict with the needs of the person, the types of treatment covered by insurance companies, and the financial resources of the patient. Although *Star Trek* depicts different dilemmas than we may have now (i.e. the United Federation of Planets doesn't offer medical insurance), conflicts over what is the best practice for medical care occur nonetheless. To understand the source of the conflicts experienced by physicians in the 24th century, I'll discuss the Prime Directive and the Hippocratic Oath, followed by biomedical ethics in the next chapter.

The Prime Directive

While reviewing episodes that include the Prime Directive, I was surprised to find this important doctrine was not even mentioned during the first twenty-one episodes of the original series. The Prime Directive first makes its appearance in "The Return of the Archons" (1967, TOS; 1:22) in a one word summary:

SPOCK: Captain, our Prime Directive of noninterference.

The preeminence of the Prime Directive is alluded to a year later in "The Omega Glory" (1968, TOS; 2:23):

KIRK [recording his computer log]: …A star captain's most solemn oath is that he will give his life–even his entire crew, rather than violate the Prime Directive.

By the way, Captain Kirk violates the Prime Directive in this episode as he does on many other occasions.

The final original series episode which refers to the Prime Directive is "Bread and Circuses" (1968, TOS 2:25). Kirk, Spock, and McCoy prepare to beam onto the planet that resembles the Roman Empire (complete with gladiator games) and they discuss how they will interact with the inhabitants.

SPOCK: Then the Prime Directive is in full force, Captain?
KIRK: No identification of self or mission. No interference with the social development of said planet.
McCOY: No references to space, or the fact that there are other worlds, or more advanced civilizations.

The Prime Directive was the vehicle *Star Trek's* creator, Gene Roddenberry, used to make a statement about the United States' involvement in the Vietnam War. The Vietnam War was a long, costly, armed conflict that pitted the communist regime of North Vietnam and its southern allies, known as the Viet Cong, against South Vietnam and its principal ally, the United States. The year after this episode aired, U.S. involvement in the war peaked. Growing opposition to the war during the 1960s led to bitter divisions among Americans. Many people felt the U.S. had wrongfully interfered with the social and political development of another country.

Twenty years later, on *Star Trek: The Next Generation,* the Prime Directive is at loggerheads with medical ethics in the episode "Symbiosis" (1988, TNG 1:22) in which Captain Picard is faced with a dilemma. In this episode the crew rescues the Ornarans who are desperate for a medication controlled by the Brekkians living on another planet.

CRUSHER: —Despite what the Ornarans have been saying, it's not a medicine. It was a medicine, but it cured the plague two hundred years ago. The plague is irrelevant now. It doesn't exist.

RIKER: Then why are they so desperate for the felicium?

CRUSHER: It's an addiction. The physical and psychological need is very real.

PICARD: Thank you.

CRUSHER: What are you going to do?

PICARD: Based on what we know so far, there's nothing I can do.

CRUSHER: You don't think drug addiction and exploitation is sufficient cause to do something?

PICARD: This situation has existed for a very long time. These two societies are intertwined in a symbiotic relationship.

CRUSHER: With one society profiting at the expense of the other.

PICARD: That's how you see it.

CRUSHER: I can synthesize a non-addictive substitute which will ease their withdrawal symptoms.

PICARD: No, I can't do that either.

CRUSHER: You can't let them have the felicium.

PICARD: Why? Because it offends against our sensibilities? It is not our mission to impose Federation or Earth values on any others in the galaxy.

CRUSHER: Well in this case, Captain, I disagree. One hundred percent.

As a physician, Dr. Crusher considers her first duty to be one of relieving suffering. Her desire to inform the Ornarans about the nature of felicium puts her role as a physician in direct conflict with her duty to the Prime Directive as a member of Starfleet.

When the Brekkians decide to give the felicium to the Ornarans, Picard realizes that the Brekkians have known all along that the drug isn't a treatment for the disease, but rather an addictive substance. Despite his belief that the Brekkians are exploiting the Ornarans, Picard feels he can't take action, because to do so would violate the Prime Directive. Likewise, realizing that starships are necessary to continue the symbiotic felicium trade, Picard decides to withhold the freighter parts that would allow the Ornarans to repair their ships. In short, assistance to either side would violate the Prime Directive. The natural course of events for the Ornarans is for their ships to deteriorate to the point where they can no longer trade with the Brekkians and must therefore learn to live without the drug.

Although drug withdrawal is an unpleasant experience, it's not as serious as the life or death scenario in "Who Watches the Watchers" (1989, TNG; 3:4), where Dr. Crusher willfully violates the Prime Directive to save a life. Liko and Oji, two Mintakans, climb up a hill to investigate the flashes of light from a malfunctioning holographic blind hiding the Starfleet observers. Liko climbs up to the blind's window and receives an electrical shock as he inadvertently touches a mechanism. Dr. Crusher watches him fall down the cliff face and rushes over to evaluate his injuries. Picard confronts Dr. Crusher in sickbay where she has beamed aboard with Liko to treat his injuries.

> CRUSHER: Before you start quoting me the Prime Directive, he'd already seen us. The damage was done. It was either bring him aboard or let him die.
> PICARD: Then why didn't you let him die?
> CRUSHER: Because we were responsible for his injuries.

The duty of a physician, to alleviate suffering, thus comes into direct conflict with the duty of a Starfleet officer to uphold the Prime Directive of non-interference in alien civilizations. Unfortunately for Dr. Crusher, she's not able to wipe Liko's short-term memory. Saving a life is the most noble of intentions; however, the Prime Directive is violated in "Who Watches the Watchers." In spite of the best efforts of Captain Picard and the crew of the USS Enterprise, the Mintakans are forever changed by their encounter with Starfleet.

In some ways the Hippocratic Oath serves as a physician's Prime Directive. It's a moral compass that guides doctors in the practice of medicine.

The Hippocratic Oath

The Hippocratic Oath was written around the fifth century B.C.E. and some form of the Oath is taken by most graduating medical students today. The ancient origins of the "Oath of Hippocrates" make it one of the oldest binding documents in history. According to the American Medical Association's Code of Medical Ethics (1996 edition), "the Oath of Hippocrates, has remained in Western civilization as an expression of ideal conduct for the physician." Today, most new doctors pledge the modern Hippocratic Oath, written in 1964 by Louis Lasagna, Academic Dean of the School of Medicine at Tufts University.

Just like the phrase "Beam me up, Scotty" never was said in the original series, the expression "First, do no harm" doesn't actually appear in either the ancient or modern versions of the Oath. Although there are multiple references to the oath on *Star Trek*, I suppose updates are likely to be made over the next few centuries to include a prohibition against genetic engineering due to the number of episodes condemning this medical practice. It's clear some form of the Oath continues to be sworn by Starfleet physicians because Kirk reminds Dr. McCoy of it in "Friday's Child" (1967, TOS 2:11).

KIRK: Bones, you took a medical oath long before you signed aboard my ship—

In the episode "First Contact" (1991, TNG 4:15) the Malcorian doctor treating an injured Commander Riker has also apparently taken the Hippocratic Oath or something very similar.

BEREL: I'm just a physician, Minister. I don't know much about affairs of state, but he is a living, intelligent being. I don't care if the Chancellor himself calls down here. I have sworn an oath to do no harm, and I will not.

I see several possible explanations for why a Malcorian doctor would have taken the Hippocratic Oath. First, this is one of the many continuity errors that have always plagued *Star Trek*. Since this episode is about first contact between the Federation and this alien species, the Malcorian doctor shouldn't be citing the Human Hippocratic Oath. A second explanation is that a physician taking an oath to do no harm is universal (pun intended). The third possibility is that Hippocrates secretly visited Malcor III and left behind his

Oath as a small token of appreciation for their hospitality. Incidentally, "First Contact" is an excellent example of Captain Picard's tendency to violate the Prime Directive when it suits him.

More plausible than the alien doctor taking the Hippocratic Oath in "First Contact" is that the Oath would be part of the programming of the ship's doctor on *Star Trek: Voyager*—who is a computer program, (or to be more precise, an "Emergency Medical Hologram"). The Doctor has apparently sworn the Oath as well. In "Heroes and Demons" (1995, VOY 1:12) The Doctor states he's taken an oath to do no harm, and in "Critical Care" (2000, VOY 7:5) it's clear that oath is the Hippocratic Oath.

> THE DOCTOR: Fortunately for these patients, I am programmed with the Hippocratic Oath. It requires me to treat anyone who's ill—

So, Starfleet doctors do swear some form of the Oath. Given the role of the Oath on *Star Trek*, it's important to look at the eight components of the 1964 Oath and their role in guiding physicians' behavior. The Oath is a guiding factor in our medical ethics and in the ethical treatment of patients. Physicians are expected to follow it regardless of whether the person has a disability or not.

"I swear to fulfill, to the best of my ability and judgment, this covenant."

1. *"I will respect the hard-won scientific gains of those physicians in whose steps I walk, and gladly share such knowledge as is mine with those who are to follow."*

At first glance this may seem like a simple respect for sharing medical knowledge and providing the best care possible by using all the medical knowledge at the physician's disposal. However, nothing is ever that simple—in life or on *Star Trek*.

In "Nothing Human" (1998, VOY 5:8), the central dilemma concerns the ethics of utilizing scientific knowledge obtained by inhumane methods. The chief engineer, B'Elanna Torres, is attacked by an alien creature that attaches itself to her. The Doctor struggles to remove the alien without killing Torres. While searching the medical database for information that may help him save Torres, The Doctor discovers a Cardassian exobiologist, Crell Moset, may have the medical expertise to assist him. Moset's medical knowledge is downloaded and a holographic representation is created to aid The Doctor in collaborating with Moset for a treatment to save Torres' life. However, a Bajoran crewman, Tabor, discovers Moset is helping The Doctor and exposes the source of Moset's medical knowledge.

> TABOR: He killed my brother, my grandfather, hundreds of people! He's a mass murderer!
> THE DOCTOR: You must be mistaken.
> TABOR: It's no mistake. Moset performed experiments on living people. Thousands of Bajorans were killed in his so-called hospital.
>   [Dialogue Omitted]
> TABOR: I can still remember the sounds his instruments made. The screams of his patients. The smell of chemicals and dead flesh. He operated on my grandfather—Exposed his internal organs to nadion radiation. It took six days for him to die. I promised myself I would never forget.

"Nothing Human" is clearly a reference to the medical experiments conducted by the Nazis at concentration camps during World War II. Whether to use the medical knowledge obtained by the Nazis continues to be debated by ethicists to this day. At the same time, the United States granted immunity from war crime prosecution in exchange for obtaining medical research results from Japanese doctors who conducted equally barbaric experiments on their prisoners of war.

Even though her life hangs in the balance, Torres has no trouble deciding that she won't allow The Doctor to use any of Moset's work. However, Captain Janeway isn't bound by the same oath or medical ethics as a physician, and she doesn't hesitate in ordering The Doctor to use whatever knowledge is necessary to save Torres' life.

Once Torres has been saved, Janeway allows The Doctor to decide whether to delete the holographic program of Crell Moset or keep it in the database. The Doctor decides to delete Moset's program.

> THE DOCTOR: I didn't come here to debate the issue with you, Crell. I came here to inform you of my decision. It is my judgment that the Medical Consultant Program and all the algorithms contained therein shall be deleted from the

database. In light of recent evidence, I cannot in good conscience utilize research that was derived from such inhuman practices.

MOSET: In good conscience. What about the well-being of your crew? You're confronted by new forms of life every day, many of them dangerous. You need me. Delete my program, and you violate the first oath you took as a physician. Do no harm.

THE DOCTOR: Do no harm. You have no right to say those words. Computer—

MOSET: You can erase my program, Doctor, but you can never change the fact that you've already used some of my research. Where was your conscience when B'Elanna was dying on that table? Ethics? Morality? Conscience? Funny how they all go out the airlock when we need something. Are you and I really so different?

THE DOCTOR: Computer, delete Medical Consultant Program and all related files.

In addition to referencing medical experiments during the Nazi regime, the episode also provides arguments against experimentation on animals. "Nothing Human" brings into question the morality of medical treatments obtained at the expense of animal and Human suffering. During the Nazi regime, people with disabilities, especially as a result of genetic abnormalities, were frequently selected as research subjects with as much opportunity to consent as a laboratory animal. Even if medical knowledge gained through unethical means eventually saves lives, is it worth the cost?

2. *"I will apply, for the benefit of the sick, all measures [that] are required, avoiding those twin traps of overtreatment and therapeutic nihilism."*

At times, those who practice medicine are confronted with the difficult choice between administering treatment that will prolong life but force the patient to continue suffering, or withholding treatment, letting nature take its course (known as *therapeutic nihilism*). Therapeutic nihilism is the idea that the body must heal itself; medications can't heal or cure anything. They only treat symptoms on the surface. In the 17th century when medicine consisted of bleeding, purging, arsenic, and mercury this concept was rather accurate. Today, therapeutic nihilism is associated with *alternative* treatments such as homeopathy and acupuncture.

In "The Wire" (1994, DS9; 2:22), a brain implant in the Cardassian tailor, Garak, begins to break down, putting Garak's life in jeopardy. In an effort to save Garak, Dr. Bashir visits Enabran Tain, head of the Obsidian order on Cardassia. (Think of the Obsidian order as the Cardassian Gestapo.) Tain confronts Bashir about whether he has his patient's best interest at heart in seeking to rid Garak of the implant.

> TAIN: ...Tell me, Doctor, how sick is Garak?
> BASHIR: He's dying.
> TAIN: And you're trying to save him.
> BASHIR: That's right.
> TAIN: Strange. I thought you were his friend.
> BASHIR: I suppose I am.
> TAIN: Then you should let him die. After all, for Garak, a life in exile is no life at all.
> BASHIR: Say what you will, my job is to keep him alive, and I need your help.

Because Garak recovers, it's easy to overlook the fact that Bashir does not consider whether his actions were in his patient's best interest. I think Bashir should have struggled more with his decision to use extraordinary means to save Garak's life. I cannot imagine my doctor making a road trip to visit someone who might know something about my medical condition even if it didn't require a space shuttle. After all, Garak tells Dr. Bashir that he activated the implant because of how miserable he was on DS9.

> GARAK: Living on this station is torture for me, Doctor. The temperature is always too cold, the lights always too bright. Every Bajoran on the station looks at me with loathing and contempt. So one day I decided I couldn't live with it anymore, and I took the pain away.

Without examining his own motives, Bashir runs the risk of overtreatment which only prolongs life. To prolong life—whether or not the increased time is quality time or even desired by the patient—is a dilemma I've experienced firsthand. My first son, Benjamin, was born with severe neurological impairments. Benjamin had few reflexes and didn't open his eyes until he was more than four months old. He had as many as ten seizures a day. As a result, I faced this conflict. I wanted to avoid overtreatment that would have only prolonged his life without alleviating his suffering. I also wanted to avoid therapeutic nihilism, as suggested by the pediatric neurologist, who thought I should leave my newborn son in the hospital and allow him to die of starvation because he couldn't swallow. I sought out a third alternative and found a doctor who suggested that Benjamin be provided with a feeding tube and palliative care. Although my son passed away before his first birthday, his short and difficult life was neither artificially prolonged nor painfully brutal.

3. "I will remember that there is art to medicine as well as science, and that warmth, sympathy, and understanding may outweigh the surgeon's knife or the chemist's drug."

The Doctor, always eager to incorporate new subroutines into his emergency medical holographic program, decides to play psychotherapist in "Retrospect" (1998, VOY 4:17) with the former Borg, Seven of Nine. Seven is assigned to work with an arms dealer, Corven, but when he pushes her out of his way to escape an exploding rifle, she assaults him—fracturing his nose. Upon further examination of Seven, The Doctor finds evidence of abnormalities.

> THE DOCTOR: She experienced an episode of acute anxiety with all the trimmings: intense apprehension, shortness of breath, dizziness. I finally managed to sedate her.
> JANEWAY: Could this have been caused by her cortical implants?
> THE DOCTOR: I don't think so. I think the problem has to do with memory suppression. I've detected a high concentration of biogenic amines in Seven's hippocampus, a substance I haven't noticed before. It's blocking portions of her memory center.

Rather than merely treating her symptoms, The Doctor attempts to find the source of Seven's reaction by helping her to recover memories of when she was with Corven on the planet. As The Doctor probes for more details, Seven recalls Corven extracting some of her Borg technology from her against her will. The Doctor becomes convinced that Seven was violated, and that this is the source of her intense reaction to Corven when he touched her later. However, Tuvok offers a note of caution:

> TUVOK: You seem to be accepting Seven's recovered memories as fact.
> THE DOCTOR: Are you suggesting otherwise?
> TUVOK: Historically, recovered memories have often proven unreliable.
> THE DOCTOR: Yes, in cases where a traumatic experience has been repressed for years. But we're dealing with a very recent memory here, which was blocked by artificial means. When I removed that mechanism, Seven remembered everything that happened.
> TUVOK: Human memory is rarely perfect.

The Doctor's attempt to help Seven emotionally recover is consistent with this part of the Oath. The Doctor's efforts didn't include hyposprays or gadgets which make those cool technology sounds, but rather he talks to, and listens to, Seven. He provides compassionate understanding of her feelings. People with psychiatric disabilities often benefit from psychotherapeutic interventions which involve counseling in addition to medication.

As demonstrated in this episode, repressed memories aren't always accurate. Unlike the crew of Voyager, as a counselor I never had the resources to verify the memories of my clients. So I did what The Doctor did; I listened to my clients and encouraged them to remember all that they could. But unlike The Doctor, I never promised a client they would feel better if the person who wronged them was punished.

I support this psychotherapy of the future depicted in "Retrospect," where there's a balance between supporting the emotional needs of Seven, with empirical verification of the events she recalls. It turns out that Seven's recollections were inaccurate; she emotionally projected her violation—assimilation by the Borg—onto the accident with the rifle. At the end of the episode, Corven dies while trying to escape Seven's false accusations. Corven's death demonstrates just how dangerous the consequences of prosecuting on the basis of so-called *recovered* memories can be. Although The Doctor may have been too quick to take Seven's narrative at face value, he didn't violate his oath by his belief in his patient and his attempt to provide compassionate understanding as well as medical care.

4. "I will not be ashamed to say "I know not," nor will I fail to call in my colleagues when the skills of another are needed for a patient's recovery."

In "Equilibrium" (1994, DS9; 3:4) Lieutenant Jadzia Dax's Trill body is rejecting her Dax symbiont for reasons Dr. Bashir cannot diagnose. Although Dr. Bashir knows that once joined—the host Trill cannot live long without the symbiont, he can't explain why Jadzia appears to be rejecting the symbiont now.

> DAX: Julian, am I in danger of rejecting my symbiont?
> BASHIR: I wouldn't worry about rejection just yet, but we do have to get your isoboramine levels back up. [To Sisko] And I suggest we take her back to the Trill homeworld and have the doctors at the Symbiosis Commission examine her.

Rather than risk treating Dax with his limited knowledge of Trill physiology, Bashir takes her back to the Trill homeworld. Dax introduces Bashir and Sisko to Timor, one of the guardians who care for the symbionts. When Dax's condition worsens, Bashir attempts to enlist Timor's help, consistent with this part of the Oath. Timor refuses to help and is obviously being coerced by some outside influence. In order to obtain the help Jadzia and Dax so desperately need, Dr. Bashir engages in some blackmail of his own, announcing his intention to reveal a Symbiosis Commission secret to the population. Please note that while Bashir adheres to part four of the Oath by seeking help on the Trill homeworld, blackmail isn't considered a part of the Hippocratic Oath and would violate the Prime Directive.

5. "I will respect the privacy of my patients, for their problems are not disclosed to me that the world may know."

In the last chapter I introduced the *Enterprise* episode "Stigma" (2003, ENT; 2:14), and the Vulcan disease, Pa'nar syndrome. During that episode, Captain Archer confronts Dr. Phlox for withholding his true motivation for attending the conference hosted by the Interspecies Medical Exchange on Dekendi. Dr. Phlox defends his decision by citing doctor-patient confidentiality.

ARCHER: And you never thought that maybe you should come to me and let me know that one of my officers has a potentially fatal disease?
PHLOX: I believe your culture embraces the concept of doctor-patient confidentiality.

Although it's unclear if the Denobulan physician has or hasn't taken the same oath as medical students on Earth, it appears they ascribe to similar medical ethics. Dr. Phlox clearly doesn't appear to think there's a conflict in keeping his patient's confidentiality, regardless of the needs of Starfleet or the Vulcan High Command. Considering how laws have a tendency to become entrenched, I can't help but wonder if HIPAA will also survive in some form into the 24th century.

6. *"Most especially must I tread with care in matters of life and death. If it is given me to save a life, all thanks. But it may also be within my power to take a life; this awesome responsibility must be faced with great humbleness and awareness of my own frailty. Above all, I must not play at God."*

The episode "Dear Doctor" (2002, ENT 1:13) takes place in a pre-Prime Directive timeline, and it provides a situation that illustrates the need for Starfleet to draft the Prime Directive. "Dear Doctor" also illustrates that the Prime Directive is consistent, at times, with the Hippocratic Oath. In this episode, the crew of the USS Enterprise rescues a Valakian man dying of a genetic disease. His planet supports two separate species: Valakians and Menk. The crew is troubled by the treatment of the Menk by the Valakians. (In many ways similar to how European settlers treated Native Americans, although there's no discussion as to who was on the planet first.) The Menk have been given land that doesn't allow them to cultivate their own crops and in the words of one crewman:

CUTLER: They force the Menk to live in compounds. They treat them almost like pets.

Dr. Phlox is asked to provide assistance to the Valakian doctors who are trying to find a cure for this rapidly mutating illness. He discovers that the condition is genetically based, and will likely wipe out the entire Valakian species in a few decades. Phlox struggles with the question: does curing the Valakians violate the natural order of the future?

ARCHER: A cure, Doctor. Have you found a cure?

PHLOX: Even if I could find one, I'm not sure it would be ethical.

ARCHER: Ethical?

PHLOX: We'd be interfering with an evolutionary process that has been going on for thousands of years.

ARCHER: Every time you treat an illness, you're interfering. That's what doctors do.

PHLOX: You're forgetting about the Menk.

ARCHER: What about the Menk?

PHLOX: I've been studying their genome as well, and I've seen evidence of increasing intelligence. Motor skills, linguistic abilities. Unlike the Valakians they appear to be in the process of an evolutionary awakening. It may take millennia, but the Menk have the potential to become the dominant species on this planet.

ARCHER: And that won't happen as long as the Valakians are around.

PHLOX: If the Menk are to flourish, they need an opportunity to survive on their own.

ARCHER: Well, what are you suggesting? We choose one species over the other?

PHLOX: All I'm saying is that we let nature make the choice.

ARCHER: The hell with nature. You're a doctor. You have a moral obligation to help people who are suffering.

PHLOX: I'm also a scientist, and I'm obligated to consider the larger issues. Thirty five thousand years ago, your species coexisted with other humanoids. Isn't that correct?

ARCHER: Go ahead.

PHLOX: What if an alien race had interfered and given the Neanderthals an evolutionary advantage? Fortunately for you, they didn't.

ARCHER: I appreciate your perspective on all of this, but we're talking about something that might happen. Might happen. Thousands of years from now. They've asked for our help. I am not prepared to walk away based on a theory.

PHLOX: Evolution is more than a theory. It is a fundamental scientific principle. Forgive me for saying so, but I believe your compassion for these people is affecting your judgment.
ARCHER: My compassion guides my judgment.
PHLOX: Captain.
ARCHER: Can you find a cure? Doctor?
PHLOX: I already have.

The need for the Prime Directive is further clarified as Captain Archer and Dr. Phlox get ready to take a shuttlepod down to the Valakian hospital (cue inspirational music).

PHLOX: Sir, it would go against all my principles if I didn't ask you to reconsider what I—
ARCHER: I have reconsidered. I spent the whole night reconsidering, and what I've decided goes against all my principles. Someday my people are going to come up with some sort of a doctrine, something that tells us what we can and can't do out here, should and shouldn't do. But until somebody tells me that they've drafted that directive I'm going to have to remind myself every day that we didn't come out here to play God.

In the end, Dr. Phlox develops a treatment which alleviates the pain and slows down the progression of the disease, thereby allowing the Valakians time to find a cure on their own—if they are able. Captain Archer refuses to provide the Valakians warp drive technology because the Valakians are decades from developing this technology on their own. In making his decision, Captain Archer recognizes that he, as well as Dr. Phlox, must not play God.

7. *"I will remember that I do not treat a fever chart, a cancerous growth, but a sick human being, whose illness may affect the person's family and economic stability. My responsibility includes these related problems, if I am to care adequately for the sick. I will prevent disease whenever I can, for prevention is preferable to cure."*

In "The Cloud Minders" (1969, TOS 3:21), the planet Ardana also has two distinct civilizations. However, this planet is divided by class rather than species. The artists and intellectuals live in the clouds in the beautiful city of Stratos. The Troglytes, the workers, are confined to the mines under the planet's surface. Two beautiful women (are there any other kind in the original series?) are contrasted in this episode. Droxine is from Stratos and lives in the clouds. Vanna is a Troglyte, works in the mines, and is one of the activist-protesters. Spock summarizes the conflict in his log:

SPOCK: This troubled planet is a place of the most violent contrasts. Those who receive the rewards are totally separated from those who shoulder the burdens. It is not a wise leadership. Here on Stratos, everything is incomparably beautiful and pleasant. The High Advisor's charming daughter Droxine, particularly so. The name Droxine seems appropriate for her. I wonder, can she retain such purity and sweetness of mind and be aware of the life of the people on the surface of the planet? There, the harsh life in the mines is instilling the people with a bitter hatred. The young girl [Vanna] who led the attack against us when we beamed down was filled with the violence of desperation. If the lovely Droxine knew of the young miner's misery, I wonder how the knowledge would affect her.

Captain Kirk and Mr. Spock are actively trying to change the order of life on Ardana. This episode, which aired during the 1960s civil rights movement, was an activist episode. The same arguments Droxine uses to justify the treatment of the Troglytes were used to justify discrimination against minorities, and people with disabilities, in the 1960s.

DROXINE: But Stratos is for advisors and studiers. What would Troglytes do here?
VANNA: Live in the sunlight and warmth, as everyone should.
DROXINE: The caverns are warm and your eyes are not accustomed to light, just as your minds are not accustomed to logic.
[A sentinel takes Vanna away.]
KIRK: Unaccustomed to light and warmth? That's necessary to all humanoids. Surely, you don't deny it to the Troglytes.

DROXINE: The Troglytes are workers, Captain. Oh surely, you must be aware of that. They mine zenite for shipment, till the soil. Those things cannot be done here.

SPOCK: In other words, they perform all the physical toil necessary to maintain Stratos.

DROXINE: That is their function in our society.

SPOCK: But they are not allowed to share its advantages.

DROXINE: How can they share what they do not understand?

KIRK: They can be taught to understand, especially in a society that prides itself in enlightenment.

DROXINE: The complete separation of toil and leisure has given Ardana this perfectly balanced social system, Captain. Why should we change it?

SPOCK: The surface of the planet is almost unendurable. To restrict a segment of the population to such hardship is unthinkable in an evolved culture.

DROXINE: The surface is marred by violence, like the Troglytes. But here in Stratos, we have completely eliminated violence.

In the 1960s, minorities, including people with disabilities, were often excluded from higher education and the arts based on the rationalization that they were mentally inferior and therefore could neither appreciate nor contribute to these activities. An inspiring example is Edward Roberts. Roberts contracted polio as a teenager and the disease left him severely disabled. Paralyzed below his neck, Roberts had some residual use of two fingers on one hand and several toes. He slept in an iron lung at night and used "frog breathing", (the common term for glossopharyngeal breathing because of the frog-like gulping technique used to push air into the lungs) during the day. Roberts fought his way into the University of California, Berkley to get his degree. During the process one of the school officials said, "We've tried cripples [sic], they don't work." In 1961 Roberts sued to be admitted to the university where he earned both a bachelor's and master's degree in political science. Thirteen years later, Roberts was appointed director of the California Department of Rehabilitation.

At the end of "The Cloud Minders," Dr. McCoy discovers that when the miners are exposed to the odorless and invisible gases from the unprocessed mineral (zenite), those gases diminish mental capacity and heighten emotions. The effect of the gas wears off once the person is no longer exposed. According to this portion of the Hippocratic Oath, prevention is preferable to cure; in compliance, McCoy delivers filter masks which will prevent the miners' mental decline and emotional instability. Kirk trades the masks to the miners for the zenite needed to cure the plague on another planet. With the masks, the miners will be in a better medical condition and will be more effective in their attempts to change the status quo. So much for the almighty Prime Directive.

8. *"I will remember that I remain a member of society, with special obligations to all my fellow human beings, those sound of mind and body as well as the infirm."*

In "Unnatural Selection" (1989, TNG; 2:7) the USS Enterprise encounters a pathogen which causes accelerated aging to the point of death. The medical director at an infected medical station implores Captain Picard to evacuate their children so they won't likewise become infected. After one child is beamed over to the starship in "styrolite in suspended animation," Chief Medical Officer Dr. Kathryn Pulaski can't find any evidence of infection. Counselor Troi senses strong telepathic abilities in the child. However, Dr. Pulaski's tests for the causes of the infection are hampered by the styrolite which protects the crew from any possible contamination. Picard is adamant that the material can't be removed without foolproof safeguards for the unknown pathogen. (In this episode *child proofing* takes on a whole new meaning.)

PULASKI: Captain, I'd like permission to put the boy in a shuttlecraft. I can study him there without risk to anyone else.

PICARD: What about you?

PULASKI: I'm prepared to take that risk. Someone has to breathe the same air he breathes, to touch him. I'm volunteering to make that test myself.

PICARD: Doctor, you have a responsibility to this ship which goes—

PULASKI [Interrupting]: I also have a responsibility to humanity.

PICARD: Starfleet guidelines about contact with quarantined—

PULASKI [Interrupting again.]: You don't have to quote the rule book. You were saying?

PICARD: Request approved.

PULASKI: Captain, you said if I—Approved?

PICARD: I recognize that you're trying to satisfy my conditions.
PULASKI: Thank you.

Dr. Pulaski's devotion to the Hippocratic Oath is apparent in her statement that she has a *responsibility to humanity*. She risks her own life in an effort to prove it's safe to evacuate the children. However, Pulaski becomes infected with the disease. The crew of the USS Enterprise go into full "save her life" mode, and by using the transporter to restore Dr. Pulaski's DNA to its pre-infected state, she's cured. The cure is provided to the personnel on the station, but since the children are the source and carriers of the infection, they can never be moved off the station.

While the Hippocratic Oath outlines the responsibility of physicians to their patients, biomedical ethics are *principles of care* based on ethical theories. For those interested in the philosophical roots of ethics theory and moral reasoning on *Star Trek*, I recommend "The Ethics of Star Trek" listed in the bibliography.

In the next chapter, I'll explore five major biomedical ethics which govern both physician treatment and medical research, using *Star Trek* episodes as illustrations. As with the discussion of the Hippocratic Oath, it will be important to evaluate how these ethics are applied to people with disabilities. Too often, there's a double standard between treatments given to someone with a disability compared with the care of those who aren't considered disabled. Biomedical ethics were created to guide better treatment of vulnerable populations such as people with disabilities.

Chapter 3
"The Line Must Be Drawn Here!"

Biomedical Ethics

Following the *Star Trek* style of quick explanation of complex ideas such as the space-time continuum, cosmic strings, or how a calibrated burst of a tachyon field will save the ship from imminent destruction, these are the five biomedical ethics and their short-hand definitions:

> *Autonomy*–freedom of choice
>
> *Beneficence*–the duty to provide a benefit
>
> *Nonmaleficence*—the obligation to refrain from doing harm
>
> *Justice*—the fair distribution of resources
>
> *Fidelity*—honesty and keeping one's promises to others

Like Romulan Warbirds, these complex ideas are cloaked—disguised by brevity. In reality biomedical ethics are multifaceted and at times present as many questions as answers. In discussing these ethics I'll look at both the physician-patient treatment relationship as well as medical research. Keep in mind, entire books have been written about biomedical ethics, so this isn't a complete discussion.

Autonomy

Autonomy means to be in control of one's choices. An example may help reveal the complexity behind what seems like a simple concept. If I become injured and need medical treatment I can choose my own doctor. However, the cost of my medical treatment will depend on whether the doctor I chose is an *in-network provider* according to my insurance company. Even within the provider networks, there may be different levels of co-pays for different doctors. Depending on my financial resources, I may be faced with going to a less expensive (and perhaps less experienced) doctor instead of the best doctor for my type of injury. If my choice of doctor is determined by my financial resources, then the insurance company could be considered to have compromised my autonomy by unduly influencing my choice in which doctor I see.

Incentives can compromise autonomy—at times unintentionally. Providing a small amount of cash to recruit research participants isn't an unusual practice. But how much money is too much, and at what point do financial incentives become large enough to jeopardize autonomy? A five dollar bill may be pretty meaningless to a high school student in the Hollywood Hills, but it may be overwhelmingly coercive to a homeless person.

Another example of how autonomy may not be clearly exercised is in the case of someone who isn't considered competent to make their own decisions. People with diminished mental abilities, which limit their understanding of consent, are protected by additional medical ethics guidelines. The problem of *compromised autonomy* is described in "The Gift" (1997, VOY; 4:2) when Seven of Nine confronts Captain Janeway with her desire to be returned to the Borg.

SEVEN: ...Your attempt to assimilate this drone will fail. You can alter our physiology but cannot change our nature. We will betray you. We are Borg.

JANEWAY: I've met Borg who were freed from the collective. It wasn't easy for them to accept their individuality, but in time they did. You're no different. Granted, you were assimilated at a very young age, and your transition may be more difficult, but it will happen.

SEVEN: If it does happen, we will become fully human?

JANEWAY: Yes, I hope so.

SEVEN: We will be autonomous, independent.

JANEWAY: That's what individuality is all about.

SEVEN: If at that time we choose to return to the Collective, will you permit it?

JANEWAY: I don't think you'll want to do that.

SEVEN: You would deny us the choice as you deny us now. You have imprisoned us in the name of humanity. Yet you will not grant us your most cherished human right, to choose our own fate. You are hypocritical, manipulative. We do not want to be what you are! Return us to the Collective!

JANEWAY: You lost the capacity to make a rational choice the moment you were assimilated. They took that from you, and until I'm convinced you've gotten it back I'm making the choice for you. You're staying here.

SEVEN: Then you are no different than the Borg.

Assuming someone cannot provide consent denies them a basic Human right. However, due to the problem of compromised autonomy among those who can't understand what they're agreeing to, we have special protections for children and those with specific disabilities (such as cognitive impairments). Federal law requires institutions that conduct research to have Institutional Review Boards (IRB) where people who aren't involved in the research review the proposed research in order to ensure procedural safeguards are followed. Institutional Review Boards protect vulnerable groups by limiting their participation if a person's consent is not truly autonomous. At the same time, IRBs don't want to limit the person's autonomy by excluding them from research participation in the name of protecting them. Research into disabilities may necessitate the participation of people with disabilities. The problem is how to determine if all participants accepting the risks in the research do so with a complete understanding of those risks.

Although Janeway isn't operating under biomedical ethics, Seven's point that her autonomy isn't being respected is justified. Janeway's actions are only ethical if Janeway believes Seven isn't completely autonomous in deciding to remain with the Borg. (Personally, I'd never want to be a Borg, even if I received Seven of Nine's hourglass figure to go with it.)

One of the problems with the principle of autonomy is that it assumes people will act in their best interest. However, as Odo points out in "Shakaar" (1995, DS9, 3:24):

ODO: It has been my observation that one of the prices of giving people freedom of choice is that, sometimes, they make the wrong choice.

In "Rapture" (1996, DS9 5:10), Captain Sisko studies a holographic image of an obe-lisk called a Bantaca spire, which he recreated from a twenty-thousand-year-old Bajoran painting. The obelisk, according to legend, leads to the lost city called B'hala. After working on the translation of the markings until after three in the morning, like any good computer user, he attempts to *save his work*. However, this noble effort is met with a *shocking* result—Sisko is knocked unconscious.

After examining Sisko, Dr. Bashir tells the captain that he's detected "odd synaptic potential" in Sisko's brain. Bashir tells Sisko to let him know immediately if he "experi-ences any other side effects such as headaches, dizziness, even nausea." Later, on Bajor, Sisko suffers an intense headache immediately before he uncovers B'hala. Religion and medicine collide as Bashir determines that Sisko's headaches are life-threatening and rec-ommends an immediate operation. Sisko refuses, unwilling to put a stop to the visions that are now about the future of Bajor.

> BASHIR: Captain, why didn't you tell me about these headaches of yours?
>
> SISKO: I guess I was too busy.
>
> BASHIR: Well, if you'd stayed busy—much longer you could have died. The area of unusual neural activity has increased another eight percent. As a result, your basal ganglia are starting to depolarize. I'm going to have to operate—try to repolarize your neural sheaths.
>
> SISKO: How will that affect my visions?
>
> WHATLEY: That's not really the issue here, is it?
>
> SISKO: [To Whatley.] It is to me. [To Bashir.] Doctor?
>
> BASHIR: Well, there's no way to tell for sure. But I assume if I can complete the procedure, your brain activity will return to normal and the visions will stop.
>
> SISKO: Then you can't do it.
>
> WHATLEY: Ben, that's ridiculous.
>
> BASHIR: If I don't operate, sir—you could die.
>
> SISKO: I understand that. But something is happening to me; something extraordinary. I have to see it through.

Later, Sisko collapses at the ceremony welcoming Bajor into the United Federation of Planets. In the infirmary, Dr. Bashir reiterates that if he doesn't operate immediately the captain will die. Since Sisko had previously refused to allow medical intervention, Bashir asks Sisko's son Jake to provide consent for the operation. Jake is aware that his father doesn't want the surgery, but he's unwilling to let his father die. I'd argue that handing the decision to Jake subverts Sisko's autonomy. The incentive to Jake of saving his father's life is clearly an overwhelming consideration. Outside of the *Star Trek* universe, an advance directive would be respected regardless of the wishes of the patient's immediate family.

Dr. Bashir tries another method of undermining his patient's autonomy in "Life Support" (1995, DS9; 3:13). In this episode Vedek Bareil is critically injured and Dr. Bashir literally brings him back to life. Before his ship malfunctioned, Vedek Bareil and Kai Winn were negotiating a peace treaty with the Cardassians. Winn is in too far over her head to continue the negotiations without Bareil telling her what to say and do. Even though his life is at stake, Bareil feels he must be present for the negotiations. Bareil therefore refuses to allow Dr. Bashir to induce a coma which would save his life until the damage by the other medical interventions has been reversed.

> BASHIR: I realize how important these talks are to Bajor, but as your physician my duty is to you first.
> BAREIL: And I have a duty to Bajor. Please, help me heal my people. It's the only thing that matters to me.
> BASHIR: There is an experimental drug called Vasokin which would increase the blood flow to your organs and might enable you to function normally for a while. But there is a great deal of risk attached.
> BAREIL: What sort of risk?
> BASHIR: In twenty-two percent of cases, Vasokin has severely damaged the patient's lungs, kidneys, even heart; sometimes the brain. In your condition, it could even be fatal.
> BAREIL: But it would allow me to function normally for the next few days?
> BASHIR: Yes. But why risk your life for a few days?
> BAREIL: I have no great desire to die, Doctor. But I am determined to carry out the will of the Prophets as long as I am able, and I cannot carry out their will if I am unconscious in some stasis tube. Please, begin the Vasokin treatment.
> BASHIR: All right. We'll start this afternoon. I only hope we don't regret this.
> BAREIL: So do I.

Dr. Bashir has no reason to doubt that Vedek Bareil is autonomous in making the decision to try the experimental drug. Bareil isn't being coerced, threatened, nor is he incompetent. Bashir fulfills his ethical duty by explaining to Bareil both the risks as well as the potential benefits of the drug. Although Bashir questions whether the Vedek's duty to Bajor requires him to take such extreme measures, Bashir recognizes that only Bareil is in the position to know whether the benefits outweigh the risks. That isn't to say Dr. Bashir gives up easily. He asks Kai Winn to release Bareil from the responsibilities of the negotiations by deception; a violation of the ethical principle of fidelity.

BASHIR: …When you see Bareil, I want you to tell him that you don't need him, that you can complete these negotiations without him.
WINN: But I do need him, Doctor.
BASHIR: I realize that. But I want you to tell him that you don't.
WINN: You seem to be asking me to lie.
BASHIR: I'm asking you to free Bareil of his obligations to you. The only way he'll accept that is if you tell him he's no longer needed, that you can go on without him. Now, if that's a lie, then so be it.
WINN: That doesn't sound like a Starfleet officer.
BASHIR: I'm a doctor first. And right now, I'm trying to give my patient his best chance to live. The only way to do that is to put him in stasis. Bareil knows that, but his desire to complete these negotiations is so strong that he's forcing me to keep him conscious and mentally alert, even though it may kill him.
WINN: None of us wants that to happen, Doctor. But if I'm not mistaken, the decision regarding Bareil's treatment is up to him.
BASHIR: Yes. As the patient, it is his right to make that choice. But I'm asking you to help me change his mind. Eminence, you're the Kai. These are your negotiations. Let this be your moment in history. Finish the talks on your own and you won't have to share the credit with anyone.

My dislike of Kai Winn continues to grow in "Life Support" as she allows Vedek Bareil to die due to her arrogance and the amazing acting by Louise Fletcher who plays Kai Winn. Kira and I are left to cry over the loss of the good-looking and charming Vedek Bareil. In the end, Dr. Bashir appears to regret having complied with Bareil's wishes to keep him alive to the point where his internal organs and half of his brain have been replaced with artificial implants. Indeed, sometimes we don't like or agree with people's choices, but the choices are still theirs alone to make.

Autonomy, Medical Research and Informed Consent

Autonomy not only plays a part in the doctor-patient relationship, it also is important to medical research. People who agree to participate in medical research should be doing so of their own free will and with full knowledge of what that agreement will involve. When people agree to participate in research, they will usually sign a form which outlines the research purpose, the risks involved, and the benefits (if any) to the participant. These forms make up what is called "informed consent."

Informed consent is central to "Scientific Method" (1997, VOY 4:7). In this episode the crew of the USS Voyager is being subjected to medical experiments by aliens they can't see. The effects of the experiments have caused everything from mild discomfort to life-threatening disease. Near the end of the episode one crewman dies as a result of their experiment when she suffers extreme adrenal stress which ruptures her arteries.

When one of the aliens, Alzen, is confronted about the use of the USS Voyager crew as *lab rats*, Alzen appeals to Captain Janeway by explaining that the experiments will benefit millions of her people. This is a classic example of *Utilitarian ethics* that was first seen in "Star Trek II: The Wrath of Khan" (1982) and "Star Trek III: The Search for Spock" (1984) in the form of "the needs of the many outweigh the needs of the few." In the *Star Trek: Voyager* episode, the argument is made in a more recognizable form—judging if an act is considered ethical by whether or not the "ends justify the means."

Alzen argues that the experiments on the crew are ethical because they advance science, thus fulfilling the ethical principle of *beneficence*. At the same time, beneficence is "doing good to others," and is tied to the idea of compassion and helping people. While advancing medical science may "help others," it's clearly not helping the Voyager crew. From Captain Janeway's perspective, not only is there no benefit to her crew, the experiments have also violated the ethical principles of *autonomy* (the crew wasn't asked to participate in the research) and *nonmaleficence* (the ethical principle that research participants must be protected from both actual harm as well as potential harm.)

ALZEN: Please understand that there's a purpose to our actions. The data we gather from you may help us cure physical and psychological disorders that afflict millions. Isn't that worth some discomfort?

JANEWAY: I'm sure you'd see things differently if your people were the ones being subjected to these experiments!

ALZEN: Just as your perspective would change if your people were the ones to live longer and healthier lives as a result. Don't forget, we've been observing you, Captain. I know the most important thing to you is the welfare of your crew. You'd even kill to protect them.

JANEWAY: If necessary.

ALZEN: Of course you would. You take care of your own, just as we do. We're really more similar than you care to admit.

JANEWAY: That's where you're wrong. What you're doing isn't self-defense. It's the exploitation of another species for your own benefit. My people decided a long time ago that that was unacceptable, even in the name of scientific progress.

The episode concludes when Janeway takes her ship on what should be a suicide course through a binary pulsar and survives the maneuver. (I knew the ship would survive because this was only the seventh episode of the fourth season.) The episode sends a strong message about the importance of autonomy to the Human race: Janeway would rather risk death than continue as a lab rat.

The concept that informed consent can compromise the outcome of a study is what has led to the use of "double-blind" studies. For example, when a drug company tests a new medication for effectiveness, the people recruited to take part in the research are told that they'll be given a pill which may be either the new drug or a placebo. Neither the person taking the medication nor the person giving the medication is told whether the pill is *real*. The term "double-blind study" refers to the fact that both the patient and researcher are *blind* as to which pill the person is being given. The theory is that the treatment and not expectations will be the only thing different between the two groups.

After the study is concluded, the researcher will be informed which group the person belonged to–treatment or placebo group– in order to see if there were any differences between the two groups. One of the differences between this kind of research and "Scientific Method" is voluntary participation as opposed to research conducted with a person's knowledge or consent. Another difference is that during drug trials no one is sticking long pins into your head to see if they can drive you over the edge.

Beneficence

The ethical principle of beneficence is the obligation of a doctor to provide care to a patient. The duty to provide treatment to anyone who's suffering, regardless of payment, is unique to the medical profession. Comedians are not required to be funny when they're not performing (some aren't funny even when they are performing.) Lawyers aren't required to represent a person just because the person has been accused of a crime, although many attorneys will provide some legal assistance on a *pro bono* ("for the good") basis. Even if I see someone crying, I'm under no obligation to provide psychotherapy just because I'm a counselor. However, a doctor of medicine has an ethical obligation to provide medical care to anyone who's ill.

In "The Breach" (2003, ENT 2:21), the Denobulan Dr. Phlox attempts to render medical treatment to Hudak, an Antaran with a fatal case of radiation poisoning. Hudak refuses to be treated by Dr. Phlox because of a long-standing hatred and distrust between Antarans and Denobulans.

PHLOX: Our two species have a complicated history. We've gone to war with the Antarans on several occasions.

ARCHER: Recently?

PHLOX: On the contrary. It's been three hundred years since our last conflict.

ARCHER: And there's still bad blood between you?

PHLOX: They've been particularly bitter disputes.

ARCHER: If you explain to him that he won't survive without your help, maybe he'd set the past aside for a few hours.

PHLOX: I seriously doubt it. He insisted I leave the room. I don't think you realize how much bad blood there is.

ARCHER: You could always sedate him and perform the treatment.

PHLOX: I have to respect his wishes.

ARCHER: Even if he wishes to die?

PHLOX: The will of the patient is the cornerstone of Denobulan medical ethics.

ARCHER: Don't you believe if you can help someone you're ethically bound to do so?

PHLOX: Hippocrates wasn't Denobulan.

ARCHER: This is an Earth ship, Doctor. I won't let that man die in my sickbay if it can be prevented.

PHLOX: Without his consent, there is nothing I can do.

ARCHER: I'm giving you an order.

PHLOX: I'm sorry, Captain, but I'm afraid I can't follow it.

This episode provides a classic ethical dilemma of the clash between beneficence and autonomy. Captain Archer states that he believes Dr. Phlox has the duty to save Hudak's life (beneficence) even if Hudak doesn't agree to allow Dr. Phlox to treat him (autonomy). Dr. Phlox believes the ethical principle of autonomy trumps both beneficence and the order of a Starfleet captain. I can't help but wonder if, even though Hippocrates wasn't Denobulan, he may have visited Denobula in addition to Malcor III.

"The Breach" provides an analogy to racial intolerance and illustrates how intolerance can lead to bad decisions. Hatred is the overriding influence in Hudak's initial refusal to allow Dr. Phlox to treat his illness. Luckily, the future on *Star Trek* is a hopeful one and Dr. Phlox convinces Hudak to undergo medical treatment by appealing to his parental desire to set a better example for his children.

PHLOX: You asked me if I had heard stories as a child about the Antarans. My grandmother lived through the last war. I would lay in my bed at night thinking about her stories, terrified that one of those evil Antarans would climb through my window.

HUDAK: I hope your confession makes you feel better, Doctor, but it doesn't change a thing.

PHLOX: You also asked me if I have children. I have five. And no, I never told them my grandmother's stories. When they asked me about the Antarans, I told them the truth, as best as I knew it. I told them about our military campaigns against your people. About how we had demonized you, turned you into a face-less enemy. I wanted them to learn to judge people for what they really are, not what the propaganda tells them.

HUDAK: How would you know who we really are?

PHLOX: I don't. But I'm proud to say that my children would consider my grandmother's attitude archaic; all of them but one. We have grown more open-minded since the last war, but there are still Denobulans who fear Antarans, even hate them. My youngest son, Mettus, was seduced by those people. I did my best to convince him he was mistaken. I told him I wouldn't tolerate the values he was embracing. It created a rift between us. Maybe I didn't do enough to reach him. Last time we spoke was nearly ten years ago. You wanted to know what my children would think if they were here now. I can tell you what Mettus would think. He would be happy to have me grant your request and let you die. But that is not the example I tried to set for my children. Why not live and set an example for yours?

Dr. Phlox doesn't violate the ethical principle of autonomy because he allows Hudak to decide whether or not to accept his medical care. Dr. Phlox also practiced the ethical principle of beneficence when he attempted to convince Hudak to allow the lifesaving treatment by sharing his personal feelings. Dr. Phlox could have allowed Hudak to die under the guise of ethically respecting his patient's choice. This would have been autonomous, but clearly not beneficent. Unfortunately, a doctor's best effort to provide care may have unintended consequences as in the case of Hugh in "I, Borg" (1992, TNG; 5:23).

In spite of the danger of having a Borg drone on board, Crusher not only saves his life, but she and La Forge inadvertently help him develop his individual nature.

LA FORGE: Third of Five, this is Dr. Crusher. Dr. Crusher, this is Third of Five.

CRUSHER: Hello.

BORG/HUGH: What is a doctor?

CRUSHER: A doctor heals the sick and repairs the injured.

BORG/HUGH: The sick and injured are reabsorbed. Others take their place.

CRUSHER: That isn't what happened to you. When we found you, you were dying. I saved your life.

BORG/HUGH: Why?

CRUSHER: It's my duty to help those who are hurt.

BORG/HUGH: You give us food.

LA FORGE: Yeah.

BORG/HUGH: Is that your duty?

LA FORGE: Yeah, that's right. Listen, Third of Five, Dr. Crusher here has repaired a lot of the damage to your biochip implants. We want to run a few tests, make sure everything's working okay.

BORG/HUGH: Tests?

CRUSHER: I'd like to show you a few diagrams and ask you some questions about them. It's very simple really.

BORG/HUGH: You will be assimilated.

LA FORGE: Yes, but before that happens, could we ask you a few questions?

BORG/HUGH: We will answer.

LA FORGE: Terrific. All right, hang on just a second here, Third of Five.

BORG/HUGH: What is your designation?

LA FORGE: Designation?

BORG/HUGH: Third of Five.

CRUSHER: You mean our names. We don't have designations. We have names. I'm Beverly. This is Geordi.

BORG/HUGH: Do I have a name?

LA FORGE: Do you want one?

BORG/HUGH: A name.

CRUSHER: I'm Beverly, he's Geordi, and you.

BORG/HUGH: You

CRUSHER: You

LA FORGE: No, no, wait a minute. That's it. Hugh. What do you think?

BORG/HUGH: You.

LA FORGE: No, not you. Hugh.

BORG/HUGH: Hugh.

People with disabilities are often subjected to the paternalistic attitudes in the medical community where doctors do what they think is in the person's best interest, at times without considering the long term consequences of the treatments because of an assumed shortened life span of the person with the disability.

Hugh develops a sense of individuality through his interactions with the crew. However, even beneficence can prove risky as we see in future episodes when we learn that teaching a Borg individuality can be more disruptive than plasma beams or temporal distortions.

Beneficence and The Prime Directive

In the movie, "Star Trek: First Contact" (1996) Dr. Crusher chooses the medical ethic of beneficence over the Prime Directive.

> DATA: Captain, this woman requires medical attention.
> CRUSHER: Severe theta radiation poisoning.
> DATA: Radiation is coming from the damaged throttle assembly.
> CRUSHER: We're all gonna have to be inoculated—and I have to get her to sickbay.
> PICARD: Doctor—
> CRUSHER: Please no lectures about the Prime Directive. I will keep her unconscious.
> PICARD: Very well. Tell Commander Riker to beam down with a search party. We need to find Cochrane.
> CRUSHER: Crusher to Enterprise; two to beam directly to sickbay.

Dr. Crusher intends to keep Lily sedated, but instead the Borg show up. So Crusher must wake Lily in order for everyone in sickbay to escape assimilation. The Prime Directive is then pretty much squashed for the entire movie. In "Star Trek: First Contact" the writers should have renamed the Prime Directive the "It's Usually A Good Idea Directive."

Beneficence and Medical Research

In medical studies, beneficence requires that the researchers provide a benefit to both those who participate in the study as well as to society at large by disseminating the information obtained through their research. The Vulcans violate medical research beneficence in "Stigma" (2003, ENT; 2:4) by not only failing to share their data with Dr. Phlox, but by allowing the stigma of Pa'nar syndrome to continue in their society. According to the *Journal of Academic Psychiatry*, the duty of beneficence goes beyond simply providing medical care and includes a responsibility to provide information to the general public for the purpose of reducing stigma.

Doctors have a *duty* to help regardless of how the patient became sick or injured. That's not to say that all medical conditions are divorced from the behavior of the patient. In the *Star Trek* future when replacement organs are artificial ones, our current debates regarding whether someone who smokes should receive a lung transplant or whether someone who drinks too much should receive a liver transplant will no longer take place.

Nonmaleficence

One aspect of *nonmaleficence* is the maxim that a physician shouldn't employ a medical treatment until he or she has demonstrated the skills to perform that procedure. Patients are to be helped; they're not tissue samples on which students learn how to practice medicine.

In "The Devil in The Dark" (1967, TOS 1:24), the USS Enterprise responds to a distress call from a mining planet where fifty miners have been killed by the monster of the week—a big and shabby alien creature. The so-called monster turns out to be a silicon-based lifeform called a Horta. The miners have been destroying the Horta's eggs which they'd thought were simple silicon spheres. The Horta traps Kirk and Spock and tries to communicate with the two Starfleet officers by burning a message into the rock floor. This attempt to communicate convinces the captain and first officer that this strange life-form is actually an intelligent and sentient being. (This is especially impressive when you consider the message was written in English by the Horta. Apparently the Horta was intuitive enough to know they didn't speak "rock.") Mr. Spock mind-melds with the creature, and learns that the Horta is in pain from the combined phaser blast by Kirk and Spock. After the mind-meld, Kirk has Dr. McCoy beam down to treat the Horta's wounds.

McCOY [OC]: Yes, Captain?
KIRK: Grab your medical kit and come down here on the double. I've got a patient for you.
McCOY [OC]: Is somebody injured? What happened?

KIRK: Never mind. Just come down to the twenty third level. You'll be led to us by tricorder readings. Kirk out.
SPOCK: Jim, I remind you that this is a silicon-based form of life. Dr. McCoy's medical knowledge will be totally useless.

Much to the surprise of everyone including Dr. McCoy, the Horta is successfully treated.

McCOY: It won't die. By golly, Jim, I'm beginning to think I can cure a rainy day.
KIRK: Can you help it?
McCOY: Help it? I cured it.

The principle of nonmaleficence doesn't require refraining from experimental treatments, only that they should be used as a line of last resort and with as much skill as possible. The risk of using an experimental treatment should also be less than the risk of not intervening at all.

Dr. McCoy is faced with a second aspect of nonmaleficence in "Star Trek VI: The Undiscovered Country" (1991). After an evening of peace talks, someone tries to assassinate the Klingon Chancellor Gorkon. Kirk and McCoy are the first Starfleet officers at the crime scene. In the room are the injured Chancellor, his military advisor, Kerla, and his Chief of Staff, Chang. In spite of Kirk's dislike of Klingons, he is desperate for McCoy to save the Chancellor's life.

McCOY: Jim, I don't even know his anatomy—His wounds are not closing.
KERLA: He's killing him!
McCOY: He's gone into some kind of damned arrest—Come on, dammit! Come on—He's not responding.
GORKON: Don't let it end this way, Captain—
CHANG: Under article number one hundred and eighty-four of your Interstellar Law—I'm placing you under arrest. You are charged with assassinating the Chancellor of the High Council.
KIRK: He tried to save him!

Chancellor Gorkon dies and Dr. McCoy is arrested for murder. At Dr. McCoy's trial, Chang cites nonmaleficence as the reason Dr. McCoy was responsible for the Chancellor's death.

CHANG: Was Chancellor Gorkon alive when you first examined him?

McCOY: Barely.

CHANG: Now be careful, Doctor. Have you ever, in your past, saved patients as 'barely' alive as he?

McCOY: I didn't have the medical knowledge I needed for Klingon anatomy.

[Dialogue Omitted]

CHANG: You say you are due for retirement. May I ask; do your hands shake?

COLONEL WORF: Objection!

McCOY: I was nervous.

CHANG: No. You were incompetent! You were incompetent, whether deliberately or as a result of age combined with drink. The court will have to determine.

McCOY: My God, man, I tried to save him! I tried to save him. I was desperate to save him! He was the last best hope in the universe for peace.

In the movie the question of whether Dr. McCoy violated the principle of nonmaleficence resides not in the use of unconventional medicine but rather whether he was incapacitated when he attempted to revive the High Chancellor. Age, alcohol, and insufficient knowledge of Klingon anatomy are possible limitations for Dr. McCoy. The final aspect of nonmaleficence is whether the doctor did his best to protect the High Chancellor against "possible harm" from his medical treatment given his limitations.

Although it may sound as though Dr. McCoy is admitting to violating the principle of nonmaleficence in the dialogue, McCoy's conduct was based on balancing the ethic of beneficence which required him to help Gorkon to the best of his ability with the ethic of nonmaleficence where he must have adequate skills to treat his patient. Unlike the Klingon court, in our courts, Dr. McCoy might be sued for medical malpractice, but he would not be accused of murder or imprisoned on Rura Penthe.

Justice

Justice is considered to be synonymous with fairness—but it's separate from the concept of equality. If I have one student in my class who's blind and reads only Braille, I could give all of my students a Braille exam. By doing so I'd be treating them all equally, but clearly not fairly. In order to observe the principle of justice I'd need to give printed exams to my sighted students and a Braille exam to the one who needs it.

In health care ethics, justice is often divided into three categories: *distributive justice* where there's a fair distribution of resources; *rights based justice* where there's respect for each person's individual rights; and *legal justice* that demonstrates respect for morally acceptable laws. Fortunately for me, there are *Star Trek* episodes that illustrate all three aspects of justice.

Fair Distribution of Resources

"Critical Care" (2000, VOY 7:5) is a made-to-order example of the ethical principle of justice as it pertains to the fair distribution of resources. In this episode, The Doctor is stolen and sold to an alien hospital ship. After he protests providing professional services to his kidnappers, the wounded start arriving and The Doctor's Hippocratic Oath kicks in, which requires him to treat the patients. Later, as medical care is denied to a patient who clearly is in need of it, The Doctor is informed by Chellick, the administrator, that the amount of medical care a patient receives is determined by a *treatment coefficient* assigned by an entity called "The Allocator."

> CHELLICK: Treatment Coefficient. The Allocator assigns one to every patient. It determines the level of care they receive.
> THE DOCTOR: How is this coefficient derived?
> CHELLICK: Through a complex formula that involves profession—skills—accomplishments.
> THE DOCTOR: How is any of that relevant to medical treatment?
> CHELLICK: An agricultural engineer is obviously more important than a waste processor.
> THE DOCTOR: Important to whom?
> CHELLICK: Society. When your resources are limited, you have to prioritize.

THE DOCTOR: So you base treatment on whether patients have particular abilities?

CHELLICK: It's much more complicated than that. The Allocator assesses the entire individual.

THE DOCTOR: And reduces his life to a number.

CHELLICK: It may seem impersonal, but it's what the Dinaali have contracted us to do.

Ever my hero, The Doctor tries to circumvent the system by redistributing medications to those who need them most rather than those with the highest treatment coefficient. A confrontation ensues when The Doctor's actions are discovered.

THE DOCTOR: Don't you have any ethical standards?

CHELLICK: You are hardly in a position to speak to me of ethics. Lying, stealing—any other crimes you wish to confess?

THE DOCTOR: I was trying to save lives.

CHELLICK: And I am trying to save a society. Do you really think Patient R-12 is going to help me do that?

THE DOCTOR: His name was Tebbis.

CHELLICK: He wasn't contributing. He was a drain on resources.

THE DOCTOR: You're not just rationing health care here. You're getting rid of the sick and the weak.

CHELLICK: If the boy had been fit, he would have survived.

THE DOCTOR: Why don't you just put a phaser to their heads?

CHELLICK: We're healers, not killers.

In an effort to force Chellick's agreement to have medication provided for patients with lower treatment coefficients, The Doctor injects Chellick with the same virus that killed Tebbis. His scheme works and Chellick agrees to reassign several patients—including himself—to a higher TC ward.

The Doctor is eventually rescued by the USS Voyager crew. Disturbed by his actions, once he's back on board he asks Seven of Nine to check out his program for anomalies.

THE DOCTOR: I was wondering if you'd mind doing me a favor. I'd like you to give me a check-up.

SEVEN: Have you been experiencing problems?

THE DOCTOR: No, but as you said, I've been off the ship for a while interfaced with an alien computer.

SEVEN: Your program appears to be operating within normal parameters.

THE DOCTOR: Really? What about over the past several days?

SEVEN: There's no indication of diminished capacity.

THE DOCTOR: No problems with my ethical subroutines?

SEVEN: None.

THE DOCTOR: I see.

SEVEN: You seem disappointed.

THE DOCTOR: While I was aboard that ship I poisoned a man.

SEVEN: Deliberately?

THE DOCTOR: Yes. I was trying to force him to let me treat patients who were dying.

SEVEN: You were prepared to sacrifice an individual to benefit a collective.

THE DOCTOR: No offense, Seven, but I don't exactly aspire to Borg ideals.

SEVEN: You were hoping your behavior was the result of a malfunction. I'm sorry Doctor, but I must give you a clean bill of health.

I disagree with Seven's analysis of The Doctor's ethical behavior. When The Doctor injected Chellick with the lethal virus he clearly violated the principles of autonomy, beneficence and nonmaleficence. The Doctor's actions may have been performing justice in a colloquial sense of the term, because he was seeking to provide care for the other patients. However it isn't possible to defend violating the other three medical ethics.

"Critical Care" (2000, VOY 7:5) is a clear indictment of the arbitrary rationing of healthcare imposed in contemporary American society by Health Maintenance Organizations (HMOs) and insurance companies. While some rationing always occurs because medical resources are not infinite, our current healthcare system gives priority for treatment not to those with the greatest medical need, but to those who can most afford care or who have the best insurance coverage.

James Kahn, who wrote the script for "Critical Care," is also a medical doctor. His personal experience was salient to the episode. In my interview with him, he said:

> ...as a matter of my daily experience not a week goes by in my clinic as a doctor that I am not involved in some dispute with an insurance company where I want to order some test or want to give some therapy to a patient and the insurance company denies it because it doesn't fit their bottom line.

Kahn said that *Star Trek* writers aspire to present moral and social dilemmas through allegories in the science fiction world. His goal in writing the script was to have one person make their argument for one side of the dilemma, the Spock argument that "Logic clearly dictates that the needs of the many outweigh the needs of the few" and have the audience agree with that premise.

> And we can agree that someone who is an agriculture specialist working to help feed the entire planet is valuable to the entire society. At the same time, he presents the opposing argument, that even if someone is only a janitor, it is not morally or ethically right to deny them health care. We would also agree with that argument. "Critical Care" does what *Star Trek* does best, spurs an examination of our values, both personally and as a society.

Recently the United States passed legislation to create national healthcare. Those familiar with the history of socialized medicine in other countries voiced their concerns regarding how the new law would be implemented in this country. Would the new system lead to something similar to treatment coefficients remains to be answered? What would the law mean for people with disabilities and people over a certain age? Keep in mind that this *Star Trek: Voyager* episode aired eight years before President Obama was elected for his first term.

According to Kahn, "Critical Care" was about more than just disabilities, older people, or class, it was the idea that you cannot ration medical care according to a numerical coefficient. His position is that everybody is entitled to medical care in order for them to "contribute whatever they can contribute" to society. And in the *Star Trek* future, that is what happens.

Respect for Human Rights

The second form of justice involves the respect for Human rights. Since I'm talking about *Star Trek*, the Universal Translator would likely change this term into something like "humanoid life rights" or "sentient life rights."

In "Phage" (1995, VOY 1:5), aliens known as Vidiians are fighting for survival against a virulent infection. However, the Vidiians combat their phage by obtaining organ transplants from unwilling donors. They lure the crew of the USS Voyager onto a planet and steal Neelix's lungs. Once Voyager's crew tracks down the thieves, Motura (the alien who is now breathing with Neelix's lungs) and Dereth (his honatta, who implanted the lungs) try to justify their actions by describing their desperation.

> JANEWAY: So now I am left with the same choice you made: Whether to commit murder to save a life, or to allow my own crewman to die while you breathe air through his lungs.
>
> MOTURA: It must be impossible for you to understand how any civilized people could come to this. Before the phage began, we were known as educators and explorers, a people whose greatest achievements were artistic. I myself am a sculptor of note on my world. All I can say is that when your entire existence is at stake—
>
> DERETH: You don't have to explain yourself, Motura.
>
> MOTURA: If the consequence of this act is a death sentence, so be it. At least it will put an end to my suffering.
>
> JANEWAY: I can't begin to understand what your people have gone through. They may have found a way to ignore the moral implications of what you are doing, but I have no such luxury. I don't have the freedom to kill you to save another. My culture finds that to be a reprehensible and entirely unacceptable act. If we were closer to home I would lock you up and turn you over to my authorities for trial, but I don't even have that ability here, and I am not prepared to carry you forever in our brig. So I see no other alternative but to let you go.
>
> Take a message to your people. If I ever encounter your kind again, I will do whatever is necessary to protect my people from this harvesting of yours.

Any aggressive actions against this ship or its crew will be met by the deadliest force. Is that clear?

DERETH: Quite.

What a "honatta" is in the Vidiian culture is never explained. Since Dereth had the medical skills to graft Neelix's lungs into Motura's body, I assume that he's something akin to a physician. Dereth's behavior violates the "humanoid rights" aspect of the justice principle because he doesn't take into account Neelix's rights, only Motura's needs. The biomedical ethic of justice requires that Dereth act fairly to both involved parties. Whether his actions compromise an equivalent *alien* ethical principle is unknown. I want to avoid being Human-centric.

The episode is resolved when Dereth uses his advanced organ transplant skills to provide Neelix with a lung donated by his Ocampa girlfriend, Kes. Even though Kes appears to be a young female in her twenties, she has been alive less than two years when she consents to the procedure. As I consider her lack of experience along with her infatuation with Neelix, I question whether she was truly autonomous in making this decision. (I always questioned her attraction to Neelix in the first place.) A second unresolved question is: Why is Dereth able to graft Kes' lung into Neelix, but cannot graft one of Neelix's lungs back into Neelix?

Legal Justice and Respect for Morally Acceptable Laws

One of my favorite *Star Trek: Voyager* episodes is "Tuvix" (1996, VOY 2:24). The story begins with a transporter accident. (Since transporter accidents have occurred in every Star Trek series, I think I'd personally avoid this form of travel.) While Tuvok and Neelix are beaming back to the ship after an *orchid reconnaissance mission* the transporter malfunctions and the two crewmen arrive on the ship combined as one person, later christened Tuvix. Captain Janeway's log entry summarizes the developing ethical dilemma nicely:

JANEWAY: Captain's log, stardate 49678.4. It's been two weeks since the transporter accident that created Mr. Tuvix—As for my relationship with Tuvix, I've found him to be an able advisor who skillfully uses humor to make his points. And although I feel a bit guilty saying it, his cooking is better than Neelix's. My taste buds are definitely happy to have him around.

After these two weeks, The Doctor is finally able to develop a plan to separate Tuvix back into Tuvok and Neelix. However, Tuvix doesn't agree to the procedure.

JANEWAY: We've just been discussing the unfortunate predicament that we're all facing, and I thought it was important to get your perspective before making a decision.

TUVIX: Are you suggesting that this is your decision to make?

JANEWAY: I am the Captain of this ship.

TUVIX: Begging your pardon, Captain, it's my life. Isn't it my decision?

JANEWAY: Aren't there two other lives to consider here? What about Tuvok and Neelix? Two voices that we can't hear right now. As Captain, I must be their voice, and I believe they would want to live.

TUVIX: But they are living in a way, inside me.

JANEWAY: It's not the same and I think you'd agree with me. They have families, friends, people who love them and miss them and want them back, just as I do.

TUVIX: But restoring their lives means sacrificing mine. Captain, what you're considering is an execution. An execution, like they used to do to murderers centuries ago. And I've committed no crime at all.

JANEWAY: Aren't you arguing for an execution too? Of Tuvok and Neelix?

TUVIX: I'm here, alive. Unfortunate as it may be, they're gone.

JANEWAY: And I have an opportunity to bring them back.

TUVIX: Don't you think that I care about Tuvok and Neelix? Of course I do. Without them, I wouldn't exist. In a way, I think of them as my parents. I feel like I know them intimately.

JANEWAY: Then you know Tuvok was a man who would gladly give his life to save another. And I believe the same was true of Neelix.

TUVIX: You're right, Captain. That is the Starfleet way. And I know there'll be some people who—who'll call me a coward because I didn't sacrifice myself willingly. Believe me, I've thought of that. But I have the will to live of two men.
Look at me, Captain. When I'm happy, I laugh. When I'm sad, I cry. When I stub my toe, I yell out in pain. I'm flesh and blood, and I have the right to live.

The Doctor refuses to perform the separation, citing the ethical principles of autonomy and nonmaleficence. He stands aside as Captain Janeway handles the transporter procedure. Although Janeway is a starship captain and therefore is not bound by biomedical ethics, she respects the need for moral justice in providing a voice for both Tuvok and Neelix—even at the expense of Tuvix (and at the expense of better tasting food.) The Doctor's refusal to participate in the procedure is ethically correct in respecting Tuvix's autonomy, but short-sighted in regards to this ethical principle of justice. Janeway is reward for her efforts with the return of her crewmen, Neelix and Tuvok, and the cost of Tuvix's cooking.

In "Similitude" (2003, ENT; 3:10), Captain Archer is given an experimental treatment for the dying chief engineer, Trip Tucker.

ARCHER: How is he?

PHLOX: His condition's unchanged. I'd like to show you something. This is one of the more interesting members of my little menagerie, a Lyssarrian Desert Larvae. Its epidermal layers secrete a viral suppressant that I use as a salve for cuts and bruises.

ARCHER: How does this relate to Trip?

PHLOX: The larvae have another, somewhat more controversial, property. When implanted with the DNA from another species it exactly replicates that species' lifecycle, albeit at a rapidly accelerated rate.

ARCHER: It becomes a clone.

PHLOX: Essentially, but one that is born, grows old, and dies in approximately fifteen days. The Lyssarrians call them mimetic symbionts. They're a closely guarded secret. Very few people know of their existence.

ARCHER: And you want to do this with Trip. Use his DNA to grow a symbiont.

PHLOX: To harvest its neural tissue for transplant. There's no guarantee that human DNA will stimulate the larvae's growth cycle, but as it stands now it may be Commander Tucker's only hope for survival. To ensure the tissue's compatibility, I'll have to wait until the symbiont reaches Commander Tucker's present physical age, then I can excise the tissue from a noncritical region of the symbiont's cerebral region. It would experience no discernible side effects and should be able to live out its normal life span.

ARCHER: Its fifteen day life span.

PHLOX: I don't make this proposal lightly, Captain, but I'm obligated to provide you with all available options.

The symbiont grows remarkably fast but the ethical dilemma is that extracting the neural tissue will kill the clone, who doesn't want to die.

Five years after "Similitude" aired, Lisa Nash made national headlines when she gave birth to her son, Adam, in 2008. Adam's conception was far from ordinary. He was conceived with a predetermined destiny: stem cells from Adam's umbilical cord were to be used in a bone marrow transplant therapy to save his sister's life. Six-year-old Molly Nash had been born with an often fatal genetic disorder called Fanconi anemia. Adam's conception used a new procedure, pre-implantation genetic diagnosis, to ensure Adam would be both free of Molly's disease and be a suitable bone marrow donor.

In late September 2008, doctors at the University of Minnesota took blood cells from Adam's umbilical cord to replace Molly's defective marrow. The treatment gave Molly an eighty-five percent chance to beat the disease. The technique raised many ethical questions, but Lisa's statement was simply: "We wanted a healthy child and it doesn't hurt him to save his sister's life."

After taking a sample from Molly's bone marrow to determine whether Adam's cells were taking hold, it was determined they were. While the clone, Sim, dies to provide the neural tissue for Tucker, Adam wasn't harmed in any way during the procedure that saved his sister's life. Yet both situations share the question of *morality* in the ethical principle of justice. In Molly's case we have to ask: Is it morally acceptable to conceive a second child for the purpose of curing the first child? Ethical dilemmas such as the decisions made regarding Sim, Tuvix, and Molly Nash are not easily resolved.

Fidelity

Fidelity is generally defined as honesty and keeping one's promises, but as a biomedical ethical principle, it has many layers. The principle of fidelity requires physicians to keep their patients' interests first in mind above all other concerns. Fidelity includes the promises of patient confidentiality. In "Imperfection" (2000, VOY; 7:2) Seven of Nine reminds The Doctor of her right to keep information about her malfunctioning cortical node from Captain Janeway.

THE DOCTOR: —I'll schedule some follow-up tests and make my report to the Captain.

SEVEN: I'd prefer to keep this between us. I don't want to worry the Captain.

THE DOCTOR: We've always kept her informed of your medical needs.

SEVEN: It was my understanding that all members of this crew have the right to doctor-patient confidentiality.

THE DOCTOR: If you want to keep this between us, that's where it'll stay.

Fidelity also prohibits physicians from attempting risky medical procedures solely to advance their professional career, earn prestige, or charge more money when a less expensive procedure would be adequate. In addition, fidelity requires the physician to maintain a patient's trust by being honest. (I may need to remind my doctor of this ethic the next time he tells me that "this won't hurt a bit" as he prepares me for an injection that we both know will hurt like blazes.) Finally, fidelity requires doctors to be respectful of the medical profession. Medical associations decree that physicians must never behave in a manner that would bring disrespect upon the practice of medicine.

In "The Expanse" (2002, ENT; 2:26), Phlox checks out the Vulcan physician's credentials and determines that the Vulcan doctor has committed deception.

PHLOX: I'm afraid this examination is over.

FER'AT: I'm nearly finished.

PHLOX: You are finished; I just checked the Vulcan database. There's only one Dr. Fer'at listed, and he's not a pathologist, he's a psychiatric analyst.

ARCHER: Soval sure is persistent. What did he want you to do? Come back with proof that I'm out of my mind?

PHLOX: You come to my sickbay under false pretenses. Where are your medical ethics?!

FER'AT: I'm just doing what I was told to.

ARCHER: Well I'm telling you to get the hell off my ship. If you wouldn't mind, Phlox, I'd like you to escort our guest to the airlock.

PHLOX: Gladly.

In other words, Vulcans can lie if they are told to do so? As Mr. Spock would say, that is fascinating.

In "Jetrel" (1995, VOY 1:15), a Haakonian scientist named Dr. Ma'Bor Jetrel contacts the USS Voyager and asks to examine Neelix. Jetrel states he fears that Neelix has a fatal disease from exposure to metreon isotopes generated by a weapon called the Metreon Cascade—a weapon Jetrel created. During a war, the Haakonians used the Cascade against the Talaxians on the moon Rinax. At first Neelix refuses to be examined by Jetrel because he doesn't trust him.

NEELIX: He's a mass murderer! When I was much younger my family and I lived on a moon called Rinax, a colony with the most temperate climate in the entire Talaxian system. Warm days, balmy nights. Until the Metreon Cascade. A melodic name, isn't it? Especially for a weapon of mass destruction.
JANEWAY: And Jetrel was somehow involved with this weapon?
NEELIX: Dr. Jetrel was the scientist who conceived the Metreon Cascade, then he led the team of scientists who built it.
JANEWAY: I see.
NEELIX: In the blink of an eye Rinax was enveloped by a deadly cloud, and those lovely days were turned into one endless frigid night. More than three hundred thousand were killed.

Jetrel tries to justify his involvement with creating the Cascade:

JETREL: It would not have made any difference. If I had not discovered the Cascade, it would have been someone else, don't you see? It was a scientific inevitability, one discovery flowing naturally to the next. Something so enormous as science will not stop for something as small as man, Mr. Neelix.
NEELIX: So you did it for science.
JETREL: For my planet, and yes, for science. To know whether or not it could be done. It's good to know how the world works. It is not possible to be a scientist unless you believe that all the knowledge of the universe and all the power that it bestows is of intrinsic value to everyone, and one must share that knowledge and allow it to be applied, and then be willing to live with the consequences.

Although it's never entirely clear whether Jetrel is simply a scientist or is also a medical practitioner, his knowledge of Talaxian physiology points to the latter. While a non-medical scientist might not be ethically prohibited from developing weapons, our society expects physicians to be healers not killers. The medical principle of fidelity is violated anytime a physician uses his or her medical knowledge in the antithesis of healing because it calls into question our trust of all medical doctors. Clearly, how can I trust my doctor if my doctor is a murderer?

After atrocities at the Guantanamo Bay detention camp came to light, the American Psychological Association was the last professional association to ban its members from working with interrogators at U.S. detention centers such as Guantanamo Bay. When the ban was issued, psychologists were brought into line with the positions of the American Medical Association and the American Psychiatric Association. Both associations declared in a May 2006 statement that "No psychiatrist should participate directly in the interrogation of a person held by military or civilian investigative or law enforcement authorities." Although the exact nature of Dr. Jetrel's discipline is nebulous, it's clear that his participation in creating the Metreon Cascade would violate the principle of fidelity if he were a physician.

At the end of the episode Dr. Jetrel confesses that Neelix doesn't have the fatal disease—the lie clearly violates of the principle of fidelity. Dr. Jetrel admits that he used the diagnosis as part of a ruse to enlist the help of the USS Voyager, because he believed the Talaxians vaporized by the weapon could be regenerated by the transporter. Tragically the valiant efforts Voyager crew fails, and the loss of so many lives remains part of Talaxian history. And Dr. Jetrel dies an unethical professional with a guilty conscience.

Fidelity and Medical Research

In "The Begotten" (1997, DS9; 5:12), Odo becomes a daddy to an infant changeling he buys from Quark. After Dr. Bashir treats the gelatinous goo which is the baby shape-shifter, Odo takes custody of the infant in a beaker. Odo talks to his new ward in an annoying non-stop soliloquy of promises including a description of how wonderful it feels to be able to take the form of a Tarkalean hawk. Odo is in the process of introducing the baby to various shapes when Dr. Mora appears. Dr. Mora is the Bajoran scientist who discovered Odo was a sentient being and helped him develop his shape-shifting abilities. My analysis of this episode addresses the question of whether Dr. Mora was ethical in how he treated Odo during the Cardassian occupation. That is, did Dr. Mora put Odo's interests ahead of his own while working with him? While working with Odo, Dr. Mora is constantly reminded of how Odo resents his treatment.

MORA: Oh, so that's what this is about. You still resent the things I did to you in order to induce you to shape-shift. Well I know they weren't pleasant for you, but really, Odo, I would hope that you would get past that by now. I am disappointed.

ODO: I have my own ideas about how to teach the changeling.

MORA: I imagine they're less invasive.

ODO: Exactly.

Odo is making very little progress with the changeling when Sisko enters and stands by the doorway while Dr. Mora is telling Odo about the pressures of his situation under Cardassian rule.

MORA: Once I realized you were sentient, the Cardassians wanted to know everything about you. I was under enormous pressure to come up with results, and I did. My technique worked. The fact that you are standing here whining about it proves it.

ODO: You enjoyed watching me suffer.

MORA: You really believe that? How pathetic. If it wasn't for me, you'd still be sitting on a shelf somewhere, in a beaker labeled "unknown sample."

ODO: If it wasn't for me, you'd be a nobody. Starfleet wouldn't hire you to judge a science fair.

[Dialogue Omitted]

ODO: Captain.

SISKO: How's it going, gentlemen?

ODO: Making progress, sir.

SISKO: I'm glad to hear it. I was just talking with Starfleet Command. They want you to establish communication with the changeling as soon as possible.

MORA: At the rate we're going, that is still a long way off.

SISKO: Better not be too long, otherwise Starfleet is going to want to take over the project.

ODO: Sir.

SISKO: As long as you're making progress, there's nothing to worry about. Oh, by the way. Starfleet wants you to file daily reports for their review.

ODO: Understood, sir.

SISKO: Carry on. [Sisko leaves.]

MORA: Now you understand the kind of pressure I was going through. I brought my old equipment from Bajor. Maybe it's time we started unpacking.

Feeling the pressure of Starfleet's scrutiny, Odo consents to use some of Dr. Mora's unpleasant techniques to induce the changeling to adopt various forms.

[The changeling is poured onto a lighted surface with a blue circle in the center.]

MORA: Odo, the changeling won't respond to anything less than six millivolts.

ODO: There must be some other way.

MORA: Spare the rod, spoil the child. Odo, without discomfort the changeling will be perfectly comfortable to remain in its gelatinous state. It'll just lie there, never realizing it has the ability to mimic other forms, never living up to its potential. Odo, six millivolts is not going to hurt it. Once it realizes there's no charge in the center, the procedure will be finished.

[Odo increases the voltage and the baby starts moving, searching for somewhere more comfortable.]

MORA: Checking to see if I'm enjoying myself?

[The baby changeling moves into the small circle in the middle of the lighted table.]

ODO: That's it. You've found it.

MORA: I smiled the first time you did that. Little did I realize you'd end up hating me for it. Well, shall we move on?

ODO: Why not?

As Odo works with the baby changeling, he develops a new respect for Dr. Mora and his methods. Odo discovers that although he resented the discomfort he suffered while

Dr. Mora attempted to determine what he was, Dr. Mora hadn't behaved unethically. Medical and research treatments aren't always pleasant. Dr. Mora had not forced Odo to shape-shift for the sole purpose of inflicting pain. Odo ultimately forgives Dr. Mora and actually thanks him for his help and faith that Odo could become more than just a sample of organic material. The episode ends with a bittersweet climax when the baby changeling dies, but not before restoring Odo's shape-shifting ability—an ability that had been taken from Odo by the Founders.

"The Begotten" illustrates that adhering to the ethical principle of fidelity is not synonymous with the most pleasant or easiest path for the medical researcher or physician. Indeed, when treating people with severe medical conditions, the treatment may be far from painless. The principle of fidelity is not synonymous with avoiding pain, but demands that the physician utilize the treatment that is in the best interest of the patient or research subject. The other lesson from this episode is that it is a tremendous amount of fun to soar through the Promenade as a Tarkalean hawk.

Ethics—The Episode

All of these ethical principles are played out in one of my favorite *Star Trek: The Next Generation* episodes, appropriately named, "Ethics" (1992, TNG 5:16). After Worf suffers an injury to his spine, he becomes paralyzed from the waist down. When Worf learns he has little chance of regaining his mobility, he goes into full Klingon mode and asks Commander Riker to assist him with Klingon ritual suicide.

> WORF: When a Klingon can no longer stand and face his enemies as a warrior, when he becomes a burden to his friends and family, it is time for the Hegh'bat. Time for him to die.
> RIKER: There must be other options.
> WORF: No, there are not. I will not live as an object of pity or shame. My life as a Klingon is over.

Riker, faced with the burden of having been asked to help Worf commit suicide, turns to Captain Picard for guidance. Riker agrees with Dr. Crusher and Counselor Troi that Worf shouldn't contemplate suicide while he still has his son, Alexander, to raise.

RIKER: I have always tried to keep an open mind, not to judge someone else's culture by my own, but for me to be a part of this ceremony—

PICARD: I understand from Dr. Crusher that Worf will never regain the use of his legs.

RIKER: That doesn't mean his life is over.

PICARD: That's a very human perspective, Will. For a Klingon in Worf's position, his life is over.

RIKER: I can't accept that.

PICARD: Will, if you were dying, if you were terminally ill with an incurable disease and facing the remaining few days of your life in pain, wouldn't you come to look on death as a release?

RIKER: Worf isn't dying and he is not in pain. He could live a long life!

PICARD: You or I could learn to live with that disability, but not Worf. His life ended when those containers fell on him. We don't have to agree with it, we don't have to understand it, but we do have to respect his beliefs.

RIKER: I can respect his beliefs—but he is asking me to take an active role in his committing suicide!

PICARD: He's asking for your help because you're his friend. That means that you're going to have to make your decision based on that friendship.

RIKER: Which leaves me back where I started.

PICARD: Will. Look, I'm sorry, I cannot help you to make this decision, but I can tell you this—Klingons choose their friends with great care. If he didn't know he could count on you, he never would have asked.

Meanwhile, Dr. Crusher discusses Worf's treatment options with Dr. Russell, the neurological specialist who has been brought in to consult. Dr. Russell is researching a pioneering technique, called *genetronics*, which replicates damaged organs from the original DNA. However, genetronics is both life-threatening and untested. Dr. Russell admits that even using holographic patients, her success rate is only thirty-seven percent. If I'm doing the math correctly that means that sixty-three percent of the "photon" patients died.

CRUSHER: You're talking about a spinal column. Even before we could replace it, we have to remove the existing one, and we don't know enough about Klingon neurological medicine to re-attach it. If something goes wrong, he'll die. I agree it has remarkable potential, but you're still in the most preliminary stages of research. No, I'm afraid I can't justify the risk to Worf. We'll have to do with more conventional approaches.

RUSSELL: You're probably right. It's too radical an approach.

Clearly, Dr. Crusher's paramount concern is nonmaleficence. She wants to pursue the treatment that poses the greatest benefit with the least amount of risk. That treatment is implantation of electrodes that will restore some—but not all—of Worf's mobility.

Worf rejects Dr. Crusher's treatment recommendations, due to his Klingon belief that living with a disability is dishonorable for a warrior. In what may seem to constitute adherence to the ethical principle of beneficence, Dr. Russell, suggests her genetronic procedure directly to Worf as an alternative to suicide. To say Crusher is *not pleased* with her colleague is an understatement:

CRUSHER: I thought we had discussed genetronics.

RUSSELL: We did.

CRUSHER: I also thought we'd decided against recommending it.

RUSSELL: You heard him. He'd rather die than live with the implants. I just gave him a better option than suicide.

CRUSHER: He's grasping for straws and you're giving him one. Now instead of dealing with his paralysis, he's going to be thinking about this miracle cure of yours.

RUSSELL: There's a real chance this could work. And if it does, it'll be a major breakthrough in neurogenetics that will change a lot of people's lives.

CRUSHER: You're using the desperation of an injured man as an excuse to try a procedure that you couldn't do under normal circumstances. I checked with Starfleet Medical. They have turned down your request to test genetronics on humanoids three times already.

Apparently Starfleet Medical has something akin to a "Human Subjects Committee" of an Institutional Review Board, and Dr. Russell hasn't been able to obtain their approval to test her theory on humanoid subjects. Dr. Crusher understands that even though Worf has consented to this experimental treatment, his autonomy may have been compromised due to the influence of his cultural beliefs, which view suicide as preferable to living with a disability.

Dr. Crusher, as Worf's primary physician, believes she must look out for his best interests, which means protecting him from Dr. Russell's cavalier attitude that Worf has nothing to lose—Klingon culture notwithstanding. If Worf dies during the procedure, Dr. Russell states that his life will contribute to her medical research. It's clear that Dr. Russell is more interested in testing her theories than in Worf's well-being. Since Dr. Russell doesn't put the best interests of her patient ahead of her own professional ambitions, she violates the principle of fidelity.

Dr. Russell's attitude that Worf has nothing to lose by agreeing to this risky experimental procedure devalues the life of anyone who has a disability or serious medical condition. In discussing her objections with Captain Picard, Dr. Crusher valiantly cites the obligation of physicians to refrain from doing harm: the principle of nonmaleficence.

> CRUSHER: The first tenet of good medicine is never make the patient any worse. Right now, Worf is alive and functioning. If he goes into that operation, he could come out a corpse.
> PICARD: This may not be good medicine, but for Worf, it may be his only choice.

Dr. Crusher, after stating in her log that she has undergone much soul-searching, eventually grants permission to go ahead with the genetronic procedure. She thereby respects Worf's *autonomy* (compromised or not) in consenting to the experimental procedure. Dr. Crusher and Nurse Ogawa assist Dr. Russell with the surgery and Worf dies on the table from heart failure. As suits the *Star Trek* universe, Worf's redundant Klingon internal organs miraculously kick in and he recovers after Dr. Crusher has already pronounced him dead. However, Dr. Crusher remains far from convinced that Dr. Russell was ethical in her behavior.

> RUSSELL: Well, I'd say your patient's recovery is going well. You're not even going to acknowledge what I did for him, are you? You just can't admit that it was my research that made this possible.

CRUSHER: I am delighted that Worf is going to recover. You gambled; he won. Not all of your patients are so lucky. You scare me, Doctor. You risk your patients' lives and justify it in the name of research. Genuine research takes time. Sometimes a lifetime of painstaking, detailed work in order to get any results. Not for you. You take short cuts, right through living tissue. You put your research ahead of your patients' lives, and as far as I'm concerned that's a violation of our most sacred trust. I'm sure your work will be hailed as a stunning breakthrough. Enjoy your laurels, Doctor. I'm not sure I could.

This conversation illustrates how medical practice ethics are not always clearly separate from medical research ethics. There needs to be a balance between the practicing physician who offers hope and the researcher who will treat patients as lab rats, even if they're the same person. Even if the patient is willing to try untested methods in hopes of a cure, the ethical physician doesn't experiment with Human subjects without first establishing safety protocols.

Various authoritative documents including the Declaration of Helsinki, the National Research Act, and *The Belmont Report*, have established guidelines for medical research. Generally speaking, a patient may consent to try unproven and even risky medical procedures provided that he or she is fully informed of the potential risks and benefits, isn't unduly influenced by others, the medical condition is life-threatening, and all conventional treatments have been exhausted and failed. These final two criteria aren't met in Worf's case; he is not in immediate danger of dying (except by his own hand), and conventional therapy wasn't attempted.

This is also the only episode where a specialist was sent to the USS Enterprise rather than transporting the patient to a starbase for treatment. If Worf's status as the only Klingon in Starfleet is the reason for this special attention, then the ethical principle of justice (fair allocation of resources) was likewise violated. Would Dr. Russell have been invited to the Enterprise to treat an ordinary crewman? On a side note, "Ethics," "The Masterpiece Society," and "The Loss" are the only episodes out of one-hundred-seventy-eight *Star Trek: The Next Generation* episodes where the *d-word* (disability) is even mentioned.

Historically, the paternalistic attitude of physicians towards people with disabilities, as exemplified by Dr. Russell's belief that Worf has nothing to lose, has demonstrated the low value of life assigned to this group of people. For example, from 1963 to 1966, a controversial medical study was conducted at the Willowbrook State School in New York during which children with cognitive disabilities were intentionally given hepatitis to see if they could then be cured with gamma globulin. For over a century mental patients, prisoners, and those with *diminished capacity* were routinely used as a source of research subjects. As a result of the many unethical experiments that were conducted, these groups of people are now provided with additional protections by IRBs which determine whether or not the proposed research can be conducted.

From a biomedical ethics perspective, one of the most controversial medical research issues today is described by the term "genetic engineering" which is the subject of the next chapter. Issues of biomedical ethics involve the lack of autonomy of the patient because these treatments are done in infancy or before. The parents make these decisions, not the patient receiving the treatment. These new therapies are also associated with higher risks than traditional treatments. They're also expensive procedures which are rarely covered by medical insurance companies. Yet, of all these concerns, of utmost importance to this book is what these treatments mean for people with disabilities now and in the future.

Chapter 4
"Looking for Lifeforms"

DATA: I just love scanning for lifeforms. Humm. Lifeforms—[computer beeps] you tiny little lifeforms—[computer beeps] you precious little lifeforms—[Data snaps his fingers]—Where are you? Do-do do. Do-do do. [more computer beeps] "Star Trek: Generations" (1994)

Genetic Engineering

On *Star Trek,* Humans aren't the only forms of life. There are Vulcans, and Klingons, and Romulans, oh my! Most of the lifeforms are humanoid—that is, they have two arms, two legs, and one head. In "The Chase" (1993, TNG 6:20), a hologram (who strongly resembles one of the Founders from *Star Trek: Deep Space Nine*) explains why so many lifeforms share a humanoid shape, other than the fact that all the actors come preassembled with this design.

HUMANOID: …Life evolved on my planet before all others in this part of the galaxy. We left our world, explored the stars, and found none like ourselves. Our civilization thrived for ages, but what is the life of one race, compared to the vast stretches of cosmic time? We knew that one day we would be gone, that nothing of us would survive. So, we left you. Our scientists seeded the primordial oceans of many worlds, where life was in its infancy. The seed codes directed your evolution toward a physical form resembling ours. This body you see before you, which is, of course, shaped as yours is shaped, for you are the end result. The seed codes also contained this message, which we scattered in fragments on many different worlds...

Alien lifeforms also have genes, which are sometimes compatible with Human genes (when the script writers want them to be.) Without this partial compatibility, we wouldn't have Mr. Spock, Deanna Troi, or B'Elanna Torres.

Genetic engineering is a favorite theme in many science fiction venues, several of which predate the original *Star Trek* series. In fact, the term genetic engineering originated in science fiction, first coined by Jack Williamson in his 1951 novel "Dragon's Island." (One year before DNA's role in heredity was confirmed.) Science fiction writers have often used genetic engineering to explain how in *their* future people have different appearances and abilities.

Since the phrase genetic engineering originated with science fiction and not science, it's impossible to find a universal definition. On *Star Trek,* genetic engineering is used as an umbrella term to encompass the real-life sciences of *eugenics, gene therapy, and germline gene therapy*, as well as *cloning.* Genetic engineering has been applied to plants, animals, and Humans. On *Star Trek* it was most often applied to humanoids.

Star Trek makes social commentaries on race, social justice, and religion as well as science. Genetic engineering is a technology where writers can show how all of these issues converge. The way genetic engineering is depicted generally reflects a projected future science based on when the story was written—as well as the surrounding controversies. When the original series aired, DNA research was a little more than ten years old. During the time *Star Trek: The Next Generation* was on the air, scientists around the world embarked on the most ambitious genetics project in history—mapping the Human genome.

Since my job here is to identify the messages about disability on *Star Trek,* starting in this chapter I will use the heading "Incoming Message" when the message is positive or accurate. When the message is either negative or inaccurate I use the heading "Red Alert!" Keep in mind that some of the negative messages are reflections of our negative beliefs about disability. Indeed, some of the messages on *Star Trek* may have been sent unintentionally.

Eugenics

Selective breeding of plants and animals has been going on for centuries. The differences among today's dog and cat breeds are the result of consciously mating animals who exhibited desired characteristics. So my short-legged Pembroke Welsh Corgi was bred to herd cows by nipping at their heels; my Border Collie had long legs so she could outrun the sheep she was bred to protect. When selective breeding was applied to Humans, the term eugenics was used.

While selective breeding is an old science, in the late 1800s Francis Galton (1822–1911) advocated that it should be applied to Humans. His writings were the beginning of the eugenics movement in the United States. Galton believed that selective breeding could improve humanity by eliminating the *undesirables* in society. It probably won't surprise anyone that Galton had a more famous cousin—Charles Darwin. Accordingly, the eugenics movement embraced *Social Darwinism* (the survival of the fittest) in their rationale. Paul Lombardo from the University of Virginia, in his essay "Eugenic Sterilization Laws," describes what happened once the eugenics idea got underway.

> In 1914, Harry Laughlin published a Model Eugenical Sterilization Law that proposed to authorize sterilization of the "socially inadequate"—people supported in institutions or maintained wholly or in part by public expense. The law encompassed the "feebleminded, insane, criminalistics, epileptic, inebriate, diseased, blind, deaf; deformed; and dependent"—including "orphans, ne'er-do-wells, tramps, the homeless and paupers." By the time the Model Law was published in 1914, twelve states had enacted sterilization laws.

Forced sterilization began in 1907 with Indiana and ended in 1981, when Oregon was the last state to repeal their law. In all, thirty-three states in the U.S. adopted forced sterilization laws during this time. In their attempts to *improve* humanity, eugenicists supported both *positive eugenics* (efforts to expand the reproduction rates of the more desirable classes of people) and *negative eugenics* (which centered on policies and laws, such as forced sterilization, to diminish childbirth among the less desirable classes).

In the fictional history presented in "Space Seed" (1967, TOS 1:22), a Eugenics War almost ended civilization on Earth. "Space Seed" begins when the USS Enterprise intercepts a ship emitting, surprisingly, a Morse code signal. Scanners detect faint heartbeats, and the crew investigates. Based on the design of the ship, it's believed to be from Earth in the 1990s, although the exact date is unknown.

SPOCK: No such vessel listed. Records of that period are fragmentary, however. The mid 1990's was the era of your last so-called World War.
MCCOY: The Eugenics Wars.
SPOCK: Of course, your attempt to improve the race through selective breeding.
MCCOY: Now, wait a minute. Not our attempt, Mr. Spock. A group of ambitious scientists. I'm sure you know the type. Devoted to logic—completely unemotional—

INCOMING MESSAGE:
Science that works with plants and animals
may not work with people.

The Enterprise crew discovers the ship has passengers—people in cryogenic sleep. The first to be revived is Khan. The dark-skinned Human (apparently his cryogenic chamber was equipped with a tanning lamp) amazes Dr. McCoy with his natural recuperative powers. Since Khan isn't forthcoming about his origins or the origins of his seventy-two shipmates, speculation continues about who these Humans are and why they've been in space for two centuries.

KIRK: ...Would you estimate him to be a product of selective breeding?
SPOCK: There is that possibility, Captain. His age would be correct. In 1993, a group of these young supermen did seize power simultaneously in over forty nations.
Kirk: Well, they were hardly supermen. They were aggressive, arrogant. They began to battle among themselves—
SPOCK: Because the scientists overlooked one fact. Superior ability breeds superior ambition.

Eventually, they discover Khan's identity along with his violent past. Kirk presents the information to the crew:

KIRK: [A historic picture of Khan is displayed on the computer screen] Name: Khan, [the picture changes] as we know him today. Name: Khan Noonien Singh.
SPOCK: From 1992 through 1996, absolute ruler of more than a quarter of your world—from Asia through the Middle East.
MCCOY: The last of the tyrants to be overthrown.

Of course, Khan attempts to take over the USS Enterprise and tries to kill Captain Kirk. And of course, even though Khan has superior physical and mental abilities, he's no match for the Enterprise crew. In the end, rather than take Khan to a reorientation center, Kirk decides to allow Khan and his crewmates to be settled on a rugged planet.

SPOCK: It would be interesting, Captain, to return to that world in a hundred years and to learn what crop has sprung from the seed you planted today.
KIRK: Yes, Mr. Spock, it would indeed.

This last scene of "Space Seed" was later the basis for "Star Trek II: The Wrath of Khan" (1982). Together these two provide the following fictitious history of eugenics.

1992 – 1996: Khan is ruler to more than a quarter of Earth.
1993: Forty nations were systematically overthrown by a group of young supermen.
The mid-1990s: The Eugenics Wars.
1996: Eighty-five genetically engineered men and women left Earth on the USS Botany Bay. Khan and seventy-two others survived over two centuries in space until found by the USS Enterprise.
2018: Sleeper ships were no longer used because space travel could be achieved without putting the crew into suspended animation.

In 2002, Mark Mosert's article "Useless Eaters: Disability as Genocidal Marker in Nazi Germany" outlined the history of eugenics, euthanasia and genocide among people with disabilities. In the 1930s, the Nazis created a positive eugenics program known as the Lebensborn program. The program provided sanctuary to unmarried German women with Aryan characteristics who were impregnated by Nazi officers. In the 1940s, the Nazis took eugenics a step further, and engaged in the large-scale murder of inferior races, people with cognitive, psychiatric, and/or physical disabilities, as well as Jews, Gays, and Gypsies (who they equated with prostitutes and were therefore inferior). After all, from the Nazi viewpoint, the best way to prevent people from having children is to kill them. According to Mosert, the German eugenics program began with the euthanasia of infants born with disabilities. The Nazis also sought to create a *master race* by selective breeding of people with Aryan characteristics (light hair and eye color.)

In "Patterns of Force" (1968, TOS; 2:21), the USS Enterprise arrives at the planet Ekos where the inhabitants are now calling themselves Nazis and are committing genocide against those from the nearby planet Zeon. Eugenics jargon is presented in this brief exchange between two Ekosians who are examining Mr. Spock:

DARAS: The Deputy Fuhrer's an authority on the genetics of racial purity. How would you classify this one?

MELAKON: Very difficult. Note the sinister eyes and the malformed ears. Definitely an inferior race.

[Dialogue Omitted]

MELAKON: Note the low forehead, denoting stupidity... the dull look of a trapped animal. You may take him now for interrogation, but I want the body saved for the Cultural Museum. He'll make an interesting display.

Although the episode is more about the dangers of absolute power than eugenics, this vignette illustrates the significant racism inherent in eugenics. The use of facial features to infer intelligence was derived from the work of men considered scientists such as Samuel George Morton (1799–1851), Louis Agassiz (1807–1873), and Paul Broca (1824–1880), who sought to find racial differences in intelligence. The arguments for and against the hypothesis linking race and intelligence continued even into the twentieth century through the works of Stephen Jay Gould (1941 – 2002), Richard Herrnstein (1930 – 1994), and Charles Murray (1943-).

More than twenty years after the Nazi planet episode aired, "The Masterpiece Society" (1992, TNG 5:13) depicted a less destructive side of the Human eugenics philosophy, albeit still with an obvious bias against it. The setting is created by Captain Picard's voice-over:

> PICARD: Captain's log, stardate 45470.1. The Enterprise has been diverted to the Moab sector to track a stellar core fragment of a disintegrated neutron star. Our science teams have been asked to monitor the planetary disruptions it may cause.

Data does what Data loves to do—he scans for lifeforms and discovers an inhabited biosphere on a planet previously thought to be uninhabited. More importantly, the planet is inhabited by Humans. At first, Captain Picard's traditional greetings are rudely ignored. However, when Picard issues a dire warning about the unlikelihood of the colony's survival, their leader, Aaron Conor, responds. Conor agrees to allow a delegation from the USS Enterprise to beam down and see if they can save the day and the biosphere. Martin Benbeck is the interpreter of the colony's founders' intentions and vocally disagrees with his leader's decision:

> MARTIN: It would be suicide to evacuate. It would destroy everything we've worked for two centuries to accomplish.
> CONOR: You see—this is an engineered society.
> RIKER: Engineered?
> CONOR: Genetically engineered. Our ancestors came from Earth to develop a perfect society. They believed that through controlled procreation, they could create people without flaws and those people would build a paradise.
> TROI: All of you have been selectively bred? Your DNA patterns chosen?
> CONOR: Eight generations of us.
> BENBECK: We have immeasurably extended the potential of humanity, physically, psychologically. We have evolved beyond—beyond—
> LA FORGE: —Beyond us.
> BENBECK: Frankly, yes. No one in this society would be blind, for example. No offense intended.
> LA FORGE: I can see you just fine, sir.

BENBECK: Yes. Well, my point was just—

CONOR: Thank you, Martin. Perhaps you've also made it clear there are still a few imperfections we're working on.

[Dialogue Omitted]

CONOR: ...My entire psychological makeup tells me that I was born to lead. I am exactly what I would choose to be. Think of it another way. Are there still people in your society who have not discovered who they really are, or what they were meant to do with their lives? They may be in the wrong job, they may be writing bad poetry. Or worse yet, they may be great poets working as laborers, never to be discovered. That does not happen here. It is, for us, an ideal existence. We will not give it up easily.

RED ALERT!
Ability, personal desires, and even talents
are all genetically determined.

Although Picard doesn't embrace eugenics, his argument against the overly predetermined nature of this society doesn't challenge its basic premise: that genetics alone determine an individual's destiny. This way of thinking leaves no role for experience or the environment in shaping a person.

PICARD: They've managed to turn a dubious scientific endeavor into dogma.

TROI: You don't approve of genetic engineering.

PICARD: It was a bad idea whose time is long past.

TROI: They seem to have made it succeed.

PICARD: They've given away their humanity with this genetic manipulation. Many of the qualities that they breed out—the uncertainty, the self-discovery, the unknown—those are many of the qualities that make life worth living. Well, at least to me. I wouldn't want to live knowing that my future was written, that my boundaries had been already set, would you?

Chief Engineer Geordi La Forge goes beyond the argument that eugenics makes life boring to the personal observation that in their society, he wouldn't have been allowed to exist. While trying to save the colony, La Forge works with their scientist, Hannah Bates, who is surprised by La Forge's opaque eyes when he removes his VISOR.

> BATES: Were you always blind?
> LA FORGE: I'm sorry. I probably shocked the hell out of you, didn't I?
> BATES: No.
> LA FORGE: I'll put it back on.
> BATES: Don't. I'm sorry. I didn't mean to embarrass you.
> LA FORGE: I've never been embarrassed by this, Hannah. Never. I was born blind. I've always been this way.
> BATES: May I see it? Your VISOR?
> LA FORGE: Sure. So, I guess if I had been conceived on your world, I wouldn't even be here now, would I?
> BATES: No. [Hannah Bates' discomfort is evident on her face and in her body language.]
> LA FORGE: No, I'd've been terminated as a fertilized cell.
> BATES: It was the wish of our founders that no one had to suffer a life with disabilities.
> LA FORGE: Who gave them the right to decide whether or not I should be here? Whether or not I might have something to contribute?

As La Forge and Bates exchange several lines of beloved *Star Trek* technobabble, he realizes that the solution to protecting the colony from the danger posed by the stellar core fragment can be solved using his VISOR technology. The irony is well defined.

> LA FORGE: Sure—with a few modifications. Oh, that's perfect.
> BATES: What?
> LA FORGE: If the answer to all of this is in a VISOR created for a blind man who never would have existed in your society. No offense intended.

Meanwhile, Troi and Conor are strongly attracted to each other. The attraction may be the result of their shared taste in dreadful solid-colored clothes. Apparently the founders of the colony failed to find a breeder with any fashion sense to include in their eugenics program. Troi realizes that she can have no future with Conor and she provides him with a strong dose of reality.

> TROI: I could fall in love with you so easily, but we both know the end of that story, don't we? How would Martin feel about introducing half-Betazoid DNA into the genetic balance?

After the disaster with the stellar core fragment is averted, Bates lies to Conor about cracks in the biosphere because she wants to leave the colony. When La Forge confronts Bates about her deception, she complains she no longer feels challenged because nothing unpredictable ever happens. She tells La Forge genetic engineering has led to monotony rather than the utopia their founders envisioned (apparently this extends beyond their sense of fashion).

> BATES: I was born to be one of the best scientific minds of my generation, and in the past five days I have encountered technology that I have barely imagined. And I've got to ask myself, if we're so brilliant how come we didn't invent any of these things?
> LA FORGE: Well, maybe necessity really is the mother of invention. You never really look for something until you need it.
> BATES: But all my needs have been anticipated and planned for before I'm even born. All of us in this colony have been living in the dark ages. It's like we're victims of a two-hundred-year-old joke. Until you came, we could only see to the wall of our biosphere. Suddenly our eyes have been opened to the infinite possibilities.

INCOMING MESSAGE:
It is our diversity and adversity
which makes us truly Human.

The list of accomplishments of people born with disabilities spans all roles in life. Stevie Wonder, who, like La Forge, was born blind, is a popular musician. President Theodore Roosevelt, who, like Conor, was a leader, was born with epilepsy, a vision impairment, and asthma. "The Masterpiece Society" clearly portrays the importance of allowing everyone to find their own way to contribute to the world. During my interview with James Kahn, one of the writers of "The Masterpiece Society," he related this episode to the law of unintended consequences. He said one of the intentional messages of the episode was, "…you think you are doing something really right, for good reasons, and things happen that you just can't anticipate."

This isn't to say that there's no place for genetic counseling in family planning. In genetic counseling, couples are advised how much they risk transmitting genetic disorders such as Tay-Sachs disease or sickle cell anemia (among others) to their child. Risks are usually described in terms of percentages because a risk isn't a certainty.

Not every disability is apparent to others. In 2008, the US Congress passed the *Genetic Information Nondiscrimination Act* which was designed to prohibit the use of genetic information in health insurance and employment. The Act prohibits group health plans and health insurers from denying coverage or charging people higher insurance premiums based solely on a genetic predisposition to developing a disease in the future. The legislation also bars employers from using a person's genetic information when making hiring, firing, job placement, or promotion decisions. The Act provides similar protections on a federal level to various state laws dating back to the 1980s. People with disabilities, whose impairments are not evident to others, are therefore free to make choices about whether or not to reveal their disability and to whom.

While selective breeding takes multiple generations to achieve, gene therapy has the potential to increase the speed at which the dual goals of eliminating undesirable traits by *gene cleansing* and creating superior Humans could be realized, at least on *Star Trek*. Anyway, that's how it's supposed to work. But on *Star Trek*, science rarely works the way it's supposed to—much like the food replicators and transporters.

Gene Therapy

When DNA is manipulated to treat a genetically-based disorder, the procedure is referred to as *gene therapy*. The idea is to identify the genes which cause diseases such as cystic fibrosis, hemophilia, muscular dystrophy, or sickle cell anemia. Then, replace the genes carrying the risky DNA with genes lacking those markers in the person's cells. Gene therapy would therefore be a means of completely preventing such diseases and the disabilities they cause. The problem is that the same technology used to address disorders could also potentially be used to create superior Humans.

Gene therapy is central to the personal and medical history of Dr. Julian Bashir, Chief Medical Officer on *Star Trek: Deep Space Nine*, and is the subject for the episode "Doctor Bashir, I Presume" (1997, DS9; 5:16). For five seasons Dr. Bashir has played spy-sleuth as he befriends Garak the Cardassian tailor, who turns out to be a former spy. Bashir is a pain in the posterior to, and then eventually best friends with, chief of engineering, Miles O'Brien. But Dr. Bashir has a dirty little secret: as a child, he was *genetically enhanced* in what the writers called "DNA resequencing."

When Dr. Zimmerman (who strongly resembles The Doctor on *Star Trek: Voyager*) arrives on Deep Space Nine, he announces that Dr. Bashir is going to be his model for a "long term medical holographic" program. Against the wishes of Dr. Bashir, Dr. Zimmerman invites Bashir's parents, Richard and Amsha Bashir, to the station for an interview. (I guess Dr. Zimmerman doesn't believe in autonomy outside of medicine.) Dr. Bashir isn't happy to see his parents because he worries his shameful secret will be exposed.

After an argument with his parents, Dr. Bashir leaves their quarters in a huff. His parents go to sickbay to assure him that they'll be careful while talking with Dr. Zimmerman.

RICHARD: And just so there's no misunderstanding, I give you my word that at no time in our interview with Dr. Zimmerman will we ever mention or even hint at the fact that you were genetically enhanced as a child.

AMSHA: Jules, you can trust us. Your father and I have kept the secret of your DNA resequencing for almost twenty-five years and we're not going to let it out now.

RICHARD: But I would just add that, despite what the authorities would like us to believe, genetic engineering is nothing to be ashamed of. You're not any less human than anyone else. In fact, you're a little more.

INCOMING MESSAGE:
Laws forbidding certain scientific procedures
won't stop them from being used.

Unfortunately for Dr. Bashir, his parents were talking to the *holographic* Dr. Bashir and Dr. Zimmerman and Chief O'Brien overheard the entire conversation.

O'BRIEN: Julian, Zimmerman is going to file a report saying that Dr. Bashir is unsuitable for computer modeling because of his suspected genetically enhanced background. Do you know what's going to happen when that report gets back to Starfleet Medical?

BASHIR: There's going to be a formal investigation which will lead to my eventual dismissal from the service.

O'BRIEN: Then it's true? You're—

BASHIR: The word you're looking for is unnatural, meaning not from nature. Freak or monster would also be acceptable. I was six. Small for my age. A bit awkward physically. Not very bright. In the first grade, while the other children were learning how to read and write and use the computer, I was still trying to tell a dog from a cat, a tree from a house. I didn't really understand what was happening. I knew that I wasn't doing as well as my classmates. There were so many concepts that they took for granted that I couldn't begin to master and I didn't know why. All I knew was that I was a great disappointment to my parents. I don't remember when they made the decision, but just before my seventh birthday we left Earth for Adigeon Prime. At first, I remember being really excited at seeing all the aliens in the hospital. Then they gave me a room and began the treatments, and my entire world began to change.

O'BRIEN: What were the treatments? Some kind of DNA recoding?

BASHIR: The technical term is "accelerated critical neural pathway formation." Over the course of the next two months, my genetic structure was manipulated to accelerate the growth of neuronal networks in my cerebral cortex, and a whole new Julian Bashir was born.

O'BRIEN: In what way did they change you?

BASHIR: Well, my mental abilities were the top priority, of course. My IQ jumped five points a day for over two weeks. Followed by improvements in my hand-eye coordination, stamina, vision, reflexes, weight, height—In the end, everything but my name was altered in some way. When we returned to Earth, we even moved to a different city, I was enrolled in a new school using falsified records my parents obtained somewhere. Instead of being the slowest learner, I was the star pupil.

O'BRIEN: And no one ever suspected?

BASHIR: Oh, there's no stigma attached to success, Chief. After the treatments, I never looked back. But the truth is I'm a fraud.

O'BRIEN: You're not a fraud. I don't care what enhancements your parents may have had done. Genetic recoding can't give you ambition, or a personality, or compassion, or any of the things that make a person truly human.

BASHIR: Starfleet Medical won't see it that way. DNA resequencing for any reason other than repairing serious birth defects is illegal. Any genetically enhanced human being is barred from serving in Starfleet or practicing medicine.

O'BRIEN: I don't think there's been a case dealing with any of this in a hundred years. You can't be sure how they'll react.

BASHIR: Oh, I am sure. Once the truth comes out I'll be cashiered from the service. It's that simple.

INCOMING MESSAGE:
Gene therapy could become source of prejudice and discrimination.
Chief O'Brien had never heard of Khan Noonien Singh.

My favorite line in the scene is "…there's no stigma attached to success." It's a commentary on the current competitive nature in our school system, which has led to some extreme parenting where children are expected to be overachievers. The terms "soccer moms" and "tiger moms" easily come to mind. It's not hard to believe that if genetic resequencing was easily available, ambitious parents would take advantage of it. It's also not hard to imagine that if genetic resequencing could remedy developmental delays, schools would put pressure on the parents to *fix* their children who are in special education. When Bashir tells his parents about the upcoming investigation, his anger at them for what was done is brought to light. The family discusses, perhaps for the first time, his parents' rationale for their decision.

RICHARD: You were falling behind.

BASHIR: I was six years old. You decided I was a failure in the first grade.

RICHARD: You don't understand, Jules. You never did.

BASHIR: No, you don't understand. I stopped calling myself Jules when I was fifteen and I'd found out what you'd done to me. I'm Julian.

RICHARD: What difference does that make?

BASHIR: It makes every difference, because I'm different! Can't you see that? Jules Bashir died in that hospital because you couldn't live with the shame of having a son who didn't measure up!

RICHARD: That's not true! We were never ashamed of you. Never.

BASHIR: I'm sorry, mother, but the truth is—

RICHARD: You don't know. You've never had a child. You don't know what it's like to watch your son. To watch him fall a little further behind every day. You know he's trying, but something's holding him back. You don't know what it's like to stay up every night worrying that maybe it's your fault. Maybe you did something wrong during the pregnancy, maybe you weren't careful enough, or maybe there's something wrong with you. Maybe you passed on a genetic defect without even knowing it.

For me this family scene is heartbreaking with those raw emotions of shame, guilt, and anger. I easily identified with Amsha because I often wondered, after the death of my son, whether or not I, too, had done something wrong during my pregnancy, or if I had a genetic defect which led to his condition.

At the end of the episode a solution is reached with Admiral Bennett which allows Dr. Bashir to remain in Starfleet and to practice medicine. His father agrees to a two-year prison sentence for breaking the law.

BASHIR: Two years? Isn't that a bit harsh?

BENNETT: I don't think so. Two hundred years ago we tried to improve the species through DNA resequencing, and what did we get for our trouble? The Eugenics Wars. For every Julian Bashir that can be created, there's a Khan Singh waiting in the wings. A superhuman whose ambition and thirst for power have been enhanced along with his intellect. The law against genetic engineering provides a firewall against such men and it's my job to keep that firewall intact.

I've made my offer. Do you accept?

RICHARD: Yes.

RED ALERT!

Eugenics is not the same thing as DNA resequencing.

In "Statistical Probabilities" (1997, DS9 6:9), we learn more about the prohibition on genetic manipulation as Bashir attempts to help a group of genetically enhanced, albeit eccentric, Humans who have been living at the Institute because of their inability to live in regular society. Jack, Lauren, Sarina, and Patrick are brought to the station by their physician, Dr. Loews.

BASHIR: They don't put people away for being genetically engineered.

JACK: No, no, no, no they just won't let us do anything that's worth doing. No, no. They are afraid that people like us are going to take over.

BASHIR: It happened before. People like us *did* try and take over.

JACK: Oh, no, no. I knew you were going to do that. I knew you were going to trot out the Eugenics Wars.

BASHIR: I'm not trotting anything out. All I'm saying is there's a reason we've been barred from certain professions. But that doesn't mean we can't be productive members of society.

JACK: Here it comes: the "We Can Still Contribute" speech. No. No, no, no, no. I will not forget what was done to me. I will not be part of a society that put me away for being too smart. No, no!

Although each has been genetically enhanced, and their intelligence would probably make someone from Mensa look stupid, each also has behaviors which limit their ability to live outside the Institute. Jack talks as if he is manic (or as if he had three too many cups of espresso), and even intentionally hurts Dr. Loews when he gets angry with her. Sarina remains silent and appears nearly catatonic. It's unclear what Lauren's limitations are, but her behavior is overly sexual when she interacts with men. Patrick is nearly childlike, paranoid, and easily manipulated by others—especially Jack.

Bashir joins his friends at dinner that evening and, throwing doctor-patient confidentiality out the airlock, discusses the arrival of his four patients, and his sympathy toward their situation.

BASHIR: All I kept thinking was, "there but for the grace of God go I."

DAX: How do you mean?

BASHIR: My parents managed to find a decent doctor to perform the DNA resequencing on me. These four weren't so lucky. They all suffered unintended side effects. By the time they were five or six, their parents were forced to come forward and admit that they'd broken the law so that their children could get treatment.

SISKO: Hmm. Perhaps they waited too long.

BASHIR: There was nothing the doctors at the Institute could do for them. These cases are so rare there's no standard treatment.

KIRA: I can't imagine it was a very stimulating environment for them.

BASHIR: That's what Dr. Loews thought when she first came to the Institute. She got permission to separate them from the other residents so that she could work with them.

ODO: Why did she bring them here?

BASHIR: She thought they might respond to meeting someone like them. Who was living a normal life. She was also hoping that one day they might be able to live on their own and be productive.

O'BRIEN: Well, let's hope they don't become *too* productive. Might make the rest of us look bad.

WORF: It is not a laughing matter. If people like them are allowed to compete freely, then parents would feel pressured to have their children enhanced so that they could keep up.

ODO: That's precisely what prompted the ban on DNA resequencing in the first place.

Using their amazing intelligence, the group from the Institute easily deduces the political situation on Cardassia and the goals of the Dominion in the so-called peace negotiations. The four patients further analyze the relative strengths and weaknesses between the

Dominion and the Federation and reach the conclusion, based on statistical probabilities, that the Federation will lose the war along with the lives of 900 billion people. Jack therefore decides it's better to give the Dominion the Federation's classified deployment plans, to reduce the number of lives lost in the conflict. Bashir points out that Jack's arrogance contributes to the fear people have of genetically engineered Humans.

> BASHIR: Wait a minute! It's one thing for us to try and avert a war, but it's quite another for us to take it on ourselves to trigger an invasion that's going to get a lot of people killed. It's not our place to decide who lives and who dies. We're not gods.
>
> JACK: Maybe not, but we're the next best thing.
>
> BASHIR: Can you hear yourself? That's precisely the kind of thinking that makes people afraid of us.

Feeling Khan-like superiority, Jack, Lauren, and Patrick tie up Bashir so they can proceed with their treasonous plans. (Well, they were only trying to contribute to society like Dr. Bashir told them they could.) Bashir thwarts the plan after he convinces Sarina, who has been left behind, to untie him. In the end, Bashir prevents the genetically enhanced Humans from committing treason. He does this in part because when Jack, Lauren, and Patrick left Sarina behind, they failed to consider how her presence could alter their plans. Bashir points out that even the most minor occurrences may cast doubt on statistical probabilities:

> BASHIR: Maybe our projections were wrong.
>
> JACK: How can you say that? We factored in every contingency, every variable. The equations don't lie. You. [Jack takes computer pads (PADDs) from Sarina.] You ruined everything. [He slams the PADDs down.]
>
> BASHIR: What do you make of that, Jack? Why didn't you anticipate that? Why didn't you factor her into your equation? [Bashir gestures toward Sarina.]
>
> BASHIR: Because you thought you knew everything, but you didn't even know what was going to happen in this room. One person derailed your plans.

One person changed the course of history. [Bashir stands next to Sarina, then turns towards Jack.] Now, I don't know about you, but that makes me think that maybe, just maybe, things may not turn out the way we thought.

Star Trek's message of hope is preserved in this episode. Statistics are only probabilities; they aren't fate. Similarly, genetic enhancements aren't absolute predictors of behavior, personality, or achievement. Genetic engineering may create people with exceptional talents, but that doesn't mean they'll be perfect Human beings. Furthermore, it's very likely that in real life, gene therapy may have unintended consequences. Although the Human Genome project has mapped the majority of our DNA, interactions between genes aren't fully understood. When I consider the number of times that Dr. Bashir violates medical ethics, I can't help but wonder if his improved eye-hand coordination cost him his sense of morality. The positive and negative implications of gene therapy for people with disabilities must be balanced with the unknown risks.

In 1990, the first FDA-approved Human gene therapy experiment in the United States occurred when four-year-old Ashanti DeSilva was treated for Adenosine deaminase deficiency. In most cases, ADA-SCID (as it's often referred to) causes premature death. At last report, (2013) DeSilva is a healthy young woman. The treatment is still experimental and highly risky. After over seventeen-thousand gene therapy attempts, there have been few successes and many have failed to correct the disease being treated. Some have caused other diseases, and tragically, some have resulted in patient deaths.

Yet, improvements in gene therapy continue to be documented. At the American Society of Hematology Annual Meeting and Exposition in January 2014, researchers Carl June and David Porter announced the results of their targeted cellular therapy where twenty-six of fifty-nine lymphocytic leukemia patients, mostly children, are now cancer-free.

Gene therapy is in clinical trials as a treatment for patients with heart failure. The report by Roger Hajjar at Mt. Sinai suggests that the gene therapy may help hearts damaged by failure heal themselves. Patients who received the gene therapy experienced eighty percent fewer cardiovascular events than those who received a placebo. As medical advances in gene therapy continue, it will bring us closer to the line dividing life-saving treatments and genetic enhancements.

Germline Gene Therapy

When manipulation of the genes occurs before birth, the procedure is no longer called gene therapy but *germline gene therapy*. Germline gene therapy may seem like science fiction, but in fact the future isn't so far away. The genetics technology called germline gene therapy in the U.S. is called *inheritable genetic modification* (IGM) in the United Kingdom. According to the U.K. Center for Genetics and Society this technology:

> ...means changing the genes passed on to future generations. The genetic changes would be made in eggs, sperm, or early embryos; modified genes would appear not only in the person who developed from the gamete or embryo, but also in all succeeding generations. IGM has not been tried in humans. It would be by far the most consequential type of genetic modification as it would open the door to irreversibly altering the human species.

In the *Star Trek* universe, germline gene therapy is depicted more than once. Using episodes from two different *Star Trek* series, I'll illustrate the purported dangers and benefits of this form of genetic engineering. The progression from eugenics to germline gene therapy is portrayed in a series of three sequential episodes from the *Star Trek: Enterprise* series: "Borderland" (2004, ENT; 4:5), "Cold Station 12" (2004, ENT; 4:6), and "The Augments" (2004, ENT; 4:7). Rather than describing each action-packed episode, I'll summarize the story as it pertains to germline gene therapy.

After the Eugenics Wars in the mid-1990s, over eighteen-hundred embryos selectively bred for superior characteristics were frozen and stored on a medical research station in space. Over a century later, Arik Soong (who strongly resembles Data, Lore, B-4, and Dr. Noonien Soong on *Star Trek: The Next Generation*) became the senior medical director of Cold Station 12, the medical storage facility from which he stole nineteen of the embryos. For those keeping track of the timeline, this was about a century before Captain Kirk encountered Khan. Theoretically these embryos are the sisters and brothers of those on the Botany Bay. Soong took the embryos to an unnamed planet in the Trialas system and began raising the resulting children. The Humans from these genetically engineered embryos were referred to as "Augments" and they called Soong "Father." Soong was captured by Earth forces ten years later, but refused to tell anyone what happened to the embryos.

Approximately ten years after Soong's imprisonment, the Augments leave their home planet in a trail of violence. The USS Enterprise goes after the Augments with Dr. Soong on board and under guard. Soong tries to convince Captain Archer the Augments are an improvement in mankind in "Borderland" (2004, ENT; 4:5):

SOONG: They're the future. They're stronger, smarter, free from sickness, with life spans twice as long as our own. You, more than anyone, should appreciate what this means.

ARCHER: Why me?

SOONG: Your father suffered from Clarke's Disease. His final years were marked with extreme pain.

ARCHER: My father has nothing to do with this.

SOONG: He didn't need to suffer. Genetic engineering could've cured him. Those who want to suppress my Augments are the same ones who condemned your father to death. Turn the ship around, Captain. Go home. Leave them alone.

The story takes on a Cain and Abel aspect between two of the Augments. Raakin was identified as the leader of the Augments by Soong, but Malik kills Raakin out of ambition. Malik frees Soong from the USS Enterprise, and their mission becomes one of stealing the other embryos and creating a world where the Augments will reign as superior beings.

When Soong discovers that Malik has killed Raakin, he's upset. For the first time, Soong begins to question what will happen when the remaining embryos are incubated to maturity. He decides to take proactive measures in "The Augments" (2004, ENT; 4:7).

MALIK: How are the embryos?

SOONG: I'll be ready to incubate the first of them in a few hours.

MALIK: You're manipulating its DNA.

SOONG: These base pairs sequences regulate the neurotransmitter levels in their brain. If I can modify them, aggression and violent behavior will be removed.

MALIK: You're changing its personality.

SOONG: I'm correcting a defect in its genome. Genetic engineering was in its infancy when you were created. They weren't able to repair all the mistakes.

MALIK: Did you fix these mistakes in the rest of us?

SOONG: I didn't know how until recently.

MALIK: What right do you have to tamper with their genome?

SOONG: Trust me. I know what I'm doing—

MALIK: You don't know that this is a defect. Maybe this is the way our creators wanted us to be.

RED ALERT!
Genetic engineering is much like "playing God."

It is in this scene that the episode moves from eugenics to germline gene therapy. The selective breeding program (eugenics) couldn't reverse all flaws in the genome. In other words, if one parent is selected based on exceptional athletic ability, it's impossible to isolate out the competitive personality or even bloodthirsty aggression that might also be characteristic in that parent. But while in prison, Soong studies genetics. He believes he's now able to identify individual genes that carry less desirable traits and replace them with genes bearing more desirable traits.

In the final battle, all of the Augments are killed when Malik destroys their ship to avoid being captured. As Soong is returned to prison, he decides to switch his focus to cybernetics. Given his name (and the actor who plays him) it's apparent that we're to believe he's an ancestor of Data's creator, Dr. Noonien Soong.

Captain Archer reflects that while Denobulans have used genetic engineering to treat diseases, they've never suffered a crisis from the misuse of the science. But Humans don't appear to be able to avoid the slippery slope.

ARCHER: None of that would have mattered in the end. It's in their nature. They were engineered to be this way. Superior ability breeds superior ambition. One of their creators wrote that. He was murdered by an Augment.

RED ALERT!
Ambition is always accompanied by violence.

Since these *Star Trek: Enterprise* episodes are a prequel to "Space Seed," the expression "superior ability breeds superior ambition" is a future echo.

The positive application of germline gene therapy is portrayed on *Voyager* in "Lineage" (2001, VOY 7:12). "Lineage" makes clear that, as on Denobula, the Federation's prohibition against genetic manipulation applies only to enhancements and not medical treatments to correct genetic disorders. The episode begins when The Doctor reveals to B'Elanna Torres and Tom Paris that they're expecting a baby. Hours after the initial examination, The Doctor contacts the still discombobulated couple with information about a genetic problem in the fetus. Torres isn't surprised to hear that her baby has inherited the same curvature of the spine that she had surgically repaired as a baby, but new options are now available.

THE DOCTOR: Fortunately, we've advanced beyond that. Genetic modification is the treatment of choice.

PARIS: If you can project an image of the spine, can you use the genetic data to show us the whole baby?

THE DOCTOR: I could. It would only be an approximation.

PARIS: Let's take a look.

TORRES: I don't know.

PARIS: Oh, come on. Aren't you curious?

TORRES: Okay.

[The Doctor projects in 3D a visual representation of how the baby will appear when she is born.]

PARIS: Oh, she's beautiful.

TORRES: Forehead ridges. [Torres' voice sounds disappointed.]

THE DOCTOR: Yes.

TORRES: But she's only one-quarter Klingon.

THE DOCTOR: Klingon traits remain dominant for several generations, even with a single ancestor.

PARIS: She looks just like her mother.

While Paris is glowing like a dilithium crystal at high warp, Torres is less enamored with the image of her unborn baby. She'd hoped any child wouldn't inherit her Klingon forehead ridges. During the episode, Torres has flashbacks to a camping trip she took with her father and cousins. Although she tells Tom that she and her father were close, the memories are painful for Torres. She feels she never fit in with the Human side of her family because of her half-Klingon lineage.

Torres becomes focused on not allowing her daughter to suffer the same feelings of isolation and discrimination. So, she visits the holodeck and plays around with various gene sequences until she gets a baby without Klingon forehead ridges. While I understand Torres is an engineer, it's not clear how she became a genetic engineer when she usually works on warp core engines.... But I digress. Torres campaigns to have The Doctor remove all Klingon aspects of her daughter's DNA.

THE DOCTOR: There's no valid medical reason to do what you're proposing.

[Dialogue Omitted]

THE DOCTOR: Why tamper with biological systems that evolved over eons?

TORRES: Like curvature of the spine?

THE DOCTOR: If I make these changes, it'll affect her appearance.

TORRES: I'm aware of that.

THE DOCTOR: Are you also aware that some of these genes influence behavior? Personality?

TORRES: None of that's as important as her health.

THE DOCTOR: What does Tom think about all this?

TORRES: I wanted to see what you thought first.

THE DOCTOR: As you can see, I'm very dubious.

TORRES: Look, I've done statistical analyses, epidemiology. At least review my work.

THE DOCTOR: All right, I'll look at it, but in the meantime I suggest you have a talk with your husband.

INCOMING MESSAGE:
Genes that control one aspect of a person's makeup
may also control other aspects as well.

Paris doesn't agree with his wife's desire to alter the genetic makeup of their baby. He is as vocal and stubborn in his views as Torres is in hers.

PARIS: Absolutely not!

TORRES: This is our child's health we're talking about!

PARIS: It's more than that. You want to change who she is, her individuality, her—You don't want her to be Klingon. That's what this is really about, isn't it? You're trying to protect her from being Klingon because you had a rough time when you were a kid.

TORRES: I was treated like a monster.

PARIS: That isn't going to happen to our daughter. Everyone on Voyager will accept her for who she really is.

TORRES: That's easy for you to say. You're human.

PARIS: Meaning what, exactly?

TORRES: Meaning you don't understand what it's like.

PARIS: Okay then, tell me.

TORRES: When the people around you are all one way and you're not, you can't help feeling like there's something wrong with you.

PARIS: Voyager isn't just one way. We've got Bajorans, Vulcans, a Talaxian.

TORRES: And one hundred and forty humans.

PARIS: Our daughter is going to have a mixed heritage just like her mother. It's something you'll have in common. Something she should be proud of. Why destroy that?

TORRES: I'm not destroying anything. Gene resequencing isn't a weapon—it's a tool—like a hyperspanner.

PARIS: She's not a machine; she's our daughter.

"Lineage" is a wonderful illustration of one of the potential ethical concerns with germline gene therapy—that of creating *designer babies*. James Kahn, who wrote "Lineage," talked about the origins of the episode where designer babies were part of the message. He recalled how he'd recently seen some 3-D ultrasounds and was impressed with the details they presented. Owing to his medical background, Kahn understood that in utero procedures could present ethical dilemmas. Kahn felt that in utero surgery to repair heart defects was juxtaposed with the Chinese practice of aborting female embryos. Aborting female embryos was one of the unintended consequences of the one-child policy. While writing the episode, Kahn reflected that only "intelligent, rich" men were usually selected as sperm donors, and the promise of elitist genes wasn't far from the problem of designer babies.

At the same time, there was a second message of self-acceptance in the episode that came from the writer's own childhood experience. He said he was looking not only at the "science fiction angle, but also…where B'Elanna was coming from with her…self-hatred of being a Klingon in a way." Kahn related it to being a Jewish child who grew up in a "kind of reactionary neighborhood" which led him to grow up with "Jewish shame." He identified with "being identified as a certain thing, which makes people look down on you in a certain way, and being ashamed of that, and then finally learning how to own that."

Kahn added that, as a physician, he believes it's ethical to use genetic engineering to cure debilitating disorders, such as cystic fibrosis, which would allow the person to live without the limitations and pain associated with these conditions.

Germline gene therapy has been used with grains such as corn and wheat. These foods have been modified in order to increase harvest yields by creating plants that are resistant to diseases and insect infestations. Don't forget the Federation's claim to Sherman's planet was considered stronger in "The Trouble with Tribbles" (1968, TOS; 2:15) because the Enterprise guarded the genetically engineered wheat known as "quadrotriticale."

One unique aspect of germline gene therapy is that this technique prevents a genetically transmitted condition from being handed down to subsequent generations. At the time I'm writing this book, the United Kingdom is debating approval of this form of genetic engineering to permit mitochondrial DNA replacement. The argument in favor of germline gene therapy is that it would give mothers at risk of mitochondrial disease the chance of having a healthy child who would no longer carry the disease. Currently, their best option is egg donation, which results in a baby who isn't genetically related to the mother. The proposed technique involves using the egg of the carrier mother and replacing her genetic markers for disease with healthy DNA from the egg of a donor mother. The arguments against the technique include the eventual use of the science to create designer babies, as well as a fear of unintended side effects. Does conferring one desirable trait create other, more harmful consequences? In addition, there could be unintended social and legal consequences of creating a baby from three people.

While it's scientifically possible for genetic engineering to prevent genetic disorders from being passed on to future generations, we don't know what other traits may be eliminated from the Human race. The emphasis on genetic engineering also conveys the message that genes solely determine a person's behavior or destiny without giving any credit to opportunities or choices.

In the episodes I've discussed so far, the role of the environment or individual choice is completely omitted from the equation. Three separate Jean-Luc Picard stories, which provide a glimpse of four different Picards illustrate that the power of *nurture* is every bit as important as that of *nature* in determining who a person becomes.

Nature Versus Nurture

In the 2002 movie "Star Trek: Nemesis," we meet two Jean-Luc Picards—the Captain Picard we've come to know and love, and his evil clone, Shinzon. (Numbering the Picards chronologically, Shinzon is Picard version 4.0). Picard and Shinzon are genetically identical, but they have led very different lives. Shinzon is as Human as Picard, but he was raised by Romulans and later exiled to be slave labor on Remus. Shinzon wants revenge on the Romulans and he wants to free the Remans.

> SHINZON: ...You don't trust me.
> PICARD: I have no reason to.
> SHINZON: You have every reason. If you had lived my life and experienced the suffering of my people, you'd be standing where I am.
> PICARD: If you had lived my life you would understand my responsibility to the Federation. I cannot allow my personal feelings to unduly influence my decisions.

INCOMING MESSAGE:
Our experiences and our environment are powerful factors
in the type of person we become.

In spite of their identical genetic makeup, Picard and Shinzon share very few personality characteristics. Picard struggles to understand how someone who's genetically identical to him could behave so differently. Data has no trouble identifying the central issues as he compares himself to the recently discovered pre-Data android named "B-4" (yes, one of the worst puns, even on *Star Trek*).

> PICARD: He said he's a mirror.
> DATA: Of you, sir?
> PICARD: Yes.
> DATA: I do not agree. Although you share the same genetic structure, the events of your life have created a unique individual.
> PICARD: If I had lived his life, is it possible I would have rejected my humanity?
> DATA: The B-4 is physically identical to me, although his neural pathways are not as advanced. But even if they were, he would not be me.
> PICARD: How can you be sure?
> DATA: I aspire, sir, to be better than I am. B-4 does not. Nor does Shinzon.

And there, in a nutshell, is the nurture argument: "the events of your life have created a unique individual."

Picard continues to struggle with the evil that pervades Shinzon's heart because he's never experienced it. He tries to appeal to Shinzon not to release the weapon that will wipe out an entire planet, Earth.

> PICARD: It can be the future. Buried deep within you, beneath all the years of pain and anger there is something that has never been nurtured. The potential to make yourself a better man, and that is what it is to be human. To make yourself more than you are—Oh yes, I know you—There was a time you looked at the stars and dreamed of what might be.
> SHINZON: Childish dreams, Captain, lost in the dilithium mines of Remus. I am what you see now.
> PICARD: I see more than that. I see what you could be—The man who is Shinzon of Remus and Jean-Luc Picard could never exterminate the population of an entire planet! He is better than that!
> SHINZON: He's what his life has made him!
> PICARD: And what will he do with that life? Waste it in a blaze of hatred? There is a better way.

SHINZON: It's too late.

PICARD: Never! Never! You still have a choice! Make the right one now!

SHINZON: I can't—fight what I am!

PICARD: Yes you can!

SHINZON: I'll show you my true nature. Our nature. And as Earth dies, remember that I will always, forever, be Shinzon of Remus! And my voice shall echo through time long after yours has faded to a dim memory.

In the end, Picard stands on Shinzon's ship, shocked by the realization that Shinzon's weapon is about to destroy himself, the Enterprise, and Earth. Data arrives and transports the captain back to the Enterprise. In the process, Data sacrifices himself in order to destroy Shinzon's weapon and ship. The momentous decision by Data to save the captain, even though it means sacrificing himself, averts what seems to be the inevitable destruction of Earth.

At the same time, what may be considered a minor decision can likewise have a significant impact on a person, as demonstrated in one of my favorite *Star Trek: The Next Generation* episodes "Tapestry" (1993; TNG; 6:15). The story begins when Picard's artificial heart is damaged during an attack on an away mission and he dies. As luck would have it, the first person Picard meets in the afterlife is the last person he wants to see: Q. The omnipotent and annoying alien who has provoked Picard since the first mission.

Picard expresses regret at the impulsive behavior in his youth that led him to need the artificial heart. Q allows Picard to relive that portion of his youth and avoid the incident. Upon returning to the present, Picard is no longer the captain of the USS Enterprise, but finds himself a Lieutenant Junior Grade in the astrophysics department. Jean-Luc Picard (version 3.0) is not a happy camper.

Q: I gave you something most mortals never experience. A second chance at life. And now all you can do is complain?

PICARD: I can't live out my days as that person. That man is bereft of passion and imagination. That is not who I am.

Q: Au contraire! He's the person you wanted to be. One who was less arrogant and undisciplined as a youth. One who was less like me. The Jean-Luc Picard you wanted to be. The one who did not fight the Nausicaan, had quite a different career from the one you remember. That Picard never had a brush with death, never came face-to-face with his own mortality, never realized how fragile life is or how important each moment must be. So his life never came into focus. He drifted for much of his career, with no plan or agenda, going from one assignment to the next, never seizing the opportunities that presented themselves. He never led the away team on Milika Three to save the ambassador, or take charge of the Stargazer's Bridge when its captain was killed. And no one ever offered him a command. He learned to play it safe. And he never, ever got noticed by anyone.

PICARD: You're right, Q. You gave me the chance to change and I took the opportunity. But I admit now, it was a mistake.

Q: Are you asking me for something, Jean-Luc?

PICARD: Give me a chance to put things back the way they were before.

Q: Before, you died in sickbay. Is that what you want?

PICARD: I would rather die as the man I was than live the life I just saw.

INCOMING MESSAGE:

Mistakes as well as accomplishments create who we are.

Q returns Picard to his original present, but this time Picard doesn't die in sickbay, Dr. Crusher is able to save him. (What would we do without Captain Picard version 1.0, after all?) The experience teaches Picard about himself and he discusses his conclusions with Riker.

PICARD: I still don't know what to make of it. Was it a dream? Was it one of Q's elaborate tricks?

RIKER: A lot of people near death have talked about strange experiences, but I've never heard one so detailed.

PICARD: And, you know, there's still a part of me that cannot accept that Q would give me a second chance, or that he would demonstrate so much compassion. And if it was Q, I owe him a debt of gratitude.

RIKER: In what sense? It sounds like he put you through hell.

PICARD: There are many parts of my youth that I'm not proud of. There were loose threads, untidy parts of me that I would like to remove. But when I pulled on one of those threads it unraveled the tapestry of my life.

Without exaggeration, when I saw this episode it was a life-changing experience. Like Captain Picard, I'd done several things in my youth of which I was ashamed. At the same time, I'm proud of the person I became. Until I watched "Tapestry," I never considered how many of those mistakes had shaped my personality and moral compass. After watching this episode I learned to enjoy surprising others by telling them that although I'm a professor with a doctorate degree, at one point in my life I was a tenth-grade dropout.

So, in addition to genes and the environment, people are shaped by the choices they make every day. Granted, not all choices will have the impact of photon torpedoes, but many of the choices we make are at least as important as our genes.

At the beginning of this section I stated there were four Captain Picards, and so far I've only introduced three. In "Encounter at Farpoint" (1987, TNG; 1:1), Captain Picard (version 1.0) feels so awkward around children he asks his newly-assigned first officer to help him present an image of geniality when interacting with the children on board the Enterprise. The fourth Picard experiences a life lived a thousand years ago on a planet called Kataan and he plays a flute. In "The Inner Light" (1992, TNG; 5:25) our Picard (Version 2.0) has a wife, Eline, a daughter, Meribor, a son, Batai Jr., and even a grandson.

In this life, he's the father of a son who's looking a little like a "failure to launch" problem. Picard is genial, understanding and, well, fatherly.

PICARD: He loves doing a lot of things—Too many. Last week, all he wanted to do was be a botanist. The week before that, a sculptor. I wish he could find some focus in his life.
ELINE: I think he has. Maybe you should talk to him.
PICARD: Batai? [Batai comes out into the courtyard.]
BATAI JR.: Father?
PICARD: I get the feeling from your mother that you have something to tell me.
BATAI JR: Yes. I was waiting for the right moment, but that will never come. I'm leaving school.
PICARD: Leaving school? No, you're not.

BATAI JR: I want to concentrate on my music. That's what I care about.

PICARD: Last year, all you cared about was mathematics. The year before that, botany. Now—

BATAI JR: Through it all, there was my music. I think you know that, Father. This is the life I want.

PICARD: Well, we'll discuss it.

BATAI JR: Thank you, father.

[Batai goes back indoors.]

ELINE: Even after all these years you still have the ability to surprise me.

Picard: If music is what he wants, why should I stand in his way? Anyway, who knows how much time he'll have to follow any dream.

People should always have the ability to follow their dreams. Our dreams and decisions, along with our genetics, environment, and happenstance all combine to shape the people we become. According to the *Star Trek* message of hope, we should always aspire to be more than we are.

Chapter 5
"Are You Out of Your Vulcan Mind?"

TROI: If you're looking for my professional opinion as ship's Counselor, —he's nuts.
"Star Trek: Generations" (1994)

Psychiatric Disabilities (Part 1)

Many of the stories on *Star Trek* take place more between the ears than among the stars. "The Man Trap" (1966, TOS; 1:1) features a scientist who, out of loneliness, becomes romantically attached to the alien creature who killed his wife (clinically this would be called a *fetish*), while Dr. McCoy experiences hallucinations in the alien's presence (*temporary psychosis*). Charlie Evans is the ultimate out-of-control teen (*oppositional defiant disorder*) in "Charlie X" (1966, TOS; 1:2). A psychiatrist, Dr. Dehner, comes aboard the USS Enterprise to study crew reactions in emergency conditions, and by the end of "Where No Man Has Gone Before" (1966, TOS; 1:3), most of the crew could use some therapy. And all that in just the first three episodes.

An examination of both the *historic* and the *current* understanding of psychiatric disabilities is important to understand how mental illnesses are depicted in the *Star Trek* universe, as well as the stigma that's still associated with them in today's world. The 1960s were an interesting historical period for psychiatry.

The 1950s set the stage for two opposing forces. In this decade, the discovery of antipsychotic medications that could control psychiatric symptoms reinforced the concept that mental illness was a physical condition. In response to the ineffective use of psychoanalysis and an increased reliance on medications with negative side effects, an international anti-psychiatry movement was started.

By the 1960s, an increasing number of mental health professionals began to question the prevailing treatment approaches, citing the lack of scientific evidence that treatment was effective. Along with the controversy over treatments, the anti-psychiatry movement brought into question the power disparity between patient and physician. The fine line between normality and revolutionary thought became political.

As the 1960's progressed, mental health practitioners began to move away from the psychodynamic practices of Sigmund Freud which included psychoanalysis, the interpretation of dreams, and the tenet that a person's development is determined by childhood events. In addition to the antipsychotic medications, new therapeutic approaches were developed such as *behavioral therapy* [see "Wolf In The Fold" (1967, TOS; 2:14)], *person-centered therapy* [see "Family" (1990, TNG; 4:2)], and *cognitive-behavioral therapy* [see "Hard Time" (1996, DS9; 4:18)].

Some episodes in the original series dealt with other aspects of psychology, such as Human development [childhood in "And The Children Shall Lead" (1968, TOS; 3:4), immaturity in "The Squire of Gothos" (1967, TOS; 1:18), parenthood in "Friday's Child" (1967, TOS; 1:11), sex in "All Our Yesterdays" (1969, TOS; 3:23), and gender in "Elaan of Troyius" (1968, TOS; 3:13)]. However, this chapter will focus on psychiatric disabilities. Some psychiatric disabilities such as obsessions, psychosis, and schizophrenia tend to invoke fear in the general public.

The differences between definitions of psychiatric disability in this century and those in the 1960s aren't entirely based on clinical evidence. When the original series went on the air in 1966, the American Psychiatric Association was preparing to revise their "Diagnostic and Statistical Manual" (DSM) for the first time since 1952. The DSM traditionally has provided the diagnostic criteria for mental disorders in the United States. However, since *Star Trek* is seen worldwide, I'll use the criteria as published in the "International Classification of Diseases and Related Health Problems" or "ICD-10" as the current version is commonly called. Furthermore, due to significant political and clinical controversies surrounding the 2013 edition of the DSM-V (some things never change), acceptance of the ICD-10 in the United States is increasing.

Due to the differences in mental health treatment and diagnosis between the 1960s and 1980s and beyond, I've separated my analysis of the original series from the later series. In addition, I've grouped the more stigmatized and less common psychiatric disabilities into this chapter. In the next chapter I'll present the anxiety and mood related disorders.

Madness, Insanity, and Going Berserk

In the original series, psychiatric disorders were not well-defined, reflecting the actual state of the field in the 1960's. Characters were referred to as "going mad" as in "City on the Edge of Forever" (1967, TOS; 1:29).

> KIRK: Captain's log, supplemental entry. Two drops of cordrazine can save a man's life. A hundred times that amount has just accidentally been pumped into Dr. McCoy's body. In a strange, wild frenzy, he has fled the ship's bridge. All connecting decks have been placed on alert. We have no way of knowing if the madness is permanent or temporary, or in what direction it will drive McCoy.

INCOMING MESSAGE:
An overdose of some medications can induce psychosis.

In "The Tholian Web" (1968, TOS; 3:9), the crew isn't only going mad, one crewman went *berserk* due to the effects of this area of space on the nervous system. The crew of the Defiant has already killed one another as a result of these spatial anomalies.

> McCOY: And the madness that affected the Defiant's crew will soon happen to the Enterprise.
> [Several Scenes Later]
> SCOTT: One of our crewmen just went berserk, but we have him under control for the moment.

RED ALERT!
When someone goes berserk,
you have to physically restrain him.

The term *insanity* was usually reserved for those with violent and criminal behavior as in "Is There In Truth No Beauty?" (1968, TOS; 3:5).

KIRK [broadcast to ship]: Captain Kirk to all ship personnel. Red Alert. An attempt was made to murder Ambassador Kollos. The murderer is dangerously insane. He is Lawrence Marvick. Be on the watch for him. Kirk out.

The messages about psychiatric disabilities in these original series shows clearly reflect the general fear of those who experience emotional disturbances.

RED ALERT!
People with mental illness are dangerous.

The best example of the fear of psychiatric conditions occurs in "Wolf In The Fold" (1967, TOS; 2:14). The dialogue provides glimpses into how psychiatry and mental illnesses were viewed in the 1960s, as well as a short course in psychobabble. When Scotty begins flirting with a local woman on Argelius II, Dr. McCoy expresses his relief that Mr. Scott will not develop a negative association regarding women.

MCCOY: ...Don't forget, the explosion that threw Scotty against a bulkhead was caused by a woman.
KIRK: Physically he's all right. Am I right in assuming that?
MCCOY: Oh, yes, yes. As a matter of fact, considerable psychological damage could have been caused. For example, his total resentment toward women.

INCOMING MESSAGE:
Trauma can produce irreversible psychological damage.

The process which would result in the psychological damage Dr. McCoy refers to is called *classical conditioning*. Ivan Pavlov developed the principles of classical conditioning which involved the pairing of one event (ringing a bell) with a second event (putting food in front of a dog) that produces a reflexive response (drooling). After a number of pairings, the reflexive response (drooling) could be triggered by the first event alone (ringing the bell). This is the famous *Pavlov's Dog* experiment.

In theory, since a woman was presumably present and responsible for the explosion, Mr. Scott may develop an association with women and explosions (and his subsequent pain from the injuries). If the association is strong enough, Mr. Scott might come to resent all women. However, in practice, classical conditioning is rarely achieved with a one-time pairing.

Unlike classical conditioning, *operant conditioning* depends on reinforcements (rewards and punishments) to shape the desired behavior. Together, classical and operant conditioning led to the development of behavioral therapy in the 1960s. While classical conditioning was limited to reflexive behaviors (such as drooling), there were relevant real-world applications for operant conditioning. One common example of behavioral therapy used operant conditioning in the form of a *token economy*. In a token economy, classroom children were rewarded for desired behaviors with a token (usually a gold star or poker chip) and later the children could exchange their tokens for privileges, toys, or candy. On the Enterprise they probably would want to exchange their tokens for a shirt that wasn't red.

Scotty is later found standing by a wall, groaning, with a bloody knife in his hand, looking at the body of a young woman he's just met. Unfortunately for him, Scotty says he can't remember what happened, and he becomes the prime suspect in the woman's murder. The chief city administrator, Mr. Hengist, takes charge of the murder investigation.

The planet's Prefect, Jaris, arrives and suggests that his wife, Sybo, can reveal whether Scotty is responsible for the woman's death through "Argelian empathic contact." Everyone goes to the Prefect's home, but Kirk offers a more scientific method of determining Scotty's recent behavior.

KIRK: Depending on your wife's empathic abilities is all very well, Prefect, but there's only one way we can find out what it is Mr. Scott cannot remember. Since you find it impossible to let us go back up to our ship, I can beam down a technician with a psycho-tricorder.

McCOY: Prefect, it will give us a detailed account of everything that's happened to Mr. Scott in the last twenty four hours.

[Dialogue Omitted]

TRACY: Lieutenant Karen Tracy reporting as ordered, Captain.

KIRK: Lieutenant, I want a twenty four hour regressive memory check made on Mr. Scott.

The episode provides no clues as to how the psycho-tricorder works. Before the equipment can be set up in the Prefect's home, Tracy is murdered. Scotty is the only person in the room when the body is discovered and, again, he has no memory of the events.

INCOMING MESSAGE:
Once someone has committed murder,
they will murder again.

Kirk asks McCoy if Scotty's head injury could be responsible for his abnormal behavior. McCoy offers a second explanation (and throws poor Mr. Scott to the wolves).

MCCOY: Hysterical amnesia. When a man feels guilty about something, something too terrible to remember, he blots it out of his conscious memory.

Hysteria was used to explain multiple psychological conditions by Sigmund Freud and is well rooted in psychodynamics. In the 1960s *hysterical amnesia* was an actual diagnosis. Hysteria was used to describe any condition that couldn't be explained by organic causes. In modern terms, it's known as a *dissociative* or *conversion* disorder. Anyone who has experienced stressful situations can attest to the body reacting to stress with a physical manifestation. When I was in graduate school, I often broke out in hives just before an exam.

Back on Argelius II, Sybo performs the empathic reading and is killed for her troubles, stabbed to death in the same manner as the other two women. With no further means of determining who's responsible for the deaths, Kirk suggests everyone beam up to the ship.

KIRK: ...On the Enterprise, we can make a recording of the registrations of Mr. Scott's conscious and subconscious mind. They will tell us what happened to him in the recent past.

In the hearing room, the computer acts much like a polygraph machine or lie detector (without the graph), verifying the accuracy of the testimony based on physiological readings. (I guess there was only one psycho-tricorder on the Enterprise.)

COMPUTER: Subject relaying accurate account. No physiological changes.

KIRK: All right. Let's hit it on the head. Scotty, did you kill Sybo?

SCOTT: No, Captain. That I'm sure of.

HENGIST: He's been saying that right along. It means no more now than it did before.

KIRK: Scotty, lie to me. How old are you?

SCOTT: Twenty-two sir.

COMPUTER: Inaccurate. Inaccurate. Data in error.

RED ALERT!
Lie detectors can prove someone's guilt or innocence.

Polygraph testing has generated considerable scientific and public controversy. Most scientists agree polygraph tests lack validity as a form of evidence regarding the truthfulness of a person's responses. Courts, including the United States Supreme Court (cf. U.S. v. Scheffer, 1998 in which Dr. Saxe's research on polygraph fallibility was cited), have repeatedly rejected the use of polygraph evidence because of its inherent unreliability.

Polygraphs are more likely to be inaccurate when the subject takes certain medications, such as beta blockers for heart conditions or antianxiety medications. As a result, people with disabilities often have the highest number of false positives when taking a polygraph. The Employee Polygraph Protection Act of 1988 generally prevents employers from using lie detector tests, either for pre-employment screening or during the course of employment.

In this episode it's Mr. Spock, not the computer, who deduces the murderer: a non-corporeal lifeform who feeds on the fear of others. "Wolf In The Fold" concludes with the entire crew receiving tranquilizers to prevent them from providing the fear the alien feeds on (or being able to take a polygraph). The alien is beamed into space in hopes that it can't hijack another corporeal form to continue its terror.

Some episodes describe beliefs that, while not mental disorders in and of themselves, can be symptoms of mental illnesses such as the grandiosity of Dr. Daystrom in "The Ultimate Computer" (1968, TOS; 2:24), or Captain Kirk's belief in his irresistible animal magnetism.

Highly Illogical (Obsessions)

Obsessions are the subject of two episodes. In "Court Martial" (1967, TOS; 1:21) Lieutenant Benjamin Finney blames Captain Kirk for filing a report about a circuit that was left open during Finney's shift. Finney believes this report stood in his way of becoming a ship's captain. Obsessed with hatred and desiring revenge, Finney fakes his own death and tampers with the computer, resulting in Captain Kirk's court-martial. When the deception is exposed, the charges against Kirk are dismissed, and Finney is offered help. Although there are few references to psychiatry in the episode, the message about the impairing nature of an obsession is clear.

RED ALERT!
The desire for revenge is a form of mental illness.

In "Obsession" (1967, TOS; 2:13), Kirk's determination to atone for a previous mistake impairs his judgment.

> KIRK: Captain's log, stardate 3619.6. One of the men in critical condition, the other is dead. And I, I am now even more convinced that this is not only an intelligent creature, but the same which decimated the crew of the USS Farragut eleven years ago in another part of the galaxy. Both Spock and McCoy are doubtful of this, and I sense they also doubt my decision to stay and fight the thing. Why am I keeping the ship here?

INCOMING MESSAGE:
Determination can be mistaken for an obsession.

Kirk doubts his decision to delay the transport of much needed medical supplies to another planet while he attempts to find the killer.

KIRK: Personal log, stardate 3620.7. Have I the right to jeopardize my crew, my ship for a feeling I can't even put into words? No man achieves Starfleet command without relying on intuition, but have I made a rational decision? Am I letting the horrors of the past distort my judgment of the present?

RED ALERT!
People with mental illness cannot accurately evaluate their own behavior.

In reality, most people with mental illness can be taught to identify behaviors resulting from their disorder. There are specific therapies that help with this process. Both Bones and Spock agree (yes, there's a first time for everything) that Captain Kirk's obsession may have made him unfit to continue commanding the Enterprise.

MCCOY: You need advice from me? You must be kidding.
SPOCK: I do not joke, Doctor. Perhaps I should rephrase my statement. I require an opinion. There are many aspects of human irrationality I do not yet comprehend. Obsession, for one. The persistent, single-minded fixation on one idea.

RED ALERT!
Obsessions always lead to irrational behavior.

Spock reviews the tapes of the USS Farragut and concludes that Kirk's hesitation to fire on the alien was inconsequential.

SPOCK: Captain, the creature's ability to throw itself out of time sync makes it possible for it to be elsewhere in the instant the phaser hits. There is, therefore, no basis for your self-recrimination. If you had fired on time and on target eleven years ago, it would have made no more difference than it did an hour ago. Captain Garrovick would still be dead. The fault was not yours, Jim. In fact, there was no fault.
KIRK: If you want to play analyst, Spock, use someone else, not me. My concern is with the ship and the crew.

RED ALERT!

Psychotherapy is not useful because
a person cannot be talked out of their obsession.

Even though Captain Kirk may think he doesn't need therapy, most people with obsessive disorders can benefit. It's important to keep in mind that most forms of obsessive-compulsive behavior are impairing in nature. The person experiences intrusive thoughts in their daily lives (obsessive thoughts) which negatively affect their behavior (compulsive actions.) Performing the actions temporarily reduces the feelings of anxiety.

Psychotherapy for obsessive-compulsive disorders usually includes cognitive-behavioral techniques. This form of therapy helps clients identify faulty logic or irrational beliefs, such as Kirk's conviction that if eleven years ago he'd fired his phaser, the outcome on the Farragut would have been different. In some ways Spock's attempt to show Kirk that his belief was illogical can be viewed as a primitive form of cognitive-behavioral therapy. In addition to psychotherapy, there are also medications which alleviate the anxiety component of the disorder, making the compulsive behaviors easier to control.

In "Whom Gods Destroy" (1969, TOS; 3:14) the Enterprise is transporting a cure for mental illness to an asylum on Elba II.

> KIRK: Captain's Log, stardate 5718.3. The Enterprise is orbiting Elba II, a planet with a poisonous atmosphere where the Federation maintains an asylum for the few remaining incorrigible criminally insane of the galaxy. We are bringing a revolutionary new medicine to them, a medicine with which the Federation hopes to eliminate mental illness for all time. I am transporting down with Mr. Spock, and we're delivering the medicine to Dr. Donald Cory, the governor of the colony.

At the asylum, Kirk and Spock meet Dr. Cory, who invites them to dinner. Dr. Cory expresses excitement about the new medication because of the violent behaviors of the patients at the facility. The fact that all the patients have different forms of mental illness is ignored. The message here is that all mental illnesses can be cured with one drug. (Giving new meaning to the term "magic bullet.")

SPOCK: A total of fifteen incurably insane out of billions is not what I would call an excessive figure. Who is the new inmate?
CORY: Garth. Garth of Izar, a former Starship fleet Captain.
[A picture of Garth is displayed on a monitor.]
KIRK: When I was a cadet at the Academy, his exploits were required reading. He was one of my heroes. I'd like to see him.
CORY: Of course.

Unfortunately, Garth has the ability to shape-shift and it's Garth—disguised as Cory who's met the landing party. During the opening credits, Kirk is placed in a cell, Spock is stunned with a phaser and dragged out of the room, and Garth destroys the medication.

KIRK: ...Now what have you done with the medicine?
GARTH: The medicine? You mean the poison. I destroyed it.

Garth's reference to the medication as poison is consistent with the anti-psychiatry movement during the 1960s. Psychiatric drugs commonly used at the time, such as Thorazine, had permanent disabling side effects and some even caused brain damage. Influential anti-psychiatry academics such as Thomas Szasz believed that medications were a form of government-sanctioned mind control. While the anti-psychiatry movement was eventually considered to have been an extreme backlash, the movement was ultimately valuable in that it exposed abusive patient practices, resulting in new patients' rights laws and ethical principles. Together, these laws and principles brought about significant changes in forced hospitalizations, the coercive use of anti-psychotic medications, and restraint of patients in mental health facilities.

Today, advances in medications now allow people with psychiatric disabilities to function without the limitations imposed by their symptoms. At the same time, much of our diagnosis of psychiatric disabilities, such as depression, is still based more on inference and observation of behavior than on empirical evidence. For instance, there's no laboratory test that identifies whether a person has low serotonin levels in their brain.

After the weekly wrestling match—Kirk defeats Kirk 2 (Garth in disguise)—and Dr. McCoy beams down to the planet to begin curing all the criminally insane patients with a new batch of medication. After Garth receives his medication, Kirk introduces himself to Garth who doesn't recognize him.

INCOMING MESSAGE:
Psychiatric medications can manage mental illnesses.

RED ALERT!
People with any form of psychiatric disability
aren't responsible for their behavior.

It's beyond the scope of this book to discuss either the legal definition of insanity or the issues involved in the so-called *insanity defense*. However, I believe it's important to consider that people with psychiatric disabilities can, on occasion, be held legally accountable for crimes. While the available statistics provide the number of people with psychiatric disabilities who are incarcerated, the same statistics too often fail to show the number of cases in which a mental illness or disability was material in the conviction. The standards for "not guilty by reason of mental disease or defect" vary from state to state.

Captain Kirk, Mr. Spock, and Dr. McCoy apparently forget they have a cure for insanity six episodes later in "The Way To Eden" (1969, TOS; 3:20), and again in the series' last episode, "Turnabout Intruder" (1969, TOS; 3:24). Maybe they needed a treatment for memory loss as well. Too bad they didn't keep track of that psycho-tricorder.

The Next Generation of Mental Health Counseling

On September 28, 1987 *Star Trek: The Next Generation* premiered with a ship's counselor on the bridge, wearing a cheerleader's uniform and go-go boots. Although Counselor Troi was a bridge officer, she was consistently referred to as "Counselor Troi" rather than "Lieutenant Commander Troi" or "Dr. Troi." The lack of both uniform and rank left me wondering about the importance of her position and respect for the counseling profession. When Troi finally donned a uniform in the middle of the sixth season, her character appeared to have suddenly increased intelligence and authority.

In the original series, Dr. McCoy attended to the physical as well as mental health needs of the crew. Troi's role as the ship's counselor was a reflection of how, over twenty years later, society had begun to embrace psychotherapy as an allied health profession.

Troi, a psychologist, was charged with caring for the mental health of the crew. The ship's physician, Dr. Crusher, attended to their physical health.

INCOMING MESSAGE:
Physicians are not the only professionals who can treat mental conditions.

The first insight into modern counseling techniques appears in "Lonely Among Us" (1987, TNG; 1:6), when Counselor Troi hypnotizes Lieutenant Worf and Dr. Crusher to recover their memories of the alien who temporarily took control of their bodies.

WORF: You wanted me, Doctor?
CRUSHER: Yes, concerning your memory blackout.
WORF: I still don't remember having one.
CRUSHER: The same thing happened to me.
TROI: I want to try hypnosis on both of you. It may restore your memory as to what happened.

Counselor Troi holds a small device which emits a flashing blue light as she hypnotizes Dr. Crusher to help her remember her previous actions. (Apparently the psycho-tricorder that disappeared was the only one in Starfleet.) The successful hypnosis allows Dr. Crusher to recall when she acted under the influence of the alien. Although this scene plays a minor role in the overall story, its inclusion sends a message that hypnosis will still be used by counselors in the future.

Most counseling techniques portrayed on the more recent *Star Trek* series are similar to current mental health practices. For example, hypnosis is currently used by some mental health professionals for treating eating disorders, smoking cessation, and other behaviors. As I discuss the various psychiatric disabilities portrayed on *Star Trek*, I'll identify their diagnostic criteria in the ICD-10, and discuss the therapeutic techniques used to treat the conditions in the episodes, as well as the current treatment options here on Earth.

Sweet Dreams and Night Terrors (Delirium)

In "Night Terrors" (1991, TNG 4:17) the enemy for the crew of the Enterprise is dream deprivation. The episode begins when the Enterprise locates a missing science vessel with only one survivor on board: a Betazoid scientific advisor in a catatonic state. The rest of the thirty-four crew members have killed each other. As the Enterprise starts to tow the science vessel to a space station, the crew discovers the ship is stuck in a Tyken's rift—almost like outer space doldrums, except, of course, there are no winds in space. The only chance of breaking free of the rift requires the crew to create an explosion.

Delirium is a syndrome which involves problems with consciousness, attention, perception, thinking, memory, emotions, physical coordination, and the sleep-wake cycle. Everyone on the Enterprise, except Data, begins to experience the symptoms of delirium.

> PICARD: It appears that I am not immune to the strange forces that are at work on this ship.
> DATA: Yes, sir.
> PICARD: It's a terrifying prospect to lose control of one's mind. When I was young, I remember watching my grandfather deteriorate from a powerful, intelligent figure to a frail wisp of a man, who could barely make his own way home. Mr. Data, it is my responsibility somehow to see that this ship is guided to safety. I will need to rely on you from now on. We may need to count on you for our very survival.
> DATA: I will do my best, sir.

Picard's reflection regarding his grandfather is an appropriate connection because delirium is more common after age sixty. (The onset of Alzheimer's disease generally occurs in younger individuals.) According to the ICD-10, all five of the following symptoms should be present for a diagnosis of delirium:

1. *Reduced ability to concentrate or remember how to do everyday tasks as well as trouble shifting attention from one task to another.*

> PICARD: Ensign, maneuver us into tractor beam range.
> RAGER: Aye, sir. [She has a blank look on her face; she does not move.]
> DATA: Is there a problem, Ensign?
> RAGER: I can't seem to remember how to enter the coordinates, sir.

2. *Seeing hallucinations, or perceptual changes that affect how things appear. The person may have a reduced ability for abstract thinking and difficulty understanding abstract ideas. Sometimes there may be temporary delusions. Often there will be a problem with short term memory, although long term memory is usually fine. The person may feel temporarily disoriented.*

TROI: We're concerned. We're afraid whatever happened on the Brittain may be starting here.

PICARD: Explain.

TROI: Well, Beverly and I have been getting unusual reports. People behaving strangely, others hearing sounds that aren't there.

PICARD: Are we talking about hallucinations?

CRUSHER: In some cases. In others just erratic behavior.

TROI: We can't track down any element that might be responsible.

PICARD: But everything started when we found the Brittain?

CRUSHER: Yes. Captain, we have to get the Enterprise away from here before it gets any worse.

3. *Changes in a person's coordination or activity level. The activity level and flow of speech may be greater or lesser than normal for that person. Sometimes they will startle more readily or respond more slowly.*

LA FORGE: Okay, all the power has been channeled to the—er—the—

DATA: The main deflector dish.

LA FORGE: Yes—Right—The deflector dish—So, what do we do now?

DATA: Data to Bridge. Mr. Worf, activate the deflector.

WORF: Aye, sir.

4. *Disturbance in the sleep-wake cycle, insomnia, or reversal of day and night levels of drowsiness. (Awake at night and sleepy during the day.) Disturbing dreams or nightmares may occur, which may continue as hallucinations after waking up.*

CRUSHER: Captain, let me ask you this—Since we located the Brittain—can you remember any of your dreams?

PICARD: I hardly ever recall dreams.

CRUSHER: Most people don't—but think—Have you even had a dream in the last ten days?

PICARD: I don't recall—

CRUSHER: I'm willing to bet you haven't. What's more, neither has anyone else on board this ship—except for Troi. [Crusher's voice sounds as though forming her words is taking an unusual amount of effort.] I began to realize that when she talked about having nightmares. I've done some additional brain tissue scans on—er—bodies—some of the bodies from the—er—the—

DATA: The Brittain, Doctor.

CRUSHER: Right—And I've also done some scans on a random cross-section from our crew. They both have the same results—a unique chemical imbalance.

PICARD: Caused by?

CRUSHER: Dream deprivation. Every night when we—we enter into—sleep—

DATA: I believe what the Doctor means is that humans enter what is known as REM sleep. Rapid eye movement. It is the level of brain wave activity at which one dreams.

CRUSHER: We have to dream in order to survive. If we don't reach REM sleep—we don't dream—we begin to lose our cognitive abilities. We find it hard to concentrate. We forget how to do the most ordinary tasks. Then we become irritable—paranoid. Some people experience hallucinations.

[Dialogue Omitted]

CRUSHER: ...There is an inevitable conclusion to this pattern, and if I can't find a way to stop it—we will all go insane.

5. *Emotional disturbances such as depression, anxiety or fear, irritability, apathy or euphoria.*

RIKER: ...I'd be a liar if I said I felt like myself—I've had to bite my tongue to keep from snapping at people. A couple of times—I've gone to my quarters and felt as if there was someone in there, waiting for me—

PICARD: I've had similar feelings. With everyone succumbing it's even more important that one of us attempt to keep control of his faculties. I want you to turn in—take a nap—I'll be on the bridge. You can relieve me in four hours.

Consistent with clinical delirium, which has a rapid onset, the crew recovers once the Enterprise breaks free from the rift and they're all able to get to sleep. Also consistent with delirium is the need for medical intervention.

INCOMING MESSAGE:
Sleep is important to a Human's well-being.
Medical intervention should be sought when insomnia is prolonged.

Delirium is usually caused by a disease process outside the brain that nonetheless affects the brain, such as an infection or high fever. And in this case the Tyken's rift.

INCOMING MESSAGE:
Boldly going nowhere will drive you insane.

After deciphering Troi's nightmares, the crew devises a solution and breaks free from the rift. Troi does not, however, consult Sigmund Freud's "The Interpretation of Dreams." The delirium is reversed after getting some much needed sleep, and before the next episode.

Psychographic Profile: Schizophrenia

Two portrayals of schizophrenia are depicted on *Star Trek: Deep Space Nine.* Schizophrenia is often described by the predominant feature of the patient's distorted thoughts. It's important to remember that, despite frequent depictions of schizophrenia as leading to murder in popular media, the majority of people with schizophrenia never become violent. Whether these *Star Trek* storylines were a reflection of the media stereotypes or a belief in those stereotypes isn't clear. According to research, less than .03 of one percent of those with schizophrenia commit murder. However, both Benjamin Sisko and Gul Dukat meet the criteria for schizophrenia. Maybe it has something to do with the Prefect's office.

The Dreamer and the Dream

According to the ICD–10, a diagnosis of schizophrenia can be made when one clear symptom out of a list of four possible symptoms is present for over one month. The first possible symptom is "thought echo, thought insertion or withdrawal, and thought broadcasting." A *thought echo* is when someone hears their own thoughts as though they were being spoken out loud. *Thought insertion* or *withdrawal* is when the person believes that someone is either inserting or removing their thoughts; that is, someone else is controlling what they think. Sisko demonstrates the symptom of *thought broadcasting,* which is when the person believes their thoughts are being heard by others; in his case, the aliens within the wormhole.

In the series premiere, "Emissary" (1993, DS9; 1:1-2), Sisko meets the wormhole aliens (a.k.a. Bajoran Prophets) and believes that as he remembers key events in his life, the wormhole aliens are seeing his memories: Jennifer on the beach—A baseball landing in a catcher's mitt—Kai Opaka—Locutus on a viewscreen—Jennifer and Sisko kissing—A newborn baby—Jake fishing—Doran on the Saratoga.

Since the images and even the conversation with the beings in the wormhole are taking place only in Sisko's mind, I could stop here because the diagnosis of schizophrenia only requires one clear symptom. However, Sisko has more symptoms.

Hearing voices is another symptom, and the voices usually provide a running commentary on the person's actions or discuss the person as though they can't hear the comments. Sisko hallucinates several times on *Star Trek: Deep Space Nine.* Most of the hallucinations are both auditory and visual, such as while he is studying the obelisk in "Rapture" (1996, DS9; 5:10).

SISKO: I was there.

KIRA: Sir?

SISKO: B'hala. It was the eve of the Peldor Festival. I could hear them ringing the temple chimes.

KIRA: You were dreaming.

SISKO: No, I was there. I could smell the burning bateret leaves, taste the incense on the wind. I was standing in front of the obelisk and as I looked up, for one moment I understood it all. B'hala, the Orbs, the occupation, the discovery of the wormhole, the coming war with the Dominion.

KIRA: You could see the future as well as the past?

SISKO: For one moment, I could see the pattern that held it all together.

KIRA: You were having a pagh'tem'far, a sacred vision.

SISKO: Hell, I don't know what I had, but it felt wonderful.

RED ALERT!
Spiritual beliefs are evidence of a psychiatric disability.

When Sisko hallucinates that he is Benny Russell in "Far Beyond the Stars" (1998, DS9; 6:13), once again the source of the hallucinations appears to be the wormhole aliens.

> BASHIR: I don't know. I'm reading some unusual synaptic potentials. Your neural patterns are similar to those you experienced last year.
> SISKO: You mean when I was having those visions about Bajor?

Sisko—through Russell—demonstrates another symptom of schizophrenia: *delusional thinking*. Delusions are false beliefs that persist even when the impossibility of the belief has been established. According to the ICD–10:

> persistent delusions...that are culturally inappropriate and completely impossible, such as religious or political identity, or superhuman powers and abilities (e.g. being able to control the weather or being in communication with aliens from another world).

That's right; when Sisko hallucinates he's Benny Russell, he's hallucinating he's a delusional person. Russell is a science fiction writer in 1953 New York and has written a story in which a "colored man" is the commander of a space station. In this pre-Civil Rights era, Russell is delusional because there's no foundation for his belief that Sisko could ever exist.

> PABST: Oh, come on, Benny. Your hero's a Negro captain, the head of a space station, for Christ's sake.
> BENNY: What's wrong with that?
> PABST: People won't accept it. It's not believable.
> HERBERT: And men from Mars are?

However, his belief the magazine will omit his story is more a reflection of the times than evidence of a paranoid thought disorder. Once Russell's hallucinations vanish, Sisko isn't sure of which person is real.

SISKO: ...But maybe, just maybe, Benny isn't the dream, we are. Maybe we're nothing more than figments of his imagination. For all we know, at this very moment, somewhere far beyond all those distant stars, Benny Russell is dreaming of us.

The idea that there would be a space station in another part of the universe wasn't considered delusional, just good science fiction.

INCOMING MESSAGE:
People with schizophrenia cannot separate
reality from their hallucinations.

The wormhole aliens appear to cause schizophrenia, at least for Sisko. He encounters the wormhole aliens again and they speak to him through Worf, Martok, Ross, and Letant in "Tears of the Prophets" (1998, DS9; 6:26). Or, in the language of the ICD-10, he hallucinates and communicates with unseen others who comment on his plans, change the setting, and they tell him what he should do.

WORF: The Sisko is of Bajor. [Wardroom]
MARTOK: It is where he belongs. [Captain's office]
ROSS: It is where he is meant to be.
SISKO: Are you telling me not to go to Cardassia? [Ops]
ROSS: The Sisko is of Bajor.
MARTOK: It is dangerous to walk a different path.
SISKO: Dangerous? In what way?
ROSS: The Sisko must not leave the chosen path.
WORF: The Sisko is of Bajor.
LETANT: It is where he belongs.

SISKO: Why is it dangerous to leave? And how will it affect Bajor? You have to tell me. [The encounter ends.]

When Admiral Ross confronts Sisko with the fact that he cannot be both the Emissary of the Prophets and remain a captain in Starfleet, Sisko choses Starfleet.

INCOMING MESSAGE:
A person who hears voices doesn't always
do what they instruct.

The final symptom of schizophrenia is *delusional perceptions*, in which the person believes they have control or influence when they don't. Sisko's belief that Lieutenant Commander Michael Eddington personally betrayed him is a good example of a delusional perception. Sisko's actions, as a result of that belief, demonstrate an obsession with capturing his former security chief in "For The Cause" (1996, DS9; 4:21).

EDDINGTON: You know what your problem is, Captain? You've made this personal. It didn't have to be. It wasn't with me. I have no animosity, no harsh feelings toward you.
SISKO: I wish I could say the same.
EDDINGTON: Does it really pay to risk yourself, your ship, your crew, on a personal vendetta? And would Starfleet approve?
SISKO: I don't need any lectures about Starfleet from you. And no matter what happens here today, it's not over between us.

This is the only one of Sisko's schizophrenic symptoms that can't be explained by his interactions with the wormhole or other aliens. Sisko's obsession with Eddington leads him to take unprecedented risks to capture Eddington at all costs.

SISKO: All right, say it.
DAX: What?
SISKO: That I have lost all perspective. That I'm turning this into a vendetta between me and Eddington, and that I'm putting the ship, the crew and my entire

career at risk, and if I had any brains at all I'd go back to my office, sit down and read Odo's crime reports.

Apparently, Sisko has some insight into the root of his Eddington obsession, as he explains to Dax:

SISKO: He played me all right, and what is my excuse? Is he a changeling? No. Is he a being with seven lifetimes of experience? No. Is he a wormhole alien? No. He's just a man, like me. And he beat me!

At the same time, Eddington uses Sisko's obsession to his own advantage. It's not uncommon for others to take advantage of someone with a thought disorder because they're easily manipulated.

EDDINGTON [hologram]: You just couldn't resist the temptation to come after me, could you, Captain.
SISKO: I like to finish what I start.
EDDINGTON [hologram]: Well, I'm afraid you're going to be disappointed, again. You won't get me, Captain. But I do have a consolation prize for you. Actually it's more of a gift.
KIRA: Incoming transmission. Sending over a document.
EDDINGTON [hologram]: It's a book. One of my favorites. "Les Miserables."
SISKO: Thank you, but I've read it.
EDDINGTON [hologram]: Recently? If not, you should read it again. Pay close attention to the character of Inspector Javert, the French policeman who spends twenty years chasing a man for stealing a loaf of bread. Sound like anyone you know?
                    [Scenes and Dialogue Omitted]
EDDINGTON [hologram]: [to Sisko] Well, Javert, let's see how deep your obsession with me is. You've got me. I can't outrun or outfight the Defiant. But, if you come after me you'll have to pay a price. You'll have to let all those helpless Cardassians spiral down to their deaths. The choice is yours.

Sisko buys into the role of Javert and becomes the villain. He orders the Defiant to detonate torpedoes carrying a gas that makes the planet on which the Maquis have built a base uninhabitable for the next fifty years. Eddington's and Sisko's crew are both shocked by Sisko's orders.

> EDDINGTON: Can't you see what's happening to you? You're going against everything you claim to believe in, and for what? To satisfy a personal vendetta?
> SISKO: You betrayed your uniform!
> EDDINGTON: And you're betraying yours right now! The sad part is you don't even realize it. I feel sorry for you, Captain. This obsession with me, look what it's cost you.

Later, Sisko takes Eddington out of prison in an attempt to stop missiles from reaching Cardassia and starting a war between the Federation and the Cardassians in "Blaze of Glory" (1997, DS9; 5:23). Eddington explains to Sisko that the captain's belief regarding his own importance is delusional and egocentric.

> EDDINGTON: You're the one who set the ground rules when you came after me, Ben. You're the one who made it personal. You could've looked the other way. You could've left the Maquis alone, but you didn't do it. You hunted us, hounded us, fought us every chance you got. And in the end, you set us up for the slaughter. I expected better of you than that. So did a lot of people. People like Cal Hudson. I bet you haven't heard that name in a while.
> SISKO: You're right about that.
> [Dialogue Omitted]
> SISKO: He [Hudson] was a good man.
> EDDINGTON: He felt the same about you. He thought you were wrong about the Maquis, but he forgave you, which is ironic considering you never forgave him. You can't forgive any of us. And not because we betrayed Starfleet, or the Federation, but because we betrayed you. That's what this is all about, your ego. Where Benjamin Sisko leads, all must follow.

Aside from Sisko's deadly obsession, his symptoms of schizophrenia are generally woven into his interactions with the wormhole aliens and, therefore, are easily dismissed. However, most of Gul Dukat's symptoms of schizophrenia are not explained by alien encounters, although we have to overlook his primary delusional belief – that he is an alien from outer space.

Prefect, Murderer, Savior

Gul Dukat commanded Deep Space Nine during the Cardassian occupation of Bajor when the station was called "Terok Nor." After Dukat's half-Bajoran daughter Ziyal was killed by his second in command, Damar, Dukat became psychotic. In retrospect, even before Dukat's hallucinations began, he showed evidence of a schizophrenic disorder characterized by distortions of thinking and perception, and by inappropriate emotions.

In "Things Past" (1996, DS9; 5:8) Dax, Sisko and Garak transport back in time and appear to those around them as Bajoran workers. Dax appears as a Bajoran *comfort woman* named Letta. Dukat's delusional thinking is evident as he tells Letta about how ungrateful he finds the Barjorans.

> DUKAT: I've wanted to increase rations in the Bajoran sector for some time now, but the resistance makes it almost impossible to show any sort of kindness to your people.
> LETTA [DAX]: You really want to help my people, don't you?
> DUKAT: Yes, of course. The Bajorans are, well, they're like my children, I suppose. And like any father, I want only what's best for them.
> LETTA [DAX]: And you still feel like that now after some of your children have tried to kill you?
> DUKAT: Bad manners are the fault of the parent, not the child. My weakness is I'm too generous, too forgiving. My heart is too big.

Dukat, who ordered the deaths of thousands of Bajorans, sounds as though he doesn't understand why the Bajorans don't send him Fathers' Day cards.

According to the ICD-10, a person with schizophrenia will generally have normal intelligence and unclouded consciousness. A person with schizophrenia may believe their actions are being controlled by outside forces, natural or supernatural, in order to influence their minds. In addition, the person believes what they think and feel is known by those around them.

In "By Inferno's Light" (1997, DS9; 5:15), during what looks like an imminent attack on Deep Space Nine, the Dominion fleet turns away from the space station and begins heading toward Cardassia. Upon seeing Dukat's ship head toward the Dominion ships, Major Kira erroneously believes that Dukat is pursing the Jem'Hadar in order to defend Cardassia.

DUKAT [on viewscreen]: Your concern is touching, Major, but I think you misunderstand me. I'm not attacking the Dominion fleet. I'm joining it.

KIRA: What are you talking about?

DUKAT [on viewscreen]: I'm afraid I have a confession to make, Major. For the past few months, I've been conducting secret negotiations between the Dominion and Cardassia. And as of last week, Cardassia has agreed to become part of the Dominion.

RED ALERT!
People with schizophrenia lie.

Dukat converses with Major Kira *as if* she was worried about his safety. It's unclear if his delusions extend to the belief that Major Kira is really worried about him or if he's just using his charming Cardassian sarcasm. His secret alliance with the Dominion adds to his grandiose belief that he's pivotal in the lives of Cardassians as well as Bajorans, not to mention the Federation. As Dukat broadcasts the news of the alliance between the Dominion and Cardassia, his sense of self-importance has grown to the status of a historical hero.

DUKAT [on viewscreen]: You might ask, should we fear joining the Dominion? And I answer you, not in the least. We should embrace the opportunity. The Dominion recognizes us for what we are: the true leaders of the Alpha Quadrant. And now that we are joined together, equal partners in all endeavors, the only people with anything to fear will be our enemies. My oldest son's birthday is in five days. To him and to Cardassians everywhere, I make the following pledge. By the time his birthday dawns, there will not be a single Klingon alive inside Cardassian territory or a single Maquis colony left within our borders. Cardassia will be made whole. All that we have lost will be ours again, and anyone who stands in our way will be destroyed. This I vow with my life's blood. For my son, for all our sons.

INCOMING MESSAGE:
Grandiosity can be a characteristic of
delusional thinking in schizophrenia.

Another characteristic of schizophrenia is *blunted emotions* where a person displays an emotional intensity that's less than one would expect under the circumstances. Dukat's dampened emotions towards his daughter and his delusions of grandeur are further established in "By Inferno's Light" (1997, DS9; 5:15).

DUKAT [on monitor]: Ziyal made her choice. As far as I'm concerned, she is no longer my daughter.
SISKO: You know, Dukat, I thought you'd changed in the last five years. I see I was wrong.
DUKAT [on monitor]: One man's villain is another man's hero, Captain. You should see the monument they're erecting in my honor at the gateway to the Imperial Plaza.
SISKO: Is that why you sold out your people to the Dominion? For a monument?

Dukat's narcissistic delusions increases in "Sacrifice of Angels" (1997, DS9; 6:6). He expresses his surprise that not only have the Bajorans failed to appreciate his magnificence, but Sisko has slighted him as well.

DUKAT: ...A true victory is to make your enemy see they were wrong to oppose you in the first place. To force them to acknowledge your greatness.

[Dialogue Omitted]

DUKAT: Perhaps the biggest disappointment in my life is that the Bajoran people still refuse to appreciate how lucky they were to have me as their liberator. I protected them in so many ways, cared for them as if they were my own children. But to this day, is there a single statue of me on Bajor?

WEYOUN: I would guess not.

DUKAT: And you'd be right. Take Captain Sisko, an otherwise intelligent, perceptive man. Even he refuses to grant me the respect I deserve.

After Damar shoots Ziyal, Dukat lies on the floor of the holding cell in a fetal position. He appears disheveled and talks to his dead daughter as if she's in the room with him.

DUKAT: We'll go back to Cardassia, Ziyal. We'll be safe there. You'll live with me. Everything will be fine.

SISKO [To Odo]: Maybe Dr. Bashir can do something for him.

DUKAT: We'll both be very happy together. I know you forgive me. After all, I am your father and I forgive you—[Odo enters the cell.]

DUKAT: My precious girl.

ODO: Easy—easy now. [Odo helps Dukat out of the cell.]

DUKAT: [To Sisko] I forgive you, too.

While Sisko is transporting Dukat on the USS Honshu to Starbase Six-Two to stand trial at a special Federation Grand Jury for war crimes, the ship is attacked by Cardassians in "Waltz" (1998, DS9; 6:11). Sisko and Dukat escape the destruction of the Honshu, crash-landing on a deserted planet. Dukat becomes increasingly unstable as he talks to his hallucinations of Kira, Weyoun, and Damar.

SISKO: There's no reason to get upset. We're just talking. Two old soldiers talking around a campfire.

KIRA [IMAGE]: I'm going to enjoy watching this. He's going to beat you, Dukat. He's going to escape and go back to DS Nine and his friends and we're all going to have a good, long laugh at your expense.

DUKAT: Enough! [Dukat shoots at where he sees Kira standing, then the wall, and down the tunnel.]

Later, Dukat presses Sisko to reveal how he feels about him. Sisko obliges by bombarding Dukat with yes and no questions and playing along with Dukat's delusions. Caught up in the debate, Dukat fails to notice that Sisko has taken possession of the same metal bar Dukat used to beat him.

SISKO: Oh believe me, you have my undivided attention. Now let me get this straight. You're not responsible for what happened during the occupation, the Bajorans are.

DUKAT: Yes, yes, exactly.

SISKO: So, why do you think they didn't appreciate this rare opportunity you were offering them?

DUKAT: Because they were blind, ignorant fools. If only they had cooperated with us, we could have turned their world into a paradise. From the moment we arrived on Bajor, it was clear that we were the superior race. But they couldn't accept that. They wanted to be treated as equals when they most certainly were not. Militarily, technologically, culturally, we were almost a century ahead of them in every way. We did not choose to be the superior race. Fate handed us our role. And it would've been so much easier on everyone if the Bajorans had simply accepted their role. But no, day after day they clustered in their temples and prayed for deliverance, and night after night they planted bombs outside of our homes. Pride—Stubborn—unyielding pride. From the servant girl that cleaned my quarters to the condemned man toiling in a labor camp to the terrorist skulking through the hills of Dahkur Province. They all wore their pride like some twisted badge of honor.

SISKO: And you hated them for it.

DUKAT: Of course I hated them! I hated everything about them! Their superstitions and their cries for sympathy, their treachery and their lies, their smug superiority and their stiff necked obstinacy, their earrings and their broken wrinkled noses.

SISKO: You should have killed them all.

DUKAT: Yes! Yes! That's right—isn't it? [His imaginary companions nod in agreement.] I knew it! I've always known it! I should have killed every last one of them. I should have turned their planet into a graveyard the likes of which the galaxy had never seen! I should have killed them all. [The metal bar crashes down on his head, and Dukat falls.]

SISKO: And that is why you're not an evil man.

RED ALERT!

Delusions disappear when refuted by facts.

After escaping from Sisko's custody, Dukat creates a religious cult in "Covenant" (1998, DS9; 7:9). Other people with schizophrenia have created similar followings.

DUKAT: They speak to me in visions. I am their Emissary.

KIRA: I don't know whether you believe what you're saying, or if you're faking it, or if you're just insane.

DUKAT: I have been touched by the hand of a god. I'm a changed man. Oh, I admit that when I first allowed myself to become a vessel for the Pah wraith, it was purely out of self-serving reasons. All I wanted was to help it enter the wormhole so it could force the Prophets out. It was nothing more than a way to exact vengeance on Sisko. But I had no idea the effect it would have on me. It was only inside of me for a very short time. But it opened my heart.

The episode takes on a Jim Jones aspect to it when Dukat attempts to lead his followers in a mass suicide. Unlike Jones, who killed over nine hundred people in the 1978 murder-suicide, Dukat is not successful because Kira is able to thwart his plan.

Mental Institutions and Treatments

It is important to keep in mind that most people with schizophrenia are not violent or dangerous like Dukat or Sisko. The majority are like the nameless stranger Dr. Bashir encounters in "Past Tense, Part I" (1995, DS9; 3:11). Bashir recognizes the symptoms of schizophrenia and is appalled the man isn't receiving proper medical care. The year is 2024.

> BASHIR: ...I mean, look at this man. There's no need for that man to live like that. With the right medication, he could lead a full and normal life.
> SISKO: Maybe in our time.
> BASHIR: Not just in our time. There are any number of effective treatments for schizophrenia, even in this day and age. They could cure that man now, today, if they gave a damn.

In 2014, psychiatric disabilities are treatable, but not curable. Research continues into both causes and treatments. These disabilities don't have one cause; the most current research demonstrates they're a complex interaction between genetic and environmental factors. Antipsychotics, the class of medications used to treat schizophrenia, are generally effective at controlling the symptoms. However, with only a decade left before the year 2024, these drugs are far from the cure Dr. Bashir mentions. One of the significant drawbacks to older antipsychotic medications was the host of side effects that often accompanied the treatment and tended to discourage people from taking them. For example, Thorazine (chlorpromazine) produces tardive dyskinesia, a potentially permanent disorder resulting in involuntary, repetitive body movements. Newer antipsychotic medications have fewer and less severe side effects. As long as a person with schizophrenia is stabilized, current treatment is generally done in an outpatient setting rather than a hospital. However, the disorder has no known cure and medications must often be taken for the rest of a person's life.

Although the antipsychotic drugs discovered in the 1950s led to a numerous research studies for the treatment of mental illnesses, the treatments haven't completely eliminated the need for mental hospitals. In some countries, it's difficult to distinguish between those institutions designed to treat psychiatric disabilities and those that are simply prisons. Mental institutions appear in every series: "Whom Gods Destroy" (1969, TOS; 3:14); "Frame of Mind" (1993, TNG; 6:21); "Shadows and Symbols" (1998, DS9; 7:2); "Endgame, Parts I and II" (2001, VOY; 7:24); "Borderland" (2004, ENT; 4:4) are examples.

In most cases, there's no need for hospitalization. In the small number of cases where a person with mental illness may require that level of treatment (for their own safety or the safety of those around them) it's generally for only a few days. The majority of people with psychiatric disabilities live, work, and socialize without revealing their disability to those around them. The portrayals of psychiatric disabilities on *Star Trek* reflect both our current prejudices and our desire to find a cure for these conditions.

The similarities in schizophrenic symptoms between Sisko and Dukat are as remarkable as the differences. Both Dukat and Sisko have delusions and inflated views of their importance. But where Sisko only made a planet uninhabitable, Dukat killed untold numbers of Bajorans.

I don't plan to let Dr. Bashir off the hook either. Bashir fails to notice the symptoms of schizophrenia in Sisko, who he sees daily. At the same time, he fails to advise Starfleet of Dukat's mental illness. Therefore, I've added medical incompetence to the list of unethical behaviors of the genetically engineered Dr. Julian Bashir. Although I think Bashir is cute with his skirt-chasing, dart-throwing, holosuite adventures and fantasies of being a spy, he's hardly a superior physician.

Chapter 6
"Captain, I Protest. I am NOT a Merry Man"

TROI: Do you want to tell me what's bothering you or would you like to break some more furniture?
"Birthright, Part 1" (1993, TNG; 6:16)

Psychiatric Disabilities (Part 2)

In many ways, emotions define us as Humans. The scarcity of emotions marks Spock, Data, Tuvok, and T'Pol as more alien than their appearances. All four characters experience emotions at some point in their star-trekking. Spock prefers his Vulcan half to his Human half. Spock experiences emotions but subjugates them with logic, except on the flower-power planet. Data's creator gives him emotions by way of a chip, which Data eventually installs in his positronic brain. For a while, Data was in the enviable position of being able to turn the chip off when it suited him. For Vulcans as well as Humans, when emotional balance is lost, there's a danger the person will become disabled by the overwhelming feelings.

"Doctor! My Capillaries are Shrinking!" (Hypochondria)

A person with hypochondria will experience disease-related symptoms, but without a physical cause. They'll often ask for investigations to determine the nature of a suspected underlying illness. Even though people with hypochondria seek confirmation of their afflictions from doctors, or in Barclay's case, the Starfleet Medical Database, they are generally fearful of drugs and their side effects. Instead, they alleviate the anxiety by seeking reassurance through multiple and frequent visits to their doctor or doctors.

In "Realm of Fear" (1992, TNG; 6:2), Barclay sees something in the transporter beam and when the tests on the transporter all come back negative, he begins to suspect that he has *transporter psychosis.*

BARCLAY: I've heard of problems. What about transporter psychosis?

O'BRIEN: Transporter psychosis? There hasn't been a case of that in over fifty years. Not since they perfected the multiplex pattern buffers.

[Scene and Dialogue Omitted]

[Barclay is in his quarters.]

BARCLAY: [pacing back and forth] Computer, access Starfleet Medical Database. Tell me about—er—describe the disorder transporter psychosis. [Barclay sits and begins clenching and unclenching his hands.]

COMPUTER: Transporter psychosis was diagnosed in the year 2209 by researchers on Delinia Two.

BARCLAY: No—no stop. All I need is, what causes it?

COMPUTER: It is caused by a breakdown of neurochemical molecules during transport, affecting the body's motor functions, autonomic systems, and the brain's higher reasoning centers.

BARCLAY: What are the symptoms?

COMPUTER: Victims suffer from paranoid delusions, multi-infarct dementia, hallucinations.

BARCLAY: Hallucinations? What kind of hallucinations?

COMPUTER: Victims experience somatic, tactile and visual hallucinations, accompanied by psychogenic hysteria. Peripheral symptoms include sleeplessness, [Barclay nods], accelerated heart rate, [he puts his hand to his chest and gasps], diminished eyesight leading to acute myopia, [he squints], painful spasms in the extremities, [more clenching and unclenching of his hands], and in most cases, dehydration.

BARCLAY: Computer, what is the treatment for transporter psychosis?

COMPUTER: There is no known treatment. [Barclay gasps and puts his face in his hands.]

INCOMING MESSAGE:

Computers have made it easy for people to self-diagnose.

During a briefing in engineering, Barclay's hypochondriacal behavior doesn't go unnoticed.

DATA: Geordi. Lieutenant Barclay appears inordinately preoccupied with his physiological condition. I have seen him check his pulse rate, as well as his visual acuity several times over the last twenty minutes.

At the conclusion of the episode, Barclay discovers that there's something in the transporter beam, and he's not experiencing transporter psychosis. However, his hypochondria continues in "Genesis" (1994, TNG; 7:19), when he visits Dr. Crusher to confirm another one of his self-diagnoses.

BARCLAY: Blurred vision, dizziness, palpitations, a stinging sensation in the lower spine. It's Terrelian Death syndrome, isn't it?
CRUSHER: I thought we agreed you'd come to me before checking Starfleet Medical Database.
BARCLAY: Yes, well, this time I'm glad I did. Maybe we can stop the cellular decay before it's too late.
CRUSHER: Reg, you don't have Terrelian Death syndrome.
BARCLAY: You—you're sure?
CRUSHER: I'm sure.
BARCLAY: [Barclay picks up Crusher's tricorder off the console and begins to scan himself.] Then maybe it is Symbalene blood burn.
CRUSHER: No, no. [Barclay hands the tricorder back to Crusher.] I don't see anything wrong with you at all. [Barclay points towards the bottom screen of the tricorder.] Wait a minute, [she sighs] there is a slight imbalance in your K three cell count.
BARCLAY: My K threes? Oh, no.
CRUSHER: Barclay, I'm sure it's nothing. Look, I'll run a microcellular scan. We'll see. This'll take a couple of minutes.

[Dialogue Omitted]

BARCLAY [Holding the medical tricorder.]: My intravascular pressure, it's going right through the roof.

CRUSHER: You're right, it is elevated. You've also got heightened electrophoretic activity.

BARCLAY: Electrophoretic activity? Is it serious?

CRUSHER: Well, based on this, I'd say you've got seventy, maybe eighty years.

BARCLAY: Eighty? Eighty years?

CRUSHER: Yes, Reg. What you've got is a mild case of Urodelan Flu. It's nothing serious. Most humans have a natural immunity to it, but the T-cell in your DNA that would normally fight off the infection is dormant.

BARCLAY: So you mean I have bad genes?

CRUSHER: You have one dormant gene out of a hundred thousand, and I can activate that gene with a synthetic T-cell to let the body attack the infection naturally. You should feel better in a couple of days.

BARCLAY: Thank you, Doctor. I feel much better.

The problem with hypochondria is that sometimes the patient is truly ill and their attention-seeking behavior clouds the doctor's judgment about the seriousness of any specific complaint. In Barclay's case, he becomes *patient zero* for a ship-wide epidemic in which the crew members devolve into lower lifeforms. But Barclay's troubles are not over once the cure is found.

BARCLAY: So, this is my fault?

CRUSHER: No. In a way it's mine. I didn't realize it at the time, but there's an anomaly in your genetic chemistry that caused the synthetic T-cell to mutate. Instead of activating one dormant gene, it started activating all of them, including your introns.

BARCLAY: And that's what—er—and that's what caused me to devolve?

CRUSHER: You and every other member of the crew. The T-cell became airborne and started to spread like a virus. You know, Reg, this is a completely new disease, and it's traditional to classify a new disease with the name of the first diagnosed patient.

BARCLAY: Oh! You mean you want to name the disease after me?

CRUSHER: That's right. How about Barclay's Protomorphosis syndrome?

BARCLAY: Barclay's Protomorphosis. It has a nice ring to it. Thank you, Doctor. [Barclay leaves.]

CRUSHER: He transformed into a spider and now he has a disease named after him.

TROI: I think I'd better clear my calendar for the next few weeks.

INCOMING MESSAGE:
People with hypochondria are truly worried about their own health.
Counseling can help with anxiety disorders including hypochondria.

Counselors in this century would generally treat hypochondria with cognitive-behavioral therapy, in a similar manner as with other anxiety disorders. One of the treatment goals for Lieutenant Barclay would be to stop self-diagnosing with the Starfleet Medical Database. I don't hold out much hope for Dr. Crusher on this one.

The Doctor also had to contend with a crewman with hypochondria—William Telfer in "Good Shepherd" (2000, VOY; 6:20).

THE DOCTOR: Mr. Telfer is a hypochondriac. I'd treat him for it, but he's afraid of medication.

JANEWAY: Have you tried counseling?

THE DOCTOR: He's afraid of that, too. All I can do is scan him and offer him reassurance.

INCOMING MESSAGE:
Sometimes reassurance can be an effective treatment for mild anxiety disorders.

While we may refer to someone as a hypochondriac in a colloquial sense, the clinical disorder infringes on the person's quality of life. While preoccupation with one's health may be annoying to others, it's even more unpleasant for the person with the hypochondriacal disorder. The anxiety over potential illness is real and frightening.

The USS Phobia

The ICD-10 describes *specific phobias* as consistent fearful reactions triggered by proximity or exposure to highly specific situations. The degree to which the phobia causes impairment depends on how easy it is for the person to avoid the phobic situation. One of the best examples of a specific phobia is Garak's claustrophobia on *Star Trek: Deep Space Nine*. In order for Garak to be diagnosed as having a simple phobia, he needs to show evidence of certain criteria.

First, anyone with a phobia has psychological or physical symptoms, which are evidence of their anxiety. In "By Inferno's Light" (1997, DS9; 5:15) Garak talks to himself while trying to work in a narrow crawl space with fiber-optic strands that are providing a flickering light source.

> GARAK: I'm sorry, but that's absolutely unacceptable. I'm under enough strain as it is, I can't have you quitting on me. Get a hold of yourself, Garak. After all, you haven't had one of these attacks in years. Yes, this is a tight enclosed space. Yes, there's not a lot of room to move. But a disciplined mind does not allow itself to be sidetracked by niggling psychological disorders like claustrophobia. Besides, this isn't like Tzenketh. The walls won't collapse in on you. Your friends are nearby, there's plenty of air, so there's nothing to be concerned about. Focus on the job. You're the only person who can contact the runabout. People are depending on you. Ziyal is depending on you. You promised her you'd come back, and that young lady has had quite enough disappointments in her life without you adding to them, so control yourself. You're stronger than this. A disciplined mind—[And the light goes out.]

RED ALERT!:
Phobias can be overcome by sheer willpower.

Garak is neither delusional nor obsessional which would preclude a diagnosis of phobia. Instead, he's clearly trying to manage his anxiety over being in a small space.

Second, the person's anxiety must be restricted to the specific situation;, in this case being in a closed space. In "Afterimage" (1998, DS9; 7:3), Garak has a panic attack, collapses, and is taken to the infirmary. Odo is with Garak in his shop when the anxiety attack occurs.

ODO: He had a claustrophobic attack in his shop.

SISKO: His shop? I don't understand. That's a good sized space.

GARAK: I know. I've been claustrophobic for as long as I can remember, but lately it seems to have gotten worse. Rooms that I once found completely tolerable now suddenly feel alarmingly cramped.

The final criterion is that the individual with the phobia tries to avoid everything connected with the trigger. Since Garak was decoding a message for Starfleet when he experienced his claustrophobia, he decides he'll no longer be able to offer that service.

GARAK: Well, I don't feel fine. Would you gentlemen mind terribly if we continued this conversation on the Promenade?

[On the Promenade.]

ODO: Better?

GARAK: A little.

SISKO: Mr. Garak, as much as I appreciate your situation, I'm not sure why you asked to see me.

GARAK: I was hoping you'd be kind enough to express my regrets to Starfleet Intelligence. When I get this way, my concentration isn't what it should be. I'm afraid I won't be decoding any transmissions for a while.

SISKO: Can I tell them when to expect you back on the job?

GARAK: I wish I could say. Believe me, I'm not happy about this either. I want to see an end to this war just as much as you. And now, if you'll excuse me, I'm going to go hem some pants. For some reason, sewing seems to calm me down.

INCOMING MESSAGE:
Performing normal activities, such as sewing,
can have a calming effect.

With all the sensitivity of a Klingon Targ, Starfleet insists that Garak continue to decode the messages. Sisko sends Ezri Dax (counselor in training) over to Garak's shop to help him. In what I can only describe as a textbook example of "How Not To Be a Counselor," here's their conversation.

EZRI: Am I interrupting?

GARAK: Ah. You must be Ezri Dax. The Captain told me that you'd be dropping by to counsel me.

EZRI: Is that all right?

GARAK: Oh, it all depends on what it involves. I'm a very private person.

EZRI: I understand. So is it helping? The sewing. Is it making you feel better?

GARAK: Thankfully, yes.

EZRI: You're lucky, nothing helps me.

GARAK: Are you claustrophobic too?

EZRI: Why would you say that?

GARAK: You just said—

EZRI: No, I get space sick. Ever since I was joined. I'm very sensitive to motion. I can even feel the station spinning.

GARAK: Really?

EZRI: It's because of what happened to Torias. He was killed in a shuttle accident.

GARAK: But why would that make you space sick?

EZRI: Because I blame myself for what happened.

GARAK: You were piloting?

EZRI: Yes. No. Depends on how you look at it. Torias was my fifth host. Didn't I say that?

GARAK: No.

EZRI: Well, he was. And I think the reason that his death has stayed with me for so long is because I just can't seem to forgive him for getting himself killed.

GARAK: But you said it was an accident. So if he's not to blame, then you're not to blame—either.

EZRI: I know—but somehow I can't help but punish myself for it.

GARAK: By getting space sick.

EZRI: Exactly.

GARAK: Don't take this the wrong way, but it sounds to me as if you're the one that needs to see a counselor.

EZRI: You're probably right. But I didn't come here to talk about myself, I came to talk about you.

GARAK: So you did.

EZRI: Do you remember anything traumatic happening to you when you were young? Something involving getting trapped in a confined space?

GARAK: If I had been that careless, my father would have left me there to teach me a lesson.

EZRI: Sounds like he was strict.

GARAK: He didn't get to be the head of the Obsidian Order without a sense of discipline.

EZRI: Did he discipline you?

GARAK: He punished me when I misbehaved. What father wouldn't?

EZRI: Tobin. My second host. He could not bring himself to discipline his children, no matter what they did. But that's another story. How did you say that your father punished you?

GARAK: He'd lock me in a closet.

EZRI: Why didn't you mention that when I asked if you'd ever been trapped in a confined space?

GARAK: I wasn't trapped. I knew he'd let me out as soon as I learned my lesson.

EZRI: Learned your lesson? Did you think you deserved to be locked in that closet?

GARAK: I could be very stubborn.

EZRI: You blame yourself. Just like I blame myself for that shuttle accident. Maybe you get claustrophobic for the same reason that I get space sick. We're both punishing ourselves for things that weren't our fault. That's it. Don't you see? We both have to let go of all this misplaced guilt.

GARAK: And if we do, our problems will simply disappear?

EZRI: Not overnight, but it's a step in the right direction.

GARAK: Well, I'll certainly give your advice some thought.

EZRI: Me too. Are you all right?

GARAK: To tell the truth, I'm starting to feel a little claustrophobic.

EZRI: Probably because we've been talking about it. Actually, I'm starting to feel a little space sick myself.

GARAK: If it's all the same to you, I think I'll go back to my sewing.

EZRI: Good idea.

GARAK: Thank you for stopping by.

EZRI: My pleasure.

In the end, Garak realizes that he has associated decoding the messages for Starfleet with guilt about betraying his fellow Cardassians. Once he examines this association, he's able to resume decoding the messages. At the same time, he continues to be claustrophobic. Unlike Ezri's inept attempt, most successful counseling for phobias involves behavioral therapy where the person is taught to relax before exposure to the phobia trigger. Counselor Troi attempts to use this approach with Reginald Barclay to overcome his fear of transporting in "Realm of Fear" (1992, TNG; 6:2).

TROI: ...Reg, you're not the first person to have anxiety about transporting. We can desensitize you to this type of fear. It's a slow and gradual process, but it works.

BARCLAY: It does? How?

TROI: Well, you might first try a relaxation technique, like plexing.

BARCLAY: Plexing?

TROI: Yes, it's a Betazoid method. The next time you feel nervous about transporting, you stimulate a neural pressure point, like this. [Troi taps behind her right ear.] There's a nerve cluster just behind the carotid artery. It stimulates the part of the brain that releases natural endorphins.

BARCLAY: Plexing. Sounds easy enough.

[Troi guides Barclay's fingers to the right place.]

TROI: Here. There.

BARCLAY: You know, I feel better already. I think I can do this.

TROI: There's no need to rush.

BARCLAY: No, no. We talked about confronting my fears. The best way out is through. You said that once, remember?

TROI: I suppose I did.

BARCLAY: I'm going to beam over there. I can do it.

INCOMING MESSAGE:

Phobias cannot be cured in just one counseling session.

Since transporter phobia is a fictitious phobia, it's appropriate that it would be treated with *plexing*—a fictitious treatment. However, the idea of combining a relaxing activity while thinking about a stress-inducing one is a common form of behavioral therapy used to treat phobias.

O'Brien supports Barclay's determination not to let his fears get the better of him. As only an Irishman on *Star Trek* can do, O'Brien shares with Barclay his story of overcoming arachnophobia.

O'BRIEN: I know how you feel about this, sir.

BARCLAY: You're afraid of transporting, too?

O'BRIEN: No. Arachnids. Sickening, crawly little things, don't you think? All those legs.

BARCLAY: Spiders? They've never bothered me.

O'BRIEN: A few years back, I was called in to re-route an emitter array at a Starbase on Zayra Four. Turns out the entire system was infested with Talarian hook spiders. You ever seen a Talarian hook spider? Their legs are half a meter long. Well, I had a choice. Do I walk away and let the emitter blow itself to hell, or do I crawl in the Jeffries tube with twenty hook spiders?

BARCLAY: What happened?

O'BRIEN: It was the hardest thing I ever did, but I got through it. After that, I was never quite as afraid of spiders.

BARCLAY: Thanks.

O'BRIEN: Energizing.

INCOMING MESSAGE:
Immersion therapy can be effective,
especially when an emitter is about to blow.

"Realm of Fear" deals with both a fictional phobia and treatment. In "Night" (1998, VOY; 5:1), The Doctor prescribes a real treatment for Neelix, a mild sedative, when Neelix suffers from another *Star Trek* original phobia.

THE DOCTOR: I've given you a mild sedative. It should control the urge to hyperventilate, and alleviate some of your anxiety.

NEELIX: Anxiety? Anxiety's what I feel when I burn a pot roast. This—this is more like—

THE DOCTOR: Dizziness? Nausea? Unspeakable dread?

NEELIX: Yes.

THE DOCTOR: Nihiliphobia; the fear of nothingness. Or in layman's terms, the fear of Nothingness. If it's any consolation, I can relate to it. I go into a void every time I'm deactivated. Emptiness, complete and utter oblivion. I'll admit it was unsettling at first. The existential horror of it all.

NEELIX: You're not helping, Doctor.

THE DOCTOR: Sorry. My point is you'll get used to it.

NEELIX: I hope so.

INCOMING MESSAGE:
Reactions to phobias can manifest as physical sensations.

The Doctor seems to have downloaded the flawed "Ezri Dax's Counseling Treatment for Phobias" program. Medication for phobias can include both short-term medications such as sedatives, as well as long-term medications such as anti-anxiety drugs. Anti-anxiety medications circumvent the feelings of anxiety associated with the trigger. Once the association between the trigger and the anxiety reaction has been broken, the person can learn to approach the trigger without anticipating feelings of fear or symptoms of panic.

For *Star Trek* fans who keep track of these things, there are three other references to phobias which bear mentioning. Barclay isn't the only Starfleet officer who has a fear of transporters. Dr. McCoy and Ensign Hoshi Sato also avoid them whenever they can. Ensign Hoshi Sato also had claustrophobia, which made wearing spacesuits rather uncomfortable for her in more ways than one. Lieutenant Malcolm Reed chose Starfleet over the Royal Navy because he had *aquaphobia*—the fear of water or drowning. And in "Star Trek" (2009), Bones states he has a phobia:

McCoy: I suffer from aviophobia. It means fear of dying in something that flies.

Aviophobia actually means the fear of flying, and it appears McCoy's admission to having this phobia is meant to be a humorous way of expressing his poor fit as a doctor on a starship, rather than admitting to an actual phobia. Considering the humor in the scene, I think my interpretation is warranted. And when Wesley asks his mother if she is afraid of the captain in "Encounter at Farpoint" (1987, TNG; 1:1), Wesley is referring to Picard's intimidating persona and not a form of *phalacrophobia*, the fear of baldness.

Mr. Broccoli's Social Phobia

Shyness is different from a social phobia. Shyness is a slight discomfort associated with meeting new people. Social phobia is a full-blown anxiety reaction to social events, associated with a fear of being judged. Generally, a person with social phobia has low self-esteem and avoids social situations because of their fear of criticism. The anxiety reaction may include flushing, trembling hands, and feeling nauseated, which is the first criteria for the diagnosis. For some people with social phobia, the symptoms may progress to panic attacks. One of the key aspects of social phobia is the high degree of avoidance the person engages in to avoid social situations, thus creating a disabling degree of impairment in work and life functioning.

The poster child for social phobia is Lieutenant Reginald Barclay, and "Hollow Pursuits" (1990, TNG; 3:21) depicts his phobia in one of the most memorable *TNG* episodes of all time. Barclay's symptoms of social anxiety are so pronounced that he makes those around him uncomfortable.

PICARD: I'm not accustomed to seeing an unsatisfactory rating for one of my crew.

RIKER: I guess the issue is whether Mr. Barclay is Enterprise material.

PICARD: I assume from your request for his transfer that you think he's not, Commander.

LA FORGE: I hate to say it but, I always thought I could work with anybody. But I just don't understand this guy. Broccoli makes me nervous, Captain. He makes everybody nervous.

PICARD: Broccoli?

RIKER: Young Mr. Crusher started that. I guess it's caught on.

PICARD: Let's just get that uncaught, shall we? There's every indication he's served competently in Starfleet for years. His ratings aboard the Zhukov were satisfactory. In fact I recall Captain Gleason speaking quite highly of him before his transfer.

INCOMING MESSAGE:

If you value diversity,
don't get rid of the person who doesn't fit in.

The second diagnostic guideline is that the anxiety must be restricted to or predominate in particular social situations. After being embarrassed by Wesley at an engineering briefing, Barclay retreats into a holodeck program. Barclay's program alleviates his social phobia because the holo-versions of his shipmates are less intimidating.

The third and final criterion is that the central characteristic of the person's social phobia will be avoidance of the types of situations which trigger the anxiety. Barclay's primary trigger for social phobia is to be in situations where his performance is being evaluated by others. This has been a long-standing problem for Barclay.

RIKER: I've reviewed Barclay's psychological profile. He's always had seclusive tendencies—it was noted at the Academy more than once—

INCOMING MESSAGE:

Social phobias are often ignored rather than treated.

La Forge orders Barclay to seek help from Counselor Troi. Since Barclay has already been interacting with his holodeck version of Counselor Troi, he's uncomfortable with the real person. When Barclay enters Troi's office, she's sitting in the same way and dressed in the same outfit as in Barclay's fantasy program. Barclay, on the other hand, acts in an entirely different manner from his behavior on the holodeck. He takes a seat on the far end of the couch sitting as far from Troi as he can get. She studies him sympathetically.

TROI: I can tell this is difficult for you.
[Barclay is only able to nod.]
TROI: Is there anything I can do to make you more comfortable?
BARCLAY [Responds too quickly.]: No!
[Troi smiles her best therapeutic smile at him.]
TROI: Have you ever been with a counselor before?
BARCLAY [swallowing]: Yes. No.
TROI [smiles]: Which one?
BARCLAY: Yes. But she—it wasn't real—really a counselor.
TROI: Most people find a counselor intimidating at first. It's okay, if you feel that way toward me.
BARCLAY: Not—at all.
TROI: Good. Close your eyes—lean back.
BARCLAY: Why?
TROI [standing]: I just want to help you relax.
BARCLAY [reacts]: You do?
[She walks by him to a light panel and turns the lights down.]
TROI: Put your feet up. It's okay. And close your eyes.
[Barclay puts his feet up and closes his eyes—tightly.]
BARCLAY: What are you going to do?
TROI: Just listen to the sound of my voice. Take a slow deep breath through your nose—and let it out through your mouth just as slowly. Good—there—that's better—isn't it?
BARCLAY: Oh, yes—oh, yes, much better. This has been—extremely helpful— [Barclay stands up.] Well, thank you for your time.
TROI: But—

[Barclay starts to back out of the room.]

BARCLAY: Really—very helpful—in through the nose, out through the mouth—
I'll practice and let you know—thank you again—

[Barclay bolts from the room, leaving Troi with a puzzled look on her face.]

INCOMING MESSAGE:
Social phobias are difficult to treat because
the person with the phobia must interact with the counselor.

While Ezri Dax wins the prize for "How Not To Be a Counselor," Reginald Barclay wins the prize for "How Not To Be a Client." The portrayal of the counseling session isn't far from the reality of how a therapist would treat someone with a social phobia. The first intervention in the treatment plan is teaching the client how to produce a relaxed state of being. The next step is to have the client maintain that state of relaxation while visualizing a situation that would normally trigger anxiety. From visualization, the counselor moves gradually to closer and closer approximations of the actual social situations that produce the most amount of fear. Often along with anti-anxiety medications to bolster the relaxation state, the ultimate goal is for the client to enter a social situation that has previously evoked a phobic reaction, while holding the relaxed state during the exposure.

While Barclay improves his social skills in this and future episodes, he never quite becomes completely comfortable outside the holodeck. However, he does learn to talk to the real Counselor Troi without running out of the room.

Wil Wheaton, the actor who played Wesley Crusher, has posted about his personal struggles with anxiety and depression on his blog (WilWheaton.net). He writes about his decisions regarding medication and psychotherapy along with his continuing struggles. Even *Star Trek* fans who don't like the character of Wesley Crusher can find Wheaton's blog inspiring because of the authentic way in which he writes about these psychiatric disabilities. Unlike Wesley Crusher, Wil Wheaton has an edgy sense of humor and his language is more Klingon than golden-child.

"Computer, End Program" (Post-traumatic Stress Disorder)

Stress reactions to battle are probably as old as war itself. For centuries, doctors recognized *battle fatigue* as a short-term reaction to extreme stress characterized by slower reaction times, indecision, and difficulty prioritizing. While battle fatigue was considered a temporary psychological condition, *shell shock* was considered to be an injury. According to Jones and Wessley, in 1910 Mott stated that during World War I doctors concluded that "mere proximity to the explosion is sufficient to cause organic changes in the brain and spinal cord by the atmospheric compression and expression." Post-traumatic Stress Disorder differs from battle fatigue and shell shock because it's considered a psychiatric disability which is neither short-term nor caused by a specific physical injury.

The second most common psychiatric disability on *Star Trek* is Post-traumatic Stress Disorder, often referred to by its abbreviation "PTSD." According to the ICD-10, in order to be diagnosed with PTSD *the person must have been exposed to a stressful event or situation that threatens their safety or is so catastrophic in nature any person would be distressed by the experience.*

In "Memorial" (2000, VOY; 6:14), Chakotay, Paris, Kim, and Neelix begin experiencing strange visions after returning to Voyager following a two week planet-scanning mission. Back on board, they all begin to remember being involved in a military operation where eighty-two civilians were killed and the bodies vaporized in order to cover up the massacre—which fits the first criterion for PTSD.

The second criterion for PTSD requires that *the person is in a state of constant remembering or re-experiencing the trauma, or that the person has intrusive flashbacks that are sudden vivid memories triggered by something associated with the trauma.* Paris and Chakotay relive the battle in their dreams, which also fits this criterion. Kim has an anxiety attack during routine maintenance. Neelix experiences auditory hallucinations and a vivid flashback which prompts him to hold Naomi Wildman behind the mess hall counter because he believes they're still under attack. After Neelix is taken to sickbay, The Doctor explains his test results.

> THE DOCTOR: His norepinephrine levels are three times what they should be. Neurochemically speaking, he's suffering from a form of post-traumatic stress disorder.
> CHAKOTAY: I dreamed I was fighting in an alien war. The same war Neelix seemed to be reliving.
> THE DOCTOR: Harry Kim was in earlier. He had an anxiety attack. I haven't spoken with Mr. Paris yet.

INCOMING MESSAGE:

Exposure to trauma will produce flashbacks,
hallucinations, and sleep disturbances.

RED ALERT!

People with PTSD are walking time bombs.

The third criteria is *avoidance, or attempts to avoid situations that are associated with the trauma.* For Neelix, this takes the form of avoiding Naomi because he doesn't feel in control of the triggers.

NEELIX: Naomi must be terrified of me after what happened in the galley.
SEVEN: She's concerned about you. She told me she wants to visit you.
NEELIX: No, not like this. I might do something to scare her again.
SEVEN: I'll give her your regards.

INCOMING MESSAGE:

People with PTSD often isolate themselves
because they think they can't be helped.

The fourth and final PTSD criterion is *the diminished ability to remember certain important aspects of the trauma, or related symptoms of psychological sensitivity including constant arousal produced by two of the following:*

- *Difficulty falling or staying asleep*
    TORRES: Sleep a little?
    PARIS: Five, six minutes.
- *Difficulty concentrating*
    PARIS: I can't concentrate on sensor readings right now.
    TORRES: Try.
- *Irritability or outbursts of anger*
    PARIS: I can't! Stop pushing me! I don't want your help! I'm sorry.
    TORRES: You know where to find me.

- *Hypervigilance*
  PARIS: Tarakis, dead ahead.
  JANEWAY: Shields. Stand by weapons. On screen. Scan for vessels.
- *Exaggerated startle response*
  THE DOCTOR: It sounds like you had an anxiety attack.
  KIM: I've never been claustrophobic before.

INCOMING MESSAGE:
PTSD is a serious condition.

As the PTSD symptoms spread to the crew of the entire ship, The Doctor administers a neural suppressant to Captain Janeway which prevents her from experiencing the memories while she seeks to find a remedy. As they retraced the flight of the shuttle, they discover the source of the PTSD symptoms. Even though the episode provides an effective depiction of the symptoms of PTSD, it turns out that the crew never took part in the battle. On the surface of Tarakis, the crew finds the source of their wartime memories in a large monument etched with alien symbols.

SEVEN: The structure contains a synaptic transmitter. I believe it was designed to send neurogenic pulses throughout this system.
JANEWAY: So anyone passing through would experience the Nakan massacre, like we did.
SEVEN: Precisely.
CHAKOTAY: Try running those symbols inscribed on the base through the translation matrix. [Reading from the translation matrix.]
Words alone cannot convey the suffering.
Words alone cannot prevent what happened here from happening again.
Beyond words lies experience.
Beyond experience lies truth.
Make this truth your own.
JANEWAY: It's a memorial. We weren't victims of a conspiracy; we were witnesses to a massacre.

INCOMING MESSAGE:
In order to prevent repeating mistakes,
we must not forget previous wrongful behavior.

Even though the alien device is the source of their memories rather than physical trauma, the symptoms the Voyager crew experience meet all the criteria for a PTSD diagnosis in this century.

"Memorial" ends without an explanation of how the crew will deal with their memories, flashbacks, or anxiety. Treatments in our century include *cognitive processing therapy* and medications for the symptoms of anxiety, depression, and sleep disorders.

Cognitive processing therapy for PTSD involves the person examining their own beliefs about safety, trust, control, self-esteem, other people, and how relationships can change as a result of a trauma. The goal is to find a balance between the person's beliefs before and after the trauma. The theory is that a person continues to *process* their traumatic memories via flashbacks until they have reconciled what happened with who they are as a person. Cognitive processing therapy is the most effective form of talk therapy for returning veterans with PTSD.

Flashbacks of the traumatic event are not necessary for a PTSD diagnosis as Ambassador Lwaxana Troi demonstrates in "Dark Page" (1993, TNG; 7:7). Ambassador Troi provides an example of the first half of the fourth criterion, *an inability to recall either partially or completely some important aspect of the period of exposure to the stressor.* Ambassador Troi is Betazoid, so the writers take a few liberties with her symptoms and introduce the "metaconscious" which Counselor Troi describes:

TROI: It's a part of the Betazoid psyche. It's a kind of filtering mechanism that protects us from psychic trauma.

Ambassador Troi becomes disabled when her blocked memories of the death of her first daughter, Kestra, are no longer filtered by her metaconscious. Although Humans don't have a metaconscious, we can block memories of traumatic events. Unfortunately, long-term obstruction of memories doesn't protect Humans from the other symptoms of PTSD; the blocking simply hides the reason for the sleep disturbances or other symptoms.

Guilt plays a significant role in the amount of time it takes to recover from a trauma and the PTSD that may result. The more the victim feels responsible, the more severe the symptoms and longer the recovery period. I can illustrate the role of guilt in traumatic events by comparing the different experiences of Counselor Troi in "Violations" (1992, TNG; 5:12), and Timmy in "Hero Worship" (1992, TNG; 5:11).

When Counselor Troi is telepathically raped by a visiting alien, her PTSD symptoms are different because Troi was victimized and she has no guilt about the attack. In "Hero Worship," Timmy believes his inadvertent touching of something on the control panel on the Vico caused the destruction of the ship. Both of Timmy's parents were killed in the accident and he's now the lone survivor. As Timmy attempts to deal with the overwhelming loss and guilt, he begins to emulate Data because androids don't experience emotions. Children with PTSD don't always fit the adult criteria of the disorder and it's often difficult to distinguish between PTSD and a normal reaction to traumatic events. When Timmy learns that his behavior had nothing to do with the accident, he's finally able to accept his parents' deaths and he abandons his android persona. Timmy's Data-emulating behavior help him cope, and although he doesn't fit all of the adult criteria, Timmy's PTSD is diagnosed by his need for these coping behaviors.

Not every traumatic event results in PTSD. In "Hero Worship" La Forge recalls a traumatic event in his childhood, one that while upsetting, didn't have long term consequences.

LA FORGE: I was caught in a fire once. I must have been, I don't know, about five, I guess. It was before I got the first VISOR. And it was only a couple of minutes before my parents found me and pulled me out. And nobody got hurt, but I tell you that was the longest couple of minutes of my life. It was a while after that before I could even let my parents get out of earshot. It was like I absolutely needed to know that they were there, you know?

Symptoms of PTSD vary with the person and the situation. In "Hard Time" (1996, DS9; 4:18), the symptoms exhibited by Miles O'Brien are different from the ones seen in "Memorial" (2000, VOY; 6:14), yet both stories share one significant feature—the traumatic events never actually happened. Rinn, the alien corrections officer, explains:

KIRA: It's me, Chief.

O'BRIEN: It can't be. It's been twenty years. You haven't changed at all.

RINN: Only a few hours passed during your correction.

O'BRIEN: I don't understand.

KIRA: Chief, I know this is going to be hard for you to accept—but you haven't been in prison. What you experienced was an artificial reality, an interactive program that created memories of things that never actually happened.

O'BRIEN: What?

RINN: The Major is correct. We punish our offenders by giving them memories of incarceration modeled to fit each offender's personality. It's more efficient and much more effective than maintaining an extensive prison system.

KIRA: Which means that what you think you experienced in prison, the things you remember, didn't happen. It wasn't real.

O'BRIEN: It's real to me, Major. It's real to me.

Although Chief O'Brien only experiences the trauma of his incarceration in his mind, the effects of his imprisonment are no less profound.

BASHIR: The bottom line is, there isn't much I can do. The Argrathi didn't just install memory implants. They ran Miles through a highly realistic time-compressed simulation of the prison experience. In his mind, he lived those twenty years. He reacted to everything that happened. He felt pain, fear, hatred. He made choices and decisions that affected the outcome. As a result, those memories are real. The only way I could rid him of the memories would be to wipe his entire memory clean, and clearly that isn't an option.

INCOMING MESSAGE:
PTSD is real and there are no simple fixes.

When the memories begin to affect O'Brien's ability to function as chief of engineering he has a confrontation with Captain Sisko.

O'BRIEN: Sir, you're blowing this all out of proportion.

SISKO: You know that's not true. What happened on Argratha affected you a lot more than you're willing to admit. And it's not going to get better overnight, no matter how much you want it to—you need help.

O'BRIEN: Please, Captain. I'm asking you as a personal favor to me, give me one more chance.

SISKO: I wish I could. But right now, in the judgment of this station's Chief Medical Officer, you're unfit for duty—which means you're on medical leave effective immediately. And if you don't begin attending counseling sessions on a regular basis, and cooperating in every other way with your physician, I will have no choice but to have you confined to the infirmary. Is that clear?

O'BRIEN: Yes, sir.

SISKO: Dismissed.

INCOMING MESSAGE:

*PTSD symptoms can be disabling to the point that
they interfere with the person's work.*

O'Brien has an argument with Bashir over Bashir's playing The-High-And-Mighty-Chief-Medical-Officer, and then returns to his quarters since he's not allowed to return to his job. Keiko tries to comfort her husband, but he explodes in anger at their daughter, Molly. O'Brien apologizes profusely and leaves to take out his anger on defenseless crates and barrels in a cargo bay. The he notices *Wall Unit 47—Weapons Locker, Authorized Personnel Only.* He taps in the code, takes out one of the six hand phasers, winds the power level to the highest setting, and puts it under his chin. He sits down on a stand and closes his eyes with the phaser at his neck. Bashir walks in as O'Brien is sitting there.

BASHIR: Chief?

O'BRIEN: Get out of here, Julian.

BASHIR: You don't want to do this, Chief.

O'BRIEN: The hell I don't.

BASHIR: Look, I don't claim to know what you're going through, but whatever it is, it's not worth dying for.

O'BRIEN: You don't understand at all. I'm not doing this for me. I'm doing this to protect Keiko—and Molly—and everyone else on the station.

BASHIR: Protect us from what?

O'BRIEN: From me. I'm not the man I used to be. I'm dangerous. I nearly hit Molly today. All she wanted was a little attention and I nearly hit her.

BASHIR: But you didn't. You're a good man, Miles Edward O'Brien. And whatever it is you think you've done wrong, you don't deserve to die.

O'BRIEN: You sound like Ee'Char.

BASHIR: Who's Ee'Char?

[Ee'Char appears in O'Brien's vision]

O'BRIEN: He's not real. He's just a memory, that's all.

BASHIR: A memory from Argratha? Who was he? Another prisoner? A guard?

O'BRIEN: He was my cell mate.

[Flashback Dialogue Omitted]

Even though he was never imprisoned with Ee'Char, O'Brien has tremendous guilt over killing Ee'Char in his mind.

BASHIR: You killed him?

O'BRIEN: And the worst part of it was, the next day the guards began feeding me again. I'd killed him for nothing, for a scrap of bread he was going to share with me.

BASHIR: But it was a mistake. You didn't mean it.

O'BRIEN: I meant it. I wanted him to die. I keep telling myself it doesn't matter. It wasn't real. But that's a lie. If it had been real, if it had been you instead of him, it wouldn't have made any difference. He was my best friend and I murdered him. When we were growing up, they used to tell us humanity had evolved, that mankind had outgrown hate and rage. But when it came down to it, when I had the chance to show that no matter what anyone did to me, I was still an evolved Human being. I failed. I repaid kindness with blood. I was no better than an animal.

BASHIR: No, no, no, no. An animal would've killed Ee'char and never had a second thought, never shed a tear. But not you; you hate yourself. You hate yourself so much you think you deserve to die. The Argrathi did everything they could to strip you of your humanity. And in the end, for one brief moment, they succeeded. But you can't let that brief moment define your entire life. If you do, if you pull that trigger, then the Argrathi will have won. They will have destroyed a good man. You cannot let that happen, my friend.

INCOMING MESSAGE:
People with PTSD are at high risk for suicide.

O'Brien allows Bashir to take the phaser from him. The *imaginary* Ee'Char bids farewell to O'Brien and disappears as he walks off. In the next scene, Dr. Bashir hands O'Brien a hypospray as they walk to O'Brien's quarters.

BASHIR: Thirty milligrams twice a day. Take it religiously for a month, and if all goes well we'll experiment with a lower dosage.
O'BRIEN: You sure this'll work?
BASHIR: It's a treatment, not a cure. It'll prevent hallucinations; take the edge off the depression. But that's all it'll do. It won't take away the memories or the feelings.
O'BRIEN: You mean the guilt.
BASHIR: Well, that'll take time.
O'BRIEN: Now's the part where you tell me I have to start seeing Counselor Telnorri again.
BASHIR: Unless you want to talk to me.
O'BRIEN: Telnorri'll be fine. Thanks, Julian; for everything.
BASHIR: What are friends for?

INCOMING MESSAGE:
People with PTSD can experience an improvement in their quality of life
when treated with medication and therapy.

As I wipe the tears out of my eyes from Molly's tender welcome home to her daddy, it's apparent to me that "Hard Time" and "Memorial" are particularly salient for military service members returning to the United States after serving in war zones. Service people who have been in prolonged battles or witnessed violent death are frequently diagnosed with PTSD. Although there is a walking-time-bombs aspect to these episodes, it may be that the writers simply wanted to convey how the person with PTSD feels about returning to civilian life. In neither episode does the person who has PTSD hurt anyone.

"Hard Time" demonstrates powerfully how PTSD relates to the personal meaning of the traumatic experience. Psychiatry has yet to explain how two people in the same life-threatening situation may react differently. One person may develop PTSD while the other is able to tolerate the event without any disabling psychiatric condition. Unlike "Memorial," "Hard Time" describes O'Brien's PTSD treatment, which includes effective medications as well as talk therapy. Until recently, medications only ameliorated some of the symptoms of PTSD such as anxiety, depression, and insomnia.

In May 2013 a report on the effectiveness of a substance similar to medical cannabis was published in *Molecular Psychiatry*. According to the report, this compound demonstrated promise in treating all the symptoms of PTSD including nightmares and flashbacks. In the United States, an increasing number of states have passed medical cannabis legislation and in 2010 the Veterans Administration issued a policy directive that physicians could no longer deny treatment to veterans who are legally medicating with cannabis. However, like many mental health issues, there are often tensions between the medical community and legislators. The issue of medical cannabis is full of controversy. Given the studies which demonstrate the effectiveness of medical cannabis, it's possible the medication Dr. Bashir gave O'Brien had THC in it.

In "The Raven" (1997, VOY; 4:6), Seven of Nine begins to hallucinate the Borg coming to reassimilate her. Seven can't reconcile the fear she experiences as a result of the hallucinations with her belief that she's not afraid because she's Borg. The Doctor hypothesizes that the hallucinations might be caused by post-traumatic stress disorder.

THE DOCTOR: Flashbacks—you could be experiencing some sort of post-traumatic stress disorder.
JANEWAY: Makes sense. You were assimilated by the Borg. You've gone through an intense, prolonged trauma.

As the story unfolds, however, the source of Seven's hallucinations is revealed to be her remaining Borg implants activated by the Voyager's proximity to the Raven. As a child, Seven was on the Raven with her parents when they were captured and assimilated by the Borg. The Doctor is able to treat Seven's PTSD through the adjustment of one of her Borg implants. If only all Humans could be cured of PTSD so easily. Of course, the cure isn't all that desirable if you have to be assimilated by the Borg first.

Although Captain Picard exhibits a few symptoms of PTSD after his abduction and rescue from the Borg, he's never depicted as a potentially violent person because of his experience and neither is Ambassador Troi. "Dark Page" provides the most sympathetic depiction of how a person with PTSD may hide suffering. People with PTSD experience a variety of symptoms, and any specific person may experience all or some of the symptoms.

"Klingon Shades of Blue" (Depression)

While anxiety disorders are the most common psychiatric disabilities in the US, depression is the most common disability world-wide. Often a person may have both. There is a continuum of severity within the depression category.

The ICD-10 describes three categories: mild, moderate and severe. In all three types, the person usually suffers from depressed mood, loss of interest and enjoyment, and reduced energy levels, which can lead to feelings of tiredness sometimes after only slight effort. In "Extreme Risk" (1998, VOY; 5:3), B'Elanna Torres exhibits all these symptoms, as well as well some of the other common symptoms of depression.

When the Malons try to grab Voyager's probe, Janeway hides the probe in a gas giant until they can retrieve it. The senior officers meet to discuss how to retrieve the probe, which is now stuck under an atmosphere so heavy one Malon ship has already imploded while trying to get close.

B'Elanna is uncharacteristically late to the meeting. She sits quietly and provides only short answers when asked for an opinion. Unlike other meetings where she volunteers more information than is always appreciated, B'Elanna is passive.

INCOMING MESSAGE:
People who are depressed often experience problems
with concentration and focus.

As Paris enthusiastically describes his hot rod shuttle fantasy, the Delta Flyer, Torres remains lost in her own thoughts. When Paris asks her if she'll help build the Flyer, Torres nods in agreement with a forced smile on her face. Janeway appears concerned about her chief engineer's lack of interest.

Later, while working with Kim, Tuvok, Paris, and Seven, Seven calls Torres' designs flawed and B'Elanna acquiesces in a most non-Klingon/non-Torres fashion. Her submissive responses elicit looks from everyone in the room.

That night when Torres delivers some specs for the Flyer, Paris confronts her about her lack of enthusiasm.

PARIS: B'Elanna, what's going on?

TORRES: Nothing.

PARIS: Well, then how come it's impossible to have a conversation with you?

TORRES: I'm sorry.

PARIS: I don't want an apology. I want an explanation.

TORRES: Tom, I'm tired.

PARIS: Asleep is more like it. You hardly said three words in that last meeting, and then when Seven changed your design you acted like, like you didn't care.

TORRES: I guess I didn't.

PARIS: I don't get it. How many times have we talked about how great it would be to do what we're doing now? To really collaborate my piloting skills and your engineering expertise. We finally get the chance to create something together from the ground up and you're not the slightest bit enthusiastic?

INCOMING MESSAGE:

People who are depressed often lack confidence
or experience diminished self-esteem.

Rather than return to her quarters to sleep, B'Elanna goes to the holodeck to play extreme patty-cake with Cardassian thugs—Klingon style.

INCOMING MESSAGE:

People who are depressed often have sleep disturbances.

The aftermath of the workout requires B'Elanna to self-administer some first aid. Still upset, she seeks out Neelix and some comfort food in the flavor of banana pancakes. But once she gets her banana pancakes, she takes only one bite and leaves.

INCOMING MESSAGE:
People who are depressed often experience a lack of appetite.

Unable to determine whether the projected micro-fractures in the Delta Flyer present a fatal flaw in the design, Torres goes to test the shuttle on the holodeck with the safety protocols turned off. By this time, I expect the computer to respond to Torres's instruction to turn off the safety protocols with, "Naturally." During the simulation, Torres is severely injured. Didn't see that coming, did you?

TORRES: Captain, what's going on?

JANEWAY: When The Doctor examined you he found evidence of internal bleeding, fractured vertebrae, contusions, cranial trauma.

TORRES: I guess the accident was pretty serious.

JANEWAY: The injuries I'm talking about didn't happen recently. Some of them are weeks, even months old.

TORRES: Well, I'm an engineer. I've had my share of bumps and bruises.

JANEWAY: But you didn't seek treatment for any of these.

TORRES: I don't run to sickbay every time I stub my toe.

JANEWAY: Some of these injuries were life-threatening, B'Elanna.

TORRES: Do I look like I'm dying?

JANEWAY: The Doctor says many of the wounds were treated by someone with the medical expertise of a first year nursing student.

TORRES: Oh, that's ridiculous.

JANEWAY: Is it? We investigated today's accident. You turned off the safety protocols during the holo-simulation. Why?

TORRES: We have a micro-fracture problem. With the safety protocols on, there's no way to be sure what would happen during a real flight.

JANEWAY: You don't really expect me to believe that, do you?

TORRES: Are you calling me a liar?

JANEWAY: According to the holodeck logs, you've been spending a lot of time there over the last few months. If I were to check, would I find that you've been running other programs without safety protocols?

After the captain gives Chakotay permission to investigate Torres' holodeck activities, he takes Torres into one of her programs.

CHAKOTAY: Oh, I recognize them all. Meyer. Nelson. Sahreen. You created a program to watch all our Maquis friends get slaughtered! What I want to know is why!

TORRES: I thought we came down here to talk about safety protocols. This has nothing to do with that.

CHAKOTAY: I'm not so sure. The logs show you only ran this program for forty-seven seconds the day after I gave you the news about the massacre. Then you shut it down and started running the most dangerous programs you could find, with the safeties off. Why?!

TORRES: This is ridiculous. I'm leaving.

CHAKOTAY: Computer, seal the doors.

TORRES: You can't do this!

CHAKOTAY: The hell I can't! You're not going anywhere until you tell me what's going on. B'Elanna, why are you intentionally trying to hurt yourself?

TORRES: I don't know.

CHAKOTAY: Are you trying to commit suicide?

TORRES: No.

CHAKOTAY: Then why?

TORRES: Because—because if I sprain my ankle, at least I feel something.

CHAKOTAY: What do you mean?

TORRES: I'm not trying to kill myself—I'm trying to see if I'm still alive.

INCOMING MESSAGE:
People with depression can become self-injurious and even suicidal.

CHAKOTAY: I don't understand.

TORRES: When you look at those corpses, how do you feel?

CHAKOTAY: Sad. Angry. Maybe a little guilty that I wasn't there to die with them.

TORRES: Not me. I don't feel anything at all.

CHAKOTAY: B'Elanna, the Maquis were like our adopted family. I can understand you trying to block out that kind of pain.

TORRES: You don't understand. It's not just the pain. I don't feel anything. Not about my dead friends, not about Tom, you, my job.

CHAKOTAY: Maybe you're afraid if you let yourself start to feel something you might not be able to stop. You can't just shut off your emotions, B'Elanna. Sooner or later you're going to have to let yourself grieve.

TORRES: Why? Just so I can go through it all over again?

CHAKOTAY: What are you talking about?

TORRES: When I was six, my father walked out on me. When I was nineteen, I got kicked out of Starfleet. A few years later, I got separated from the Maquis. And just when I start to feel safe you tell me that all of our old friends have been slaughtered. The way I figure it—I've lost every family I've ever had.

CHAKOTAY: B'Elanna, you have a new family now, here on Voyager and you're not going to lose us. You're stuck with us.

TORRES: You can't promise me that.

INCOMING MESSAGE:
People with depression often have bleak
and pessimistic views of the future.

Depression, like anxiety, is a real disability but one that's hidden from casual observation. The hidden nature of the disability may prevent others from understanding how debilitating the condition is to the person who's experiencing it. While Torres is able to continue to function in her job as chief engineer, a major depressive episode may prevent someone from working if it's severe enough.

Janeway may have looked depressed in "Night" (1998, VOY; 5:1), but she was only having a Starfleet style pity party. Unlike Torres, Janeway's isolation is not presented with any other depression symptoms.

Depression is most often treated with psychotherapy, medication, or both. An experimental therapy, known as *transcranial direct current stimulation*, or tDCS, involves a low-level charge about 1/400th of that used in electroshock treatment. Unlike electroshock (also called electroconvulsive therapy or ECT), which is administered for a few seconds to patients under anesthesia, tDCS is given for 20 to 30 minutes continuously while patients are conscious. This new treatment has fewer side effects; ECTs often cause severe memory loss and a restricted range of emotions.

Furthermore, a study by researchers at the Hebrew University of Jerusalem have found that changes in one type of non-neuronal brain cells—microglia—underlie the depressive symptoms brought on by exposure to chronic stress. This research promises that new drugs can be developed that will treat depression faster than our current ones. In the meantime, never underestimate the medicinal effects of banana pancakes with maple syrup.

Chapter 7
"This Is Not a Synthehol Kind of Night"

TROI: Look. He wouldn't even talk to me unless I had a drink with him. And then it took three shots of something called tequila just to find out he was the one we're looking for. And I've spent the last twenty minutes trying to keep his hands off me. So don't go criticizing my counseling techniques—It's a primitive culture—I'm just trying to blend in.
"Star Trek: Generations" (1994)

Addiction in the 24th century: Alcohol, Drugs, and the Holodeck

In the psychedelic 1960s, morality plays were the basis for the outer space adventures on the groovy USS Enterprise. The shows depicted the classic, but square, struggle of good versus evil, and good always won. The black and white thinking that addictions are an evil gradually faded to shades of gray on *Star Trek: The Next Generation* as the crew became addicted to the holodeck and a game. Since Starfleet officers were too cool to develop drug addictions, that role was saved for those who were *out of this world.*

Genetic predispositions to psychiatric disabilities are relevant to the discussion of addictions. Inasmuch as alcohol, drugs, and addictive behaviors might be a form of self-medication, people with increased sensitivity to stresses due to disability are at higher risk for addictions. Research has also shown that people marginalized owing to disability, poverty, or other stigmas are more likely to be diagnosed as having an addiction while the same behaviors may be considered merely as eccentricities among those who are affluent.

Captain Picard's crew drank synthehol; Captain Kirk's crew was drinking the real McCoy. Actually it was McCoy who was most often drinking and offering others a snort. Nowhere was this distinction between alcohol and synthehol more apparent than when Scotty appeared in "Relics" (1992, TNG; 6:2), and Data found him something *green* to drink after Mr. Scott complained about the synthehol.

Definitions of addiction depend on the model, similar to the models and definitions of disability covered in the first chapter. I'll illustrate four major models from their corresponding time periods with four different series.

Moral Model

The oldest model of addiction is the *moral model* on which our criminal justice system was founded. The 19th century opium dens and early 20th century speakeasy became associated with other socially undesirable behaviors such as crime, wickedness, domestic violence, and laziness. Rather than proposing treatment methods for addictions, the moral model viewed punishment as a more appropriate response.

In "This Side of Paradise" (1967, TOS; 1:25), the Enterprise is sent to an Earth colony on a distant planet bombarded with deadly Berthold rays. According to Kirk's log, Starfleet recently discovered that Berthold rays cause tissue disintegration within about three years. However, the Enterprise crew discovers that not only has Elias Sandoval survived, so have the colonists he led. In fact they're healthier than before they left. The source of their improved health comes from exposure to flower spores. The spores also produce a nearly euphoric sense of well-being.

On the planet Spock is reunited with Leila Kalomi, the colony's botanist who, for six years, has had unrequited love for the Vulcan. Leila's costume is one of the most conservative of any female guest star on the original series. Maybe the director felt the spores provide something akin to beer goggles, so the beautiful Leila didn't need a censor-testing costume.

The use of a flower as a drug symbol may indicate the writers were making an analogy regarding opium. On the other hand, references to the effects of the spores are more similar to marijuana. In the 1960s, most members of the medical profession believed that marijuana use caused a person to become lazy, with no desire to participate in social situations and activities. This condition was called "amotivational syndrome." Evidence was derived from case histories and observational reports; however, controlled studies later failed to support the existence of amotivational syndrome. The episode illustrates all four basic tenets of the moral model of addiction.

1. *Drugs are evil.*

Leila promises to reveal to Spock how the colony has survived the deadly Berthold rays after Spock inspects the vegetable garden. They walk up to a group of pink flowers.

> SPOCK: You've not yet explained the nature of this thing.
> KALOMI: Its basic properties and elements are not important. What is important is it gives life, peace, love.
> SPOCK: What you're describing was once known in the vernacular as a happiness pill. And you, as a scientist, should know that that's not possible.
> KALOMI: Come. I was one of the first to find them. The spores.
> SPOCK: Spores?
> [As they approach the pink flowers, Spock is sprayed with spores from the flower. Spock's head and shoulders are covered with flower power and his face contorts with pain. The pain causes him to drop his tricorder, double over, and finally drop to the ground on his knees.]
> SPOCK: No—[Agony fills his voice.]
> KALOMI [Surprised.]: It shouldn't hurt—
> SPOCK: No—I can't—please—don't! [More agony.]
> KALOMI: Not like this. It didn't hurt us.
> SPOCK: I am not like you. [Spock is on the ground with his hands on his head. Then suddenly the pain is gone from Spock's face.]

Spock not only proclaims his love for Leila. He kisses her. Repeatedly. And if that isn't enough to convince everyone that these spores are evil, Spock is out of uniform, smiling, while hanging upside down from a tree branch when Kirk finds him after the commercial break. The horror of it all!

Soon Kirk is the only person on both ship and planet not infected by the spores. The stoic Captain Kirk, alone, recognizes the danger the effects from the spores represent.

SPOCK: It's a true Eden, Jim. There's belonging and love.

KIRK: No wants. No needs. We weren't meant for that. None of us. Man stagnates if he has no ambition, no desire to be more than he is.

SANDOVAL: We have what we need.

KIRK: Except a challenge.

Kirk's recognition that the colonists lack the motivation to move beyond subsistence living is a good illustration of amotivational syndrome; the colonists have only planted enough crops to sustain themselves.

2. *Drug abusers are anti-social and should be punished.*

KIRK: Mr. Spock. Are you out of your mind? You were told to report to me at once.

SPOCK: I didn't want to, Jim.

KIRK: You? Yes, I can see that. Miss Kalomi, you'll have to come back to the settlement and prepare to transport up to the ship.

SPOCK: There'll be no evacuation, Jim, but perhaps we should go back and get you straightened out.

KIRK: Mr. Sulu, Mr. Spock is under arrest, and he's in your custody until we get back to the Enterprise.

SPOCK: Very well. Come with me.

[Spock takes Leila's hand and leads the group to a clump of the plants, where they all get sprayed with spores. Sulu and Kelowitz get a shower of flower power, but Kirk is barely spritzed.]

KIRK: What's—

SPOCK: Mr. Sulu understands, don't you, Mr. Sulu?

SULU: Yes, I see now. Of course we can't remove the colony. It'd be wrong.

Refusing to obey orders is insubordination and Kirk accordingly decides to have Spock arrested. However, despite the potential for court-martial, Kirk finds his crew to be increasingly insubordinate as more and more of them come under the influence of the spores. Even the redshirts standing in line for the transporter disobey his orders.

3. *Drug abusers choose to use drugs. Drug abusers are weak or have moral deficits of character.*
Kirk sits in his captain's chair as he begins a log entry on the deserted USS Enterprise.

> KIRK: Captain's log, stardate 3417.7. Except for myself, all crew personnel have transported to the surface of the planet. Mutinied. Lieutenant Uhura has effectively sabotaged the communications station—I don't know how to get my crew back—how to counteract the effect of the spores. I don't know what I can offer against paradise.

Kirk's log depicts ambiguity about whether or not the crew chose to be infected by the spores; otherwise it wouldn't make sense that Kirk is trying to offer them something more enticing to get the crew to return from the planet. At the same time, mutiny against the captain is not only a court-martial offense—the charge transforms Kirk's crew into criminals. Spock is the first Enterprise crew member infected, and isn't given a choice about being sporified. Leila exposes him without his consent. But Spock takes his turn, by leading Sulu and Kelowitz to the flowers, where they're showered with the power. Kirk is barely decorated with the spores. Either the confetti gun is malfunctioning, or there should have been more ammo when firing at the almighty Captain Kirk.

4. *Addicts are "weak" but can overcome a compulsion to use with willpower.*
After Kirk is sprayed with the spores, he returns to his quarters to pack and join the colony, putting his green wraparound shirts in his Samsonite. As Kirk removes a medal from the safe the smile leaves his face. The music changes to dramatic as he slams the case shut.

In the transporter room, Kirk prepares the Samsonite for transport, and his anger flashes again. (Cue dramatic music again.) That flash of anger cures Kirk from the effects of the spores. Kirk surmises he can overcome the influence of the spores by producing strong negative emotions.

> KIRK: No. [Louder.] No! I—can't—leave! [Kirk punctuations the last word by slamming his fist down on the transporter controls. He exhales and his face reflects a sudden expression of relief.]
> [Calmly he says to himself.] Emotions—Violent emotions—Needs anger.

[Kirk looks at the suitcase and then begins dictating a log entry.]

Captain's log, supplemental. I think I've discovered the answer, but to carry out my plan entails considerable risk. Mr. Spock is much stronger than the ordinary human being. Aroused, his great physical strength could kill. But it's a risk I'll have to take.

Kirk's detox of Mr. Spock can be viewed as an example of 1960s tough love. Aware of the dangers in his plan, Kirk arms himself with a metal bar.

KIRK: All right, you mutinous, disloyal, computerized, half-breed, we'll see about you deserting my ship.

SPOCK [In a too calm voice]: The term half-breed is somewhat applicable, but computerized is inaccurate. A machine can be computerized—not a man.

KIRK: What makes you think you're a man? You're an overgrown jackrabbit—an elf with a hyperactive thyroid.

[Additional Insults and Retorts Omitted]

[Finally, Spock is sufficiently provoked and while striking at the captain bends the metal bar with one blow. Spock proceeds to throw Kirk around the transporter room with ease. Fortunately, Kirk is able to dodge the blows that damage the walls and after yet another weekly brawl, as Spock is about to hit him with what appears to be a metal table.]

KIRK: Had enough? I didn't realize what it took to get under that thick hide of yours. Anyhow, I don't know what you're so mad about. It isn't every first officer who gets to belt his Captain several times.

SPOCK: You did that to me deliberately.

KIRK: Believe me, Mr. Spock—it was painful in more ways than one.

SPOCK: The spores—they're gone. I don't belong anymore.

KIRK: You said they were benevolent and peaceful. Violent emotions overwhelm them—destroy them. I had to make you angry enough to shake off their influence. That's the answer, Mr. Spock.

SPOCK: That may be correct, Captain, but trying to initiate a brawl with over five hundred crewmen and colonists is hardly logical.

Once freed from the effects of the spores, even the colony's founder recognizes the negative effects of the spores in the second reference to amotivational syndrome.

SANDOVAL: We've done nothing here. No accomplishments, no progress. Three years wasted. We wanted to make this planet a garden.

The analogy between "This Side of Paradise" and addiction isn't perfect. An addiction requires repeated exposures to the drug, but we're shown only one encounter between each crew member and the spores. It appears the spores never wear off. Withdrawal from the influence of the spores produces no physical cravings or other symptoms of detoxification. However, the episode accurately portrays the belief in *amotivational syndrome* and the message that feeling groovy all the time leads to stagnation.

According to the moral model of addiction, people who use drugs are criminals and should be in prison. As a result there are no treatments that use the moral model in their approach. The belief is that prisons control both the person's access to drugs as well as protect society from their criminal behaviors, such as theft. Incarcerated long enough without access to drugs, people will go through drug withdrawal and their addictions come to an end.

Despite centuries of marijuana use as an herbal remedy, the Controlled Substances Act of 1970 classified marijuana along with heroin and LSD, as a Schedule I drug, where drugs are categorized if they have the relatively highest potential for abuse and no accepted medical use. However, an increasing number of states have since legalized medical marijuana, putting state laws at odds with federal laws in the United States. In 2013, Colorado and Washington legalized marijuana for recreational purposes beginning in 2014.

Alcohol legalization and prohibition have an uneven history in the United States. After the failure of nationwide alcohol prohibition in the 1920s, the moral model of addiction was gradually replaced with the medical model. The medical model was first applied to alcoholism and later to drugs. It has been also applied to compulsive activities such as overeating, gambling, and shopping, with opposing opinions as to whether or not it applies.

Medical Model

The medical model views addiction as a complex illness that involves the combination of several biological mechanisms. The medical model recognizes both physical and psychological dependency as the basis for addiction. A person can be psychologically dependent without being physically dependent, but not the other way around. Physical dependency, sometimes called *chemical dependency*, is when a person develops a tolerance to the drug. Building tolerance means that the person will need to increase the amount of drug or alcohol intake in order to experience the same desired effects. Once dependence has been established, the person will experience withdrawal symptoms when they discontinue use.

With psychological dependency there's a reinforcing experience to the drug or activity (e.g. shopping, gambling, and video games) which generates the desire to repeat the experience. So while a person may become physically dependent on alcohol, he or she may become psychologically dependent on gambling. The chemical changes in the brain are why addiction is referred to as a *brain disease*. In the case of psychological dependence, the pleasurable activity increases the amount of endorphins in the brain, which reinforce the person's desire to repeat the activity. The medical model states that:

1. *The drug has an effect on the brain which alters the person's mood.*
2. *Over time the person will develop tolerance to the drug and require more of it for the same effects.*
3. *When the person stops using the drug, they will experience withdrawal symptoms and cravings for the drug.*
4. *The person is psychologically and/or physically addicted to the drug.*
5. *The person cannot end the addiction without treatment.*

To determine if Captain Janeway is addicted to coffee I'll use the medical model of addiction. The first criterion is that coffee must be a mind-altering substance. The active ingredient in coffee is caffeine, and caffeine is a central nervous stimulant. In other words, it stimulates the brain, increases focus, alertness, and reduces sleepiness. Other criteria can be expanded upon by using a common diagnostic tool for alcoholism known as the CAGE diagnostic questionnaire.

The CAGE was developed in 1984 by Dr. John Ewing at the Bowles Center for Alcoholic Studies at the University of Chapel Hill, NC. It is based on the medical model of addiction. Two "yes" answers indicate the individual may have a harmful use or addiction disorder. The underlined letter in each question is how the acronym CAGE was developed. In order to determine if Captain Janeway's coffee drinking could be considered an addiction, I will evaluate the evidence for each question.

CAGE: Diagnostic Questionnaire

1. *Have you ever felt you needed to <u>C</u>ut down on your drinking?*

Captain Janeway voiced her self-imposed limit on drinking coffee in "Timeless" (1998, VOY; 5:6) and her rationale for violating it.

> JANEWAY: Normally, I draw the line at a pot of coffee, but tonight is a special occasion.

Since Janeway has felt the need to limit her coffee drinking, I would score the answer to this question as *yes*.

2. *Have people <u>A</u>nnoyed you by criticizing your drinking?*

It appears that Janeway is annoyed by Chakotay's observation that she's drinking too much coffee in "Hunters" (1998, VOY; 4:15).

> CHAKOTAY: You know, you drink too much of that stuff.
> JANEWAY: Really?
> CHAKOTAY: If I'm not mistaken that's your third cup this morning.
> JANEWAY: Fourth. And on a day like today it won't be my last. Coffee - the finest organic suspension ever devised. It's got me through the worst of the last three years. I beat the Borg with it—

Janeway clearly feels justified in her coffee consumption. Perhaps her annoyance is more about the familiar tone Chakotay takes in speaking to her. Without more evidence, I'd score this question as *maybe*.

3. *Have you ever felt <u>Guilty</u> about drinking?*

In "The Cloud" (1995, VOY; 1:5) Neelix does his best to induce feelings of guilt in Janeway regarding her coffee consumption.

> JANEWAY: Neelix. Do we have any coffee left?
>
> NEELIX: No, but we have something even better.
>
> JANEWAY: I don't want something even better. I want coffee.
>
> NEELIX: It's made from a proteinaceous seed I discovered on an expedition
>
> JANEWAY: Never mind. I'll use one of my replicator rations for coffee.
>
> NEELIX: That would not be appropriate, Captain.
>
> JANEWAY: I beg your pardon?
>
> NEELIX: You need to set an example for the crew.
>
> JANEWAY: Well, thank you for reminding me. [Her words are dripping with sarcasm.]
>
> NEELIX: You're welcome. After all, if you want the crew to begin to accept natural food alternatives instead of further depleting our energy reserves, you need to encourage them by your own choices, don't you?
>
> JANEWAY: Fine. Give me your even-better-than-coffee substitute.
>
> NEELIX: And how about some Takar loggerhead eggs with that this morning?
>
> JANEWAY: Just coffee.
>
> NEELIX: It's a tiny bit richer blend than you're used to, but you'll learn to love it.
>
> [Neelix pours a thick glop, about the consistency of molasses, into her cup.]

Coffee becomes a motivating force as Janeway orders the ship to change course and enter a nebula.

> JANEWAY: Are you thinking we could collect these omicron particles to provide an additional antimatter reserve, Lieutenant?
>
> TUVOK: Precisely.
>
> JANEWAY: Senior bridge officers, report for duty. Commander, set a new course. There's coffee in that nebula.

However, everything doesn't go as anticipated when they become trapped in an energy barrier. Instead of increasing their energy reserves, they expend more energy chasing the particles. Janeway's disappointment is obvious.

> JANEWAY: ...How much of our energy reserves did we lose, Ensign?
> KIM: Eleven percent, Captain.
> JANEWAY: I'm just going to have to give up coffee. That's all there is to it.

Although Neelix does his best to induce Janeway to feel guilty about her coffee drinking, the question is whether Janeway feels guilty about her coffee drinking. Although this episode was only halfway through the first season, with six and a half more seasons ahead, at this point I'd score this question *no*. Her comment about giving up coffee is related to the power reserves on the ship and not a belief that her coffee drinking is a problem.

4. *Have you ever felt you needed a drink first thing in the morning (Eye-opener) to steady your nerves or to get rid of a hangover?*

Voyager becomes stuck in an area of sub-space described as analogous to a boat stuck on a sandbar in "Bride of Chaotica!" (1999, VOY; 5:12). Three days into the ordeal, Janeway's nerves are frazzled. With limited controls and only a few replicators operational, Neelix has his hands full in the galley when Janeway enters.

> JANEWAY: Coffee, black.
> NEELIX: Sorry, Captain. We lost two more replicators this morning—
> [Janeway puts her hands on Neelix's chest in an intimidating manner.]
> JANEWAY: Listen to me very carefully because I'm only going to say this once— Coffee—Black.
> NEELIX: Yes, ma'am. [Neelix walks over to the replicator and orders.] Coffee, black.
> [Neelix turns his attention back to the captain.] While I've got your attention, there
> are—
> JANEWAY: Coffee first. [Janeway takes a long drink from the mug. Her face relaxes as she swallows the coffee.] Now, what's the problem?

In this scene, Janeway appears to have crossed the line from wanting coffee to needing coffee. As a result, I would score this question *yes*. With two *yes* answers (questions one and four), Captain Janeway should be evaluated further regarding her coffee drinking.

Current treatments for a coffee or caffeine addiction include medications to alleviate the painful headaches, which typically accompany withdrawal. In addition, the person may need medication for agitation, nervousness, insomnia, nausea, and irritability. The person may find that, without the stimulant effects of the coffee, they require more sleep than before, but this side effect generally subsides with time and sleep. Caffeine addictions are rarely fatal for Humans, but trellium can turn peace-loving Vulcans into violent zombies.

Trellium turns out to be Vulcan crack for T'Pol on *Star Trek: Enterprise*. In "Anomaly" (2003, ENT; 3:2), T'Pol is exposed to trellium-D, a mineral used to insulate starships against the spatial distortions in the Expanse. Later, in "Impulse" (2003, ENT; 3:5), the harmful effects of trellium-D on Vulcans are discovered. Trellium-D causes disruption to the synaptic pathways that allow Vulcans to control their emotions. Sadly, the discovery isn't made soon enough to save the lives of the Vulcans on the Vulcan ship, Seleya. However, the effects of trellium-D aren't over for the Enterprise's Vulcan subcommander as she explains her addiction to Dr. Phlox in "Damage" (2004, ENT; 3:19):

PHLOX: There's a good deal of residual trellium in your bloodstream. How long have you been doing this?

T'POL: Three months.

PHLOX: I need to know precisely what has been happening.

T'POL: When I was exposed to trellium aboard the Seleya, it affected me in a way that I wasn't prepared for.

PHLOX: As I recall, you were homicidal and paranoid.

T'POL: The initial effects were overwhelming, but as they began to wear off I discovered I was able to access certain emotions. I wanted more. I began to experiment by ingesting small amounts of trellium. I devised a way to inject it into my bloodstream.

PHLOX: You must have known it was dangerous. Trellium exposure is deadly to Vulcans. It eats away at the neural pathways.

T'POL: I thought, in small amounts, it would be safe. At first, I was able to control the new emotions. My interactions with the crew improved.

PHLOX: Commander Tucker, for example. When did you realize you were becoming addicted?

T'POL: Two days ago. The damage to E deck made it impossible to access the cargo bay. I began experiencing agitation, anxiety, withdrawal symptoms.

PHLOX: You're not experiencing them now.

T'POL: I was able to retrieve the trellium. I was almost killed in the process.

PHLOX: [Administers a hypospray.] This will help stabilize your synaptic pathways, but the withdrawal symptoms will return in a few days. It's going to take time. It won't be easy.

T'POL: I understand.

Although T'Pol ends her addiction to trellium-D, she never regains her previous Vulcan level of emotional control due to the damage to her neural pathways. In "E²" (2004, ENT; 3:21), T'Pol learns from her future self that she'll never fully recover from the effects of her addiction to trellium-D.

In addition to medications to treat the physical side effects of withdrawal, various counseling techniques are commonly used in this century on Earth. Addiction is difficult to treat, and there's a good deal of controversy about the best approaches to treatment of drug and alcohol addiction. In general, counseling focuses on modifying maladaptive behavior. Counselors who specialize in addiction recovery explore with the person how to cope with the experiences, memories, or events that emotionally overwhelm them without relying on drugs and alcohol. Once a person becomes abstinent, the client and therapist can set short and long term goals, which include employing new coping skills, rebuilding damaged relationships, accepting responsibility and releasing guilt. Relapse prevention strategies should also be included as a part of the treatment plan.

Alcoholics Anonymous developed the first relapse prevention program—a twelve-steps system for recovery. Alcoholics Anonymous eventually led to the creation of a myriad of other twelve-step programs, including Narcotics Anonymous, Overeaters Anonymous, and Gamblers Anonymous. Twelve-step relapse prevention programs recognize that it's important to make sobriety as social as addictions in order for people to be the most successful. Although the founders of Alcoholics Anonymous were physicians, when the Big Book of Alcoholics Anonymous was written in the 1930s, the authors lacked the scientific means to support their beliefs.

Research within the last few decades has shown that people who become addicted to alcohol are physiologically different than those who don't. Certain populations, such as twenty-five to forty percent of people from Japan, twenty-five percent of Han Chinese, and fifteen to thirty percent of Koreans, have a nonfunctional form of the enzyme *aldehyde dehydrogenase*, the enzyme that breaks down alcohol in the liver. People who have this condition are at higher risk of intoxication with smaller amounts of alcohol. However, it doesn't unilaterally predict addiction to alcohol.

Social Model

The *social model* of addiction recognizes that drug use is a learned behavior and that other people may influence addictive behavior through modeling. Treating gambling as a drug has led to understanding gambling as an addiction, which can be defined with the social model of addiction.

The components of the social model include:

- *Drug use is a learned behavior*
- *People use drugs because drug use is modeled by others*
- *Peer pressure*
- *Environmental effects lead to drug use (advertising, etc.)*

"The Game" (1991, TNG; 5:6) appears to illustrate the social model of addiction, and in some ways answers the question: *Are video games addictive?* In the episode, Riker meets an alien woman on Risa—the pleasure planet. She entices Riker to play a virtual reality game using a device that sits on the face and uses the player's brainwaves to move discs into funnel-shaped objects. As the player succeeds in this virtual Frisbee golf, the pleasure centers of the player's brain are stimulated as a reward.

The first few criteria are easily identified in the episode. Playing the game is a learned behavior and soon almost everyone on the Enterprise has replicated one of the headsets to play. Wesley Crusher is now a Starfleet Academy cadet on leave to visit his family and friends on the Enterprise when he befriends the pretty Ensign Robin Lefler. As the young couple visits Ten Forward, they see people everywhere playing the game and the modeling is evident. It seems that everyone, including his mother is trying to pressure the goody-two-shoes Wesley and his girlfriend into playing the game.

Concerned about how obsessed everyone on the Enterprise has become with the game, the two young Starfleet stars discover that the game is doing more than just giving the player a good feeling upon mastering the goal. It's affecting the players' brain chemistry.

LEFLER: It's stimulating the septal area.

WESLEY: That's the pleasure center of the brain. Whatever this thing does, it must feel pretty good.

LEFLER: No wonder it's so popular.

WESLEY: Look at this. Serotonin levels are way off. Let's run a neurochemical analysis.

LEFLER: I'm seeing widespread bonding to neuroreceptors.

WESLEY: Correct me if I'm wrong, but this looks like a psychotropic reaction.

LEFLER: Are you saying you think the game's addictive?

WESLEY: What's going on in the prefrontal cortex?

LEFLER: Doesn't that area control higher reasoning?

WESLEY: Yeah, it sure does. I'd better go talk to the captain.

Wesley sounds the alarm when he visits Captain Picard to reveal the diabolical nature of the game and its addictive effects on the crew.

WESLEY: I did some preliminary tests on the game, and what I found leads me to believe that it may have some harmful side effects. Specifically, sir, I think it's psychotropically addictive.

PICARD: Addictive? What have you discovered?

WESLEY: The game initiates a serotonin cascade in the frontal lobe of the brain. Now I know that's nothing conclusive, but it could explain why everyone is so attracted to it. And at the same time, it stimulates the brain's reasoning center. I don't know what that's all about.

After Wesley leaves the captain's ready room, Picard turns and puts on the game headset to "make it so" with the discs. At this point the analogy to the social model falls apart because the game is revealed to be an alien mind-control device.

Video games on Earth are not mind-controlling even if they can be a waste of time. (The possibility that the Ktarian also work for X-Box or Nintendo should not be ruled out.) Modern video games are advertised, there's peer pressure, and the behavior is modeled by others. However, the first criterion, that playing video games act as a drug in the brain, hasn't been medically established. Video games played to the exclusion of social relationships, or affecting the employment of the player, may fall into the category of harmful use, but it's not an addiction as clinically defined.

The similarities between gambling and gaming are tenuous at best. Gamblers wager more and more money, increasing their risk of disaster in order to achieve the thrill they seek. When playing video games, the lost points will not determine whether or not the player can pay the rent or provide other necessities.

Biopsychosocial Model

The *biopsychosocial model* integrates the biological, psychological and social factors which increase the likelihood a person will develop an addiction. The model uses a continuum which ranges from habit, to harmful use, to addiction. The model focuses on the various factors leading to addiction rather than separating out drugs, alcohol, or behaviors. The person copes with distress by using their drug/behavior as a method of experiencing pleasure or avoiding stress. Biologically speaking, endorphins are nature's feel-good brain chemicals that are activated when a person is injured as well as when we ingest certain chemicals, such as alcohol or drugs. The brain also increases the amount of endorphins when we experience something thrilling or dangerous, like being chased by the Borg. Unfortunately, endorphins are also susceptible to tolerance; either the level of risk must increase, or the amount of time spent in the behavior must increase, in order to receive the same sensation. Remove the ability to engage in the behavior and the person may become anxious, even to the point of panic attacks or other physiological sensations. Addiction is defined as the point at which the person is unable to control the drug/behavior even though harmful consequences result.

Biological Factors

While others may have wasted time on the holodeck, the poster child for holodeck addiction is Lieutenant Junior Grade Reginald Endicott Barclay III. Barclay's drug is escaping into the holodeck and interacting with his holo-crew on his own terms in the programs he creates.

Barclay isn't the same person on and off the holodeck. In the opening scene of "Hollow Pursuits," (1990, TNG; 3:21) holo-Troi comments on how Barclay impresses her after watching Barclay dominate holo-La Forge and holo-Riker.

> HOLO-TROI [In a soft, sensual voice.]: I feel your confidence, your arrogant resolve. It excites me.

While on the holodeck, Barclay's service number probably ends in 007; in Cargo Bay Five he's awkward, stuttering, and late for his shift. Again.

It would appear that Barclay has a biological predisposition to anxiety. Barclay's anxious tendencies can be seen in his social phobia ["Hollow Pursuits"], transporter phobia ["Realm of Fear" (1992, TNG; 6:2)], and his hypochondria ["Genesis" (1994, TNG; 7:19)]. Engaging in holodeck programs allows Barclay both to escape from the stresses of dealing with his coworkers on the ship and to relax. In both "Hollow Pursuits" and "Pathfinder" (1999, VOY; 6:10) Barclay even prefers to sleep on the holodeck rather than his own quarters.

Social Factors

At the beginning of "Hollow Pursuits," Barclay doesn't have any friends. La Forge becomes project leader and Barclay becomes his project—by order of Captain Picard. La Forge enters Ten Forward to look for Barclay and ends up talking to Guinan about the engineer.

> LA FORGE: Maybe I'm not making myself clear, Guinan. Barclay—well—he's always late. The man's nervous. Nobody wants to be around this guy.
> GUINAN: If I felt that nobody wanted to be around me, I'd probably be late and nervous too.
> LA FORGE: Guinan—that's not the point.
> GUINAN: Are you sure? Excuse me. [She leaves to serve a customer.]

La Forge locates Barclay in the holodeck and enters it with one of Barclay's programs running. Barclay's stress levels peak like an EM burst when he sees La Forge in person on the holodeck in Barclay's Enterprise/Gainsborough program, complete with sword fights.

In Ten Forward, Barclay explains to La Forge that his holodeck activities are his only means to escape from his shyness and social discomfort. What better place to discuss an addiction than in a bar, right?

LA FORGE: Hey, Barclay, I've spent a few hours on the holodeck too, you know. Now, as far as I'm concerned what you do in the holodeck is your own business, as long as it doesn't interfere with your work.

BARCLAY: You're—you're not going to tell anyone about this?

LA FORGE: I don't think everybody would appreciate your imagination like I do. It is kind of unusual, recreating people you already know.

BARCLAY: Well, it was just—I needed to blow off some steam because one—one of the officers had been getting on my back.

LA FORGE: Let me guess.

BARCLAY: It was you, and I just couldn't tell you what I wanted to tell you to your face—so it just sort of got out of control.

Barclay's acknowledgement that his holodeck activities have gotten out of control further strengthens the addiction aspect of his behavior. In addition, Barclay clearly recognizes how his social discomfort is alleviated while on the holodeck. According to the biopsychosocial model of addiction, Barclay's shyness and lack of social network puts him at an increased risk of developing an addiction to reduce his discomfort in social situations.

BARCLAY: It's—it's—I—when I'm in there—I'm just more comfortable. You don't know what a struggle this has been for me, Commander.

LA FORGE: I'd like to help, if I can.

BARCLAY: Being afraid all the time—of forgetting somebody's name—not knowing what to do with your hands. I mean, I'm the guy who writes down things to remember to say when there's a party. And then when he finally gets

LA FORGE: You're just shy, Barclay.

BARCLAY: Just shy. Sounds like nothing serious—doesn't it? You can't know.

Rather than deny the magnitude of Barclay's addiction, La Forge orders Barclay to work with Counselor Troi. When Barclay has a holodeck addiction relapse in "Pathfinder" (1999, VOY; 6:10) he explains to Counselor Troi about playing poker with the Voyager crew on the holodeck.

BARCLAY: I hoped that the poker game would help calm my nerves so that I could get a decent night's sleep before the briefing but, when I got home that night I couldn't keep my mind off Voyager. I needed to get back to the holodeck.

[Dialogue Omitted]

BARCLAY: For some reason, I never slept in my apartment as comfortably as I did in my holographic quarters. I suppose I felt more at home on Voyager.

Barclay denies he has had a relapse as he describes to Counselor Troi about how he coped with embarrassing Commander Harkins at a meeting with Admiral Paris.

TROI: How did you deal with your feelings afterwards?

BARCLAY: What do you mean?

TROI: Well, did you talk to Commander Harkins after the meeting? Apologize?

BARCLAY: Well, no, I wanted to—er—fine tune my plan, so—I—er, just went right back to work.

TROI: Be more specific. What exactly did you do?

BARCLAY: Well, I needed someone to—er—bounce ideas off of—someone to help focus my thoughts.

TROI: Sounds reasonable. I suppose you consulted with some of your Pathfinder colleagues.

BARCLAY: Well, not exactly.

TROI: You went back to the holodeck, didn't you?

BARCLAY: They're the only people that I can talk to—

TROI: They're not people—

BARCLAY: I know, but they—they help me with my work.

[Dialogue Omitted]

TROI: Commander Harkins invited you to his home. You went to the holodeck instead.

BARCLAY: It's not what you're thinking, Deanna. This isn't a relapse of my holo-addiction.

Obviously Harkins doesn't agree with Barclay's assessment.

HARKINS: Before I brought you onto my team I reviewed your file. You've struggled with holo-addiction before. From where I stand it looks like you've had a relapse.

BARCLAY: I know it... it may look that way.

HARKINS: I think you need counseling.

Harkins' attempts to persuade Barclay to socialize more outside the holodeck indicate that the commander may know more about psychology than the Mutara Interdimensional Deep Space Transponder Array. (Sometimes it appears script writers are being paid by the syllable.)

Psychological Factors

Back on the Enterprise ("Hollow Pursuits"), Riker, La Forge and Troi witness sources of Barclay's anxiety as they search the holodeck for Barclay's whereabouts with his program running. Barclay's holo-Riker is considerably shorter than the first officer, as Troi points out to Riker:

TROI: You are very tall. It might be threatening to some people.

Troi refuses to allow Riker to end the holodeck program using a psychological rationale.

TROI: If Barclay is having difficulty facing reality, to suddenly destroy his only means of escape would be brutal and could do considerable damage.

However, Troi loses her professional distance and psychological point of view when she encounters her own holodeck character.

> TROI: It could provide us with valuable information about what's troubling him. You know, there's nothing wrong with a healthy fantasy life, as long as you don't let it take over.
> RIKER: You call this healthy?
> TROI: You're taking it so seriously. It's not without its element of humor.
> [As the words leave her mouth, the trio sees holo-Troi wearing a one-shoulder, Grecian style green gown. Troi's mouth drops open in shock, while Riker and La Forge look amused.]
> HOLO-TROI: I am the goddess of empathy. [She puts her arms forward as though to embrace them.] Cast off your inhibitions and embrace love, truth, joy.
> LA FORGE: Oh. My. God.
> HOLO-TROI: Discard your facades and reveal your true being to me.
> TROI: Computer, discontinue—
> RIKER: —Computer, belay that order! We want to get more insight into what's been troubling the poor man, remember? Quite a healthy fantasy life, wouldn't you say?
> [Riker and La Forge are smiling and La Forge nods his head in agreement.]

Addictions treatment focuses on both the actual problem behaviors as well as developing new skills to cope with the sources of stress that contribute to the addiction. Unlike treatments developed using the medical or social model of addiction, the biopsychosocial model doesn't require the person to become abstinent from their drug/behavior. Treatment goals under this model focus on regaining control of the person's drinking, eating, or, in Barclay's case, holodeck activities.

In my interview with University of Rochester Professor Sarah Higley I learned that she invented the term *holo-addiction* when she wrote "Hollow Pursuits." She told me that she created the episode to explore:

> how a man could become addicted to the holodeck in the way we have become addicted to the Internet or to virtual worlds—except that the Internet and virtual

reality hadn't been developed publicly....I had no idea I was being prescient. This was pre-Internet, and online gaming was largely undeveloped in 1991, much less Second Life, a virtual world that fascinates me now for many of the same reasons that drove me to write "Hollow Pursuits. And just like the holodeck, it is wildly addicting and a sobering exposure of all sorts of closeted fantasies.

With the advancements being made in virtual reality technology, holo-addiction may one day become recognized by the psychiatric community. Perhaps Barclay will write that book on holo-addiction after all.

Safe Harbor and Prevention

Although addiction can be a disabling condition which impairs a person's health and well-being as well as the ability to work and socialize, addiction is still considered a self-inflicted disorder and as a result there's often less compassion for people with addictions. In addition, there are fewer legal protections. For example, the Americans with Disabilities Act provides protection against discrimination for psychiatric disabilities except for alcoholism, substance abuse and behavioral addictions such as gambling. At the same time, there is what's called the *safe-harbor* provision within the law. If a person seeks treatment for an addiction, the safe-harbor provides that the person can't be terminated from their job while they are in treatment. However, firing a person for being under the influence of alcohol or drugs is permissible.

Addiction is considered to be a preventable disability in all models of addiction presented in this chapter. However, despite the creation of prevention programs, the number of people with harmful use or addictions hasn't been reduced worldwide. One of the best known prevention programs in the United States is the Drug Abuse Resistance Education or D.A.R.E. as it's generally called. Police officers began delivering the D.A.R.E program to schools in 1985. Research on the effectiveness of D.A.R.E. has failed to find any substantial reduction in the number of people who become addicted to drugs, join gangs, or commit violent acts. In what sounds like a public service announcement for D.A.R.E., Tasha Yar explains to a naïve and self-righteous Wesley about the evils of drug addiction in "Symbiosis" (1988, TNG; 1:21).

WESLEY: ...What I can't understand is why anyone would voluntarily become dependent on a chemical.

DATA: Voluntary addiction to drugs is a recurrent theme in many cultures.

YAR: Wesley, no one wants to become dependent. That happens later.

WESLEY: But it does happen. So why do people start?

YAR: On my home planet, there was so much poverty and violence, that for some the only escape was through drugs.

WESLEY: How can a chemical substance provide an escape?

YAR: It doesn't, but it makes you think it does. You have to understand, drugs can make you feel good. They make you feel on top of the world. You're happy, sure of yourself, in control.

WESLEY: But it's artificial.

YAR: It doesn't feel artificial until the drug wears off. Then you pay the price. Before you know it, you're taking the drug not to feel good, but to keep from feeling bad.

WESLEY: And that's the trap?

YAR: All you care about is getting your next dosage. Nothing else matters.

WESLEY: I guess I just don't understand.

YAR: Wesley, I hope you never do.

This drug lecture provides a classic example of the importance of prevention in the medical model of addiction.

There are times when it seems that everything is referred to as an addiction, even on *Star Trek*. For example, the Jem'Hadar are not clinically addicts even though they are said to be addicted to Ketracel-White in "Hippocratic Oath" (1994, DS9; 4:3).

GORAN'AGAR: ...There is a drug that all Jem'Hadar must have in order to live. We call it Ketracel-White.

BASHIR: An isogenic enzyme.

GORAN'AGAR: You know about it?

BASHIR: I know that the Jem'Hadar have been genetically engineered by the Dominion to be addicted to what you call Ketracel-White. And that by controlling the supply of the drug, the Founders maintain control over you.

GORAN'AGAR: The Vorta. They are the ones who control the drug. They are the ones we came here to escape.

The Jem'Hadar's physical dependence on Ketracel-White is closer to the dependence on insulin for a person with diabetes. Ketracel-White produces no pleasurable sensations or high. The Jem'Hadar don't develop tolerance, which requires that they increase the dosage. Similar to withholding insulin from a person with diabetes, death results from not taking Ketracel-White, although it's neither immediate nor painless.

It seems impossible to write about addictions on *Star Trek* without acknowledging that some people consider *Star Trek* an addiction. In my (not so) humble opinion, if any hobby or interest becomes harmful to your life, personal relationships, or health, then it would be wise to find balance between your interests and your life. For some people, it may be necessary to seek assistance in finding that balance. *Star Trek* fans should not be punished; they are usually really nice people even if the spore exploding flowers are hateful.

There are other examples of activities which are not considered addictions on *Star Trek* but rather entertainment, routines, or habits. Senior officers on *Star Trek: The Next Generation* frequently play poker together. There are no Dabo or Tongo addictions on *Star Trek: Deep Space Nine*. On *Star Trek: Voyager*, crew members take up Vulcan kal-toh, and even though it's described as a game of logic, patience and balance, Ensign Kim refers to the game as addictive in the colloquial sense of the word. The Voyager crew often relaxes at Sandrine's in Marseilles with a pool table in holodeck program Paris III. And even though Bashir and O'Brien spend more time in the holosuite on Deep Space Nine than Barclay does on the holodeck aboard the Enterprise, the pair's adventures are never considered addictions. Silly? Yes. Addictions? No.

I'll leave it up to others to determine if Counselor Troi has a chocolate addiction, or whether it's simply her favorite food. I have exempted Porthos from analysis since he's neither a member of Starfleet nor humanoid. Therefore, the question regarding whether or not the adorable beagle's affection for cheese constitutes harmful use or an addiction will go unanswered.

Chapter 8

"Please State the Nature of Your Medical Condition"

Physical Disabilities

According to *Star Trek*, people will still have disabilities in the future. *Star Trek* generally provides a positive view of people with disabilities, and conveys empowerment for anyone with a disability or *difference*. But at times the messages on *Star Trek* reflect today's stigma toward people with physical impairments.

"The Ship Has Been Disabled" (Mobility Impairments)

Seven people appear in wheelchairs on *Star Trek*, each with a message about mobility impairments. As most fans know, the first pilot for the series was "The Cage" (written in 1964), which was later sliced and diced into "The Menagerie Part I and Part II" (1966, TOS; 1:12 & 1:13). The story begins as the USS Enterprise arrives at Starbase 11 after Spock told Captain Kirk that Fleet Captain Christopher Pike had requested to meet with him. Pike was the previous commander of the Enterprise and Spock served as Pike's first officer for eleven years.

A mystery unfolds as the Enterprise arrives at the starbase. Commodore Mendez and his aide, Lieutenant Piper, explain that due to injuries sustained during a maintenance accident, Pike has been hospitalized with burns and paralysis. Although it's impossible that Pike sent the message, it's also known that Vulcans cannot lie. Kirk points out that Spock is only half Vulcan, and the other half is Human. The astonishing implication is that Humans are quite capable of deception.

PIPER: We're forced to consider every possibility, sir. We can be certain Captain Pike cannot have sent a message. In his condition he's under observation every minute of every day.

MENDEZ: And totally unable to move, Jim. His wheelchair is constructed to respond to his brain waves. Oh, he can turn it, move it forwards, or backwards slightly.

PIPER: With the flashing light, he can say yes or no.

MENDEZ: But that's it, Jim. That's as much as that poor devil can do. His mind is as active as yours and mine, but it's trapped inside a useless vegetating body. He's kept alive mechanically, a battery-driven heart.

INCOMING MESSAGE:

Physical disabilities can occur without brain impairments.
The brain, unlike the heart, can't be replaced by an artificial mechanism.

Chronologically, the first *Star Trek* wheelchair was shown on *The Menagerie*. It's a box-like device which encases Pike's body from the floor to above his elbows, almost halfway up to his shoulders.

INCOMING MESSAGE:

The more restrictive and isolating the assistive technology,
the harder it is to include the person with a disability.

"The Menagerie" ends happily with Captain Pike being returned to the forbidden Talos Four where the Talosian Keepers provide him with the illusion of a healthy body. Pike is reunited with Vina, the woman he met many years ago when he first visited Talos Four.

In a farewell message to the Kirk, the Keeper provides what I consider to be a prediction of the development of virtual reality.

KEEPER: Captain Pike has an illusion, and you have reality. May you find your way as pleasant.

Virtual reality interfaces are already being developed that may provide new choices for people with severe physical disabilities. For instance, virtual reality exercises have proven to be effective in retraining muscle coordination with stroke survivors. Virtual reality games have also been developed to teach social skills to people with *autism spectrum disorders*. Research also suggests that in the future, virtual reality interfaces will provide people who are severely impaired the ability to perform work that they're currently unable to accomplish. Believe it or not, virtual reality has more applications than just awesome video games.

INCOMING MESSAGE:

In the future, mobility will not be limited by a person's physical body.
Virtual reality may present an opportunity for people with severe disabilities
to interact without physical limitations.

The second person seen in a wheelchair appears in "Too Short A Season" (1988, TNG; 1:17). An elderly and frail Admiral Jameson is in an enclosed wheelchair similar to Captain Pike's, but with his upper torso free to move.

The famous physicist, Stephen Hawking, appears as himself in "Descent, Part I" (1993, TNG; 6:26). While playing poker with Data, Albert Einstein, and Sir Isaac Newton, Hawking is the third person seen sitting in a wheelchair on *Star Trek*. Dr. Hawking has Amyotrophic Lateral Sclerosis, which has resulted in all but complete paralysis. He has only enough muscle control to press a button with his right hand. He uses the button to control his computer. This computer interface allows Hawking to control his wheelchair, communications board, and even his home appliances. In the poker scene, Hawking is seated in his electric wheelchair and his notebook computer is positioned in front of him. There's a robotic arm which holds his cards.

INCOMING MESSAGE:
Computers can talk for people with disabilities.
There was no reason to program the holodeck to eliminate Hawking's wheelchair.
Having a disability doesn't mean you can't have a sense of humor.

Ensign Melora Pazlar is the fourth person to use a wheelchair, which she calls her "electric trolley car." Dr. Bashir replicates the device for Pazlar in "Melora" (1993, DS9; 2:6). Wheelchairs are obviously obsolete by the time Deep Space Nine is operating.

DAX: I haven't seen one of these in three hundred years. I'm surprised it was even on file in the replicator's data bank.
BASHIR: It isn't. Ensign Pazlar sent me the specifications.

INCOMING MESSAGE:
Wheelchairs will not be needed in the 24th century,
unless you're from a low-gravity planet.

Ever the overachiever, Dr. Bashir tweaked the wheelchair—much to Pazlar's disappointment.

PAZLAR: I see you have my trolley car ready to go.
BASHIR: As requested.
DAX: Can I help?
PAZLAR: I'm fine, thank you.
[She goes carefully down the steps and sits in the chair.]
PAZLAR: That's better. You've modified it.
BASHIR: Yes. I wanted to give you as much mobility as I could.
PAZLAR: I've been practicing on the model I requested for a month.
BASHIR: Well, it's no problem. We can replicate the other design.
PAZLAR: No, I'll just have to adapt.

INCOMING MESSAGE:
It can be annoying to a person with a disability
to be provided with more assistance than requested.

The balanced, realistic portrayal of Pazlar's internal struggles between dependence and independence are likely due to the insights of the screenplay writer, Evan Carlos Somers

(1958 – 2010). Somers, like Ensign Pazlar, used a wheelchair for mobility. At the age of sixteen, Somers had a diving accident which resulted in quadriplegia.

Somers wrote three episodes of *Star Trek: Deep Space Nine* and one episode of *Star Trek: Voyager*. At the age of forty-five he filmed the documentary: *The Seeker* (2005). In his documentary, Somers sought out information about how close medical science was to a cure for spinal cord injuries. Prior to his death at age fifty-two in 2010, Somers wasn't only a screenplay writer, but also a professor of screenwriting at Santa Monica College in California. Among his accomplishments were a Bachelor's degree in Psychology, a Master's degree in Communication, and the Joan Young Media Access Award.

Emory Erickson, "The Father of the Transporter," is the fifth person who uses a wheelchair. While technically this occurred before Captain Pike's accident, the episode "Daedalus" (2005, ENT; 4:10) was shown about forty years later. The wheelchair in this episode looks much like contemporary wheelchairs in the first decade of the 21st century.

When the *Star Trek* timeline was crashed off the side of the cliff along with the 1965 Corvette convertible in "Star Trek" (2009), Kirk's mother is wheeled into a shuttle from the USS Kelvin. There are striking similarities between her wheelchair and the one at the end of the movie where reboot-Captain Pike is the seventh and final character seated in a wheelchair on *Star Trek*. Pike's wheelchair in "Star Trek" (2009) is minimalistic compared to the one his character sat in on the original series forty-five years previously. Apparently differences between the two timelines are not limited to Spock and Uhura smooching.

INCOMING MESSAGE:
Advancement with assistive technology will increase
the inclusion of people with disabilities.

In "Star Trek Into Darkness" (2013), Pike no longer uses the wheelchair, but is able to walk with a cane. Apparently, Pike is still recovering from his injuries after he was rescued in "Star Trek" (2009). When Kirk files a false report with Starfleet, Pike is given back command of the Enterprise—cane and all. Tragically, Pike is killed before he resumes his seat in the captain's chair.

INCOMING MESSAGE:
Command experience is more important than physical impairments.
People with physical disabilities are still capable of fulfilling important roles.

Lieutenant Worf's spinal cord was crushed during an accident in the cargo bay in "Ethics" (1992, TNG; 5:15). However, no one proposed Worf use a wheelchair for mobility. Instead, Dr. Crusher proposed to restore partial mobility with a different type of treatment.

CRUSHER: ...We've discussed a variety of surgical procedures. I'm afraid none of them will repair the spinal cord, but we have found a way for you to regain much of your mobility. We can implant a series of neural transducers in your lower torso and legs. They're designed to pick up the electrical impulses from your brain and stimulate the corresponding muscles. With a little work, you can eventually regain sixty to seventy percent of your motor control.
RUSSELL: The first step would be to fit your legs with motor assist units like this one. They're a training device. Once you've mastered using them, we can move on to the implants.
[She puts a band around his leg.]
RUSSELL: Now try to move your leg.
[Worf's leg jerks off the table, and disgust registers on his face.]
CRUSHER: No, no, that's good for a first try. It will take some time before you get used to manipulating the—
WORF: No! [He rips the band off.] I will not live like that.
CRUSHER: These are very sophisticated devices. With enough time, they will give you—
WORF: Sixty percent of my mobility. No, I will not be seen lurching through corridors like some half-Klingon machine, the object of ridicule and disgust.

The motor bands on Worf's legs are similar to the assist bands that Ensign Pazlar uses on Deep Space Nine. Apparently, in addition to the lack of a treatment that would restore all of Worf's mobility, Dr. Crusher also lacked a cure for Klingon warrior-vanity.

INCOMING MESSAGE:
Acceptance of a disability and acceptance of treatment are connected.
In the future, there will be other options for restoring mobility than wheelchairs.

Technology that improves mobility is moving away from perfecting the wheelchair, which requires a *sitting* position, to devices which instead allow the person to move around in a *standing* position. Standing provides better cardiovascular health and offers the ability to make eye-to-eye contact. Two of the most promising developments are powered exoskeleton robotic suits (think "Iron Man" movie) and internal (implanted) or external (worn) electrode stimulators (think "Ethics" and "Melora" episodes).

"Pon Farr" (Endocrine System)

The main function of the endocrine system is to maintain internal balance, known as *homeostasis*, through the release of hormones. Humans experience various times in their lives when the internal balance is off-kilter, such as during puberty or menopause. After completing their first mission, Captain Archer states in "Broken Bow" (2001, ENT; 1:1) that Dr. Phlox will remain on board the Enterprise because he has developed a fondness for the Human endocrine system. I guess hormonal changes can be entertaining to those observing—as opposed to those experiencing the effects.

Humans aren't the only ones to experience periodic hormonal imbalances. Vulcans also experience hormonal fluctuations. Spock undergoes the "pon farr" in "Amok Time" (1967, TOS; 2:1).

SPOCK: It is a thing no out-worlder may know except those very few who have been involved. A Vulcan understands, but even we do not speak of it among ourselves. It is a deeply personal thing. Can you see that, Captain, and understand?
KIRK: No, I do not understand. Explain. Consider that an order.
[Dialogue Omitted]
SPOCK: ...if any creature as proudly logical as us were to have their logic ripped from them as this time does to us. How do Vulcans choose their mates? Haven't you wondered?
KIRK: I guess the rest of us assume that it's done quite logically.

SPOCK: No. No. It is not—we shield it with ritual and customs shrouded in antiquity. You humans have no conception. It strips our minds from us. It brings a madness which rips away our veneer of civilization. It is the pon farr—the time of mating. There are precedents in nature, Captain. The giant eelbirds of Regulus Five, once each eleven years they must return to the caverns where they hatched. On your Earth—the salmon. They must return to that one stream where they were born, to spawn or die in trying.

KIRK: But you're not a fish, Mr. Spock. You're—

SPOCK: No. Nor am I a man. I'm a Vulcan. I'd hoped I would be spared this—but the ancient drives are too strong. Eventually, they catch up with us, and we are driven by forces we cannot control to return home and take a wife. Or die.

INCOMING MESSAGE:
Hormones affect the brain's function.
Hormonal imbalances can be embarrassing.

When the young Vulcan engineer, Ensign Vorik, begins pon farr in "Blood Fever" (1997, VOY; 3:15), the private and embarrassing nature of the event is revisited.

THE DOCTOR: ...You're going through the pon farr, aren't you?

VORIK: That's an extremely personal question, Doctor.

THE DOCTOR: Yes, I'm aware that Vulcans prefer to keep their mating practices very much to themselves. There's almost nothing in the medical database beyond a few observations made by Starfleet doctors over the years. Your symptoms, the chemical imbalance and loss of emotional control are consistent with those observations. Have you been eating and sleeping normally?

VORIK: I knew there was something wrong. I was hoping it wasn't this.

THE DOCTOR: I assume this is your first pon farr? There's nothing to be embarrassed about. It's a normal biological function. I'll do what I can to help you through it, but I'll need a little more information.

VORIK: We do not discuss it.

THE DOCTOR: I'm afraid you'll have to. You have a severe imbalance in your brain chemistry. If it gets much worse, it could become life threatening. Now I need to know how Vulcans deal with this condition.

VORIK: We go home. Every seven years of our adult life, Vulcans experience an instinctual, irresistible urge to return to the homeworld and take a mate.

INCOMING MESSAGE:
Life cycle changes due to hormonal imbalances
may create a condition of temporary disability.

Vorik is in the unenviable position of being too far away from Vulcan to be able to return there and take a mate. Logically, he must therefore mate with someone on Voyager. Vorik focuses his energies (or hormones) on mating with Lieutenant Torres, who soundly rejects him as only a Klingon can—by dislocating his jaw.

INCOMING MESSAGE:
People should respect the privacy of others including their medical conditions.
Never touch a Klingon without permission.

The Doctor doesn't respect Vorik's confidentiality (a violation of the fidelity ethic) and seeks the opinion of the senior Vulcan on board, Lieutenant Commander Tuvok.

THE DOCTOR: I'm concerned about Ensign Vorik's cortical readings. One returns to normal levels, then another one spikes. It's chaotic. As if the brain's regulatory system had simply shut down. I can't tell if he's making any progress with these meditations. I thought maybe you could suggest other possible treatments.

TUVOK: I cannot.

THE DOCTOR: Is that because you don't know, or because you don't want to discuss it?

TUVOK: For both of those reasons there is little help that I can offer. It is inappropriate for me to involve myself in Ensign Vorik's personal situation.

THE DOCTOR: For such an intellectually enlightened race, Vulcans have a remarkably Victorian attitude about sex.

TUVOK: That is a very human judgment, Doctor.

THE DOCTOR: Then here's a Vulcan one. I fail to see the logic in perpetuating ignorance about a basic biological function.

TUVOK: There is nothing logical about the pon farr. It is a time when instinct and emotion dominate over reason. It cannot be analyzed by the rational mind, nor cured by conventional medicine. Anyone who has experienced it understands that it must simply be followed to its natural resolution.

INCOMING MESSAGE:

Hormones can affect a person's judgment.

When Vorik touches Torres, he "transmits" his pon farr to her as well. As both of them are affected, they end up in ritual Vulcan combat that resolves Vorik's pon farr.

INCOMING MESSAGE:

Hormonal imbalances can be treated with
medication and behavioral or dietary therapies.

Vulcans aren't the only aliens to experience hormonal imbalances. Ambassador Lwaxana Troi, daughter of the Fifth House, Holder of the Sacred Chalice of Rixx, Heir to the Holy Rings of Betazed (oh, and Counselor Troi's mother), experiences the Betazoid equivalent to menopause called "the phase" on "Manhunt" (1989, TNG; 2:19).

TROI: My mother is beginning a physiological phase. It's one that all Betazoid women must deal with as they enter mid-life.

RIKER: Yes, it's something Troi warned me about when we first started to see each other. A Betazoid woman, when she goes through this phase, quadruples her sex drive.

TROI: Or more.

RIKER: Or more? You never told me that.

PICARD: Well, under the circumstances, I think it would be prudent if I were to make myself less available for the duration of this journey.

[Dialogue Omitted]

TROI: You cannot apply human style logic to this, Captain. A Betazoid woman in the phase would be shocked and deeply resentful, should you spurn any such advances. She would take it personally.

INCOMING MESSAGE:

It's important to remember emotional stability may be compromised when hormones are imbalanced.

Luckily for Picard, the ambassador becomes enamored with a holodeck figure until it's time for her to leave the ship.

Common disorders of the Human endocrine system such as Graves' disease, Cushing's syndrome, and diabetes don't appear on *Star Trek*. Perhaps by the time warp travel has been achieved, medical science will have developed cures for these chronic medical conditions. Indeed, the only endocrine disorders depicted on *Star Trek* are both temporary and part of normal development. In other words, much to the chagrin of all the parents in the universe, there'll never be a cure for puberty.

"If You Prick Me, Do I Not Leak?" (Blood and Immune Systems)

Dr. McCoy diagnoses himself with *xenopolycythemia* in "For The World Is Hollow And I Have Touched the Sky" (1968, TOS; 3:8). This rare blood disease causes excessive proliferation of red blood cells in the Human body. With only one year to live, McCoy, not Kirk, gets the girl. (Apparently Kirk only gets the girl when her outfit must be glued in place.) Not only does McCoy get the girl, he marries the Fabrini leader and finds a cure for his illness.

CHAPEL: Excellent, Doctor. The white corpuscle count is back to normal.

[McCoy groans.]

SPOCK: Your hemoglobin count is back to normal, Doctor, which indicates that the flow of oxygen to each cell of your body is back up to its abundantly energetic level.

MCCOY: Thank you, Mr. Spock, for bringing back the knowledge of the Fabrini.

KIRK: Dr. McCoy, the Fabrini descendants are scheduled to debark on their promised planet in approximately three hundred and ninety days. I think that we could manage to be in that vicinity at that time, if you wanted to thank the Fabrini personally.

INCOMING MESSAGE:

Cures can be found at any time and any place.

According to the "Star Trek Concordance," xenopolycythemia as characterized by excessive proliferation of red blood cells is similar to the Human condition "polycythemia," which causes sluggish blood flow to the extremities, and clots which can lead to heart attack or stroke. On Earth, polycythemia is not contagious; it is usually caused by a genetic mutation, or is secondary to other conditions that increase blood production hormones or reduce oxygen levels in the bloodstream.

Antibiotics became widely available in the 1940s, and by the 1960s physicians were already aware that the overuse of these drugs could develop antibiotic-resistant bacteria. When a group of space-hippies comes on board the Enterprise in "The Way To Eden" (1969, TOS; 3:20), Dr. McCoy finds that one of their members is a carrier of an untreatable disease.

MCCOY: ...There's a nasty little bug evolved in the last few years, Jim. Our aseptic, sterilized civilizations produced it. Synthococcus novae. It's deadly. We can immunize against it, but haven't learned to lick all the problems yet.

KIRK: Does he have it? What about the others?

MCCOY: All the others are clear. He doesn't have it. He's a carrier. Remember your ancient history? Typhoid Mary? He's immune, as she was, but he carries the disease and spreads it to others.

INCOMING MESSAGE:

Sometimes a person can appear healthy and still be a disease carrier.

People who are carriers of a disease have a responsibility to those around them.

(Keep these in mind the next time you board an airplane or spaceship.)

In "The Pirates of Orion" (1974, TAS; 2:1), there's an infectious outbreak among the Enterprise crew which at first appears no more serious than pneumonia. However, it's only minor among Humans.

> McCoy: Jim, choriocytosis is a strange disease. In races with iron-based blood, it's practically nothing, but in other—
> Kirk: Get to the point, Bones.
> McCoy: Spock has contracted the disease. It's fatal to Vulcans.
> Kirk: Are you sure?
> McCoy: I've triple-checked, Jim. I wish to God I was wrong. Spock's blood is copper-based. The infection enters the blood stream, and encases the cells so they can't carry oxygen.

The interference in the ability for the blood cells to carry oxygen through the body makes *choriocytosis* similar to sickle cell disease. Spock survives when the Enterprise is able to capture the Orion pirates and obtain the cure for Spock's illness.

INCOMING MESSAGE:
Some genetic disabilities affect people differently.

"Life Support Systems" (Respiratory and Pulmonary Systems)

In "Journey to Babel" (1967, TOS; 2:10), the Enterprise is carrying diplomats to an interplanetary conference where they'll consider the petition of the Coridan planet to be admitted to the Federation. On board is Mr. Spock's father, Ambassador Sarek. Sarek collapses suddenly while Captain Kirk is questioning him about the murder of a Tellarite on board the Enterprise.

> McCoy: As far as I can tell from instrument readings, our prime suspect has a malfunction in one of the heart valve [sic]. It's similar to a heart attack in a human. But with Vulcan physiology, it's impossible to tell without an operation. Mrs. Sarek, has he had any previous attacks?
> Mrs Sarek: No.

SAREK: Yes. There were three others. My physician prescribed Benjisidrine for the condition.

INCOMING MESSAGE:

Even Vulcan men often hide their medical conditions from their wives.

Spock suggests to Dr. McCoy a type of heart surgery that would save Ambassador Sarek's life. The problem is that the surgery requires a large amount of Vulcan blood to be available and there's not a sufficient supply on the ship. Anticipating this objection, Spock directs McCoy to a drug which has been used on a species similar to Vulcans that accelerates the production and replacement of the blood. Spock proposes to have Dr. McCoy administer the drug to him so he can supply enough blood for the surgery.

MCCOY: It could damage you internally. It could kill you. I'm sorry, Spock. I can't sanction it.

MRS SAREK: And I refuse to permit it. I won't risk both of you.

SPOCK: Then you automatically condemn Sarek to death. And you, Doctor, have no logical alternative either. If you do not operate, Sarek will die. You now have the means to perform the operation. I am volunteering myself as the blood donor. I'll be at my station until you require me.

INCOMING MESSAGE:

Good medicine requires a balance between risks.
When the risk of doing nothing is greater
than the risk of doing something—do something.

Meanwhile, Captain Kirk is attacked and wounded by an Andorian delegate. The mounting drama is captured by Mr. Spock's log entry.

SPOCK: Captain's log, stardate 3843.4. First Officer Spock in temporary command. The captain has been critically wounded by one of the delegates to the Babel conference. The ship is on alert status. We are still being followed by the intruder vessel.

[In sickbay]

MCCOY [To Kirk]: It's a bad wound. Punctured left lung. A centimeter or so lower, it'd have gone through the heart.

INCOMING MESSAGE:

Captains and Humans need both their hearts and lungs to be puncture-free.

When Sarek's condition deteriorates further, McCoy must operate, with Spock providing the blood during the surgery. However, Spock goes into full Starfleet-mode on the doctor and refuses to relinquish command because of the critical situation: one murdered Tellarite, one Andorian thug in the brig, and a ship that's silently shadowing the Enterprise.

INCOMING MESSAGE:

A father should be careful about disapproving of his son's career decision;
one day the son might need to provide a blood transfusion.
Sometimes the needs of the many outweigh the needs of the few.

Kirk and McCoy conspire to convince Spock the captain can take back his command (a violation of the fidelity ethic because of the deception it involves). Of course, the Enterprise is saved, the spy is revealed, and both Sarek and Spock make it through the operation.

INCOMING MESSAGE:

Loyalty to Starfleet is good; but a father's life is more important.
One cannot give a blood transfusion while commanding a starship.

Sarek isn't the only one to experience problems with his cardiovascular system. In "Samaritan Snare" (1989, TNG; 2:17), we first learn of Picard's artificial heart when the heart needs to be replaced.

PICARD: Complete waste of time.
WESLEY: Pardon?

PICARD: I shouldn't be taking this trip at all. I should be back on board the Enterprise.

WESLEY: Why are you coming with me to Starbase Five One Five, sir?

PICARD: Well, it's certainly not my idea. I'm sorry, Ensign, I didn't mean to take it out on you. I just hate the prospect of another damned cardiac replacement.

WESLEY: Cardiac replacement? I didn't know.

PICARD: Well, now you do.

WESLEY: A parthenogenetic implant?

PICARD: What else would it be? My heart was injured and a replacement was necessary. That would have been it, except that the replacement is faulty.

WESLEY: Why would anyone use a faulty replacement?

PICARD: Just pilot the shuttle, Ensign.

[Omitted Scenes and Dialogue]

PICARD: Just not overly thrilled at the prospect of having my innards becoming the subject of Starfleet gossip.

WESLEY: Of course not, sir. Why didn't you just have Dr. Pulaski perform the operation? I'm sure you could've trusted her to keep it quiet.

PICARD: Let's say I have personal reasons and leave it at that, shall we?

INCOMING MESSAGE:

What may not seem embarrassing to an outsider,
may be embarrassing to the person with a disability.
In the future, there will still be problems with quality control.

In addition to Picard, Rom's and Quark's mother, Ishka, is given an artificial heart by Dr. Bashir after she has a heart attack in "Profit and Lace" (1998, DS9; 6:23).

INCOMING MESSAGE:

In the future artificial hearts will be common.

While it's possible to substitute an artificial heart for a biological heart in a Human, apparently lungs are not as easily replaced in Talaxians. In "Phage" (1995, VOY; 1:5) Neelix's lungs are stolen.

JANEWAY: Can't we fit him with a pair of artificial lungs?

THE DOCTOR: His respiratory system is directly linked to multiple points along his spinal column. It's too complex to replicate. I may be able to surgically reattach the organs if we get them back. In the meantime I'll have to search for other options.

To prolong Neelix's life, The Doctor constructs holographic lungs to provide the same function; however to use them Neelix must remain motionless. To save Neelix's life, the Vidiians who stole his lungs transplant one of Kes' lungs into Neelix.

INCOMING MESSAGE:
Organ transplants will still be a medical option
when artificial organs are not available.

In "The Ambergris Element" (1973, TAS; 1:13), the captain and first officer are transformed by Aquans into water-breathing creatures.

MCCOY: Medical log, stardate 5506.2. Captain Kirk and First Officer Spock were rescued forty eight hours ago. They have no recollection of what happened to them after they were attacked, but medical examinations show an unidentified substance in the bloodstream has affected their entire metabolism and changed them into water-breathers. Their internal structure is completely transformed, and even their eyes are covered with a transparent film like the second eyelid of a fish. So far all efforts to return them to normal have failed.

The Enterprise uses its phasers to change the epicenter of a quake, saving the aliens' underwater city. The grateful Aquans reciprocate, sharing their ancient records which provide the information necessary to create a medicine to reverse the mutations. Returning Kirk and Spock to normal is important since it might prove difficult for even the crew of the Enterprise to take orders from a captain living inside an aquarium.

INCOMING MESSAGE:
Be kind even to aliens who have mutated you.
Sometimes it is better to seek a cure than to adjust to the disability.

The Human heart and lungs can develop many ailments which result in disability even without alien interference. *Star Trek* provides two examples of respiratory treatments that may become available in the future.

In "When It Rains..." (1999, DS9; 7:21), the location of Deep Space Nine puts it at the center of the war between the Dominion and Starfleet. Dr. Bashir experienced with the limitations of battlefield medicine prepares for future crises.

BASHIR: It's very difficult to keep a supply of synthetic organs on hand in a battlefield situation. You never know how many livers you're going to need, or how many hearts.

ODO: I can imagine. But what does that have to do with me?

BASHIR: Well, the Holy Grail of organ replacement is to be able to find a way to inject the patient with undifferentiated tissue so that it can become whatever organ is needed. The only problem is—

ODO: Doctor, get to the point.

BASHIR: I need to borrow a cup of goo.

ODO: Excuse me?

BASHIR: Please? I'll give it back. You see—I need to study your morphogenic matrix so that I can synthesize organic tissue that can change form the way your cells do.

ODO: To use for organ replacement.

BASHIR: Exactly.

ODO: Can't you just scan me or something?

BASHIR: I need a sample. It's for a good cause.

ODO: All right, Doctor.

[Odo puts his finger into the beaker and pours off part of himself.]

INCOMING MESSAGE:
Artificially grown organs may be used in the future to replace injured ones.
Major medical breakthroughs often occur during times of war.

While we don't have any changelings in this century (unless you count politicians), the idea that science could "grow" artificial organs is experimentally possible. According to Claire Barrett in Dezeen magazine, in 2013:

> Like other forms of 3D printing, living tissue is printed layer by layer. First a layer of cells is laid down by the printer, followed by a layer of hydrogel that operates as a scaffold material; then the process repeats. The cells fuse, and the hydrogel is removed to create a piece of material made entirely of human cells. This is then moved to a bioreactor, where the tissue continues to grow—as it would in nature—into its final form.

The Voyager crew is ordered to find an Earth probe in "Friendship One" (2001, VOY; 7:21), only to discover the probe has landed on a planet where its high antimatter radiation levels are making the inhabitants, the Uxali, sick. One of the Uxali scientists attacks Ensign Kim and is stunned as Kim and Chakotay make their escape. Back on Voyager, the Uxali scientist, Ortin, is treated for his respiratory distress in sickbay.

SEVEN: The first phase of your therapy is complete. How do you feel?
OTRIN: I can breathe more easily.
SEVEN: Your lungs were damaged by the radiation. The nanoprobes are repairing them.

INCOMING MESSAGE:
Respiratory distress can be a disability.
Relieving a person's suffering is the best form of diplomacy.

The nanoprobes Otrin received were Borg technology, donated by Seven of Nine. Nanotechnology is currently being developed in this century. Robert Freitas Jr., founder of the Nanofactory Collaboration, states that with diligent effort, the first fruits of advanced nanomedicine could begin to appear in clinical treatment sometime during the 2020s.

"No Response to Our Hail" (Hearing and Deafness)

Vulcans and Ferengi are known to hear better than Humans ("Return to Tomorrow," 1968, TOS; 2:20 and "Siege of AR-558," 1998, DS9; 7:8) while Cardassians have less acute hearing ("Distant Voices," 1995, DS9; 3:18.) In "Star Trek: Nemesis" (2002) it's revealed that Picard was treated for an inherited hearing disorder.

> SHINZON: When I was very young I was stricken with an odd disease. I developed a hypersensitivity to sound. Even the slightest whisper caused me agony. No one could do anything about it. Finally I was taken to a doctor who had some experience of Terran illnesses and he diagnosed me with Shalaft's syndrome—Do you know it, Captain?
>
> PICARD:—Yes.
>
> SHINZON: Then you know it's a very rare syndrome. Genetic. Apparently all the male members of a family have it—eventually I was treated and now I can hear as well as you can, Captain—

The disorder described may be akin to *hyperacusis* (also spelled *hyperacousis*) which is characterized by an oversensitivity to sound frequencies in certain ranges. Someone with severe hyperacusis would have trouble tolerating even everyday sounds that would not be unusually loud to others.

INCOMING MESSAGE:
Some genetic disorders can be treated successfully.
Hearing disorders can be genetic.
Clones will have the same genetic disorders as the person cloned.

In the first chapter, I explored the question of when a disability could become an asset by discussing "Is There In Truth No Beauty?" The query reappears in "Loud as a Whisper" (1989, TNG; 2:5).

Deaf with a capital "D" is used by the Deaf community to identify a person who is both hearing impaired and embraces their Deaf identity. Members of the Deaf community view deafness as a difference in Human experience rather than a disability.

Riva, the famous Federation mediator, is Deaf. Howie Seago, the actor who played Riva is a Deaf actor. Due to his deafness, Riva travels with an entourage of three people—one woman (Harmony/Balance) and two men (Scholar/Artist and Passion/Warrior)—who are his "chorus." Riva's telepathic communication with his chorus provides voices for his thoughts.

PICARD: Then Riva the mediator

HARMONY/BALANCE: Is Deaf.

PICARD: Deaf?

HARMONY/BALANCE: Born, and hope to die.

PICARD: And the three of you speak for him?

CHORUS: Yes.

SCHOLAR/ARTIST: We serve as translators. We convey not only his thoughts, but his emotional intent as well. I am the Scholar. I represent the intellect, and speak in matters of judgment, philosophy, logic. Also, I am the dreamer, the part that longs to see the beauty beyond the truth which is always the first duty of art. I am the poet who—

PASSION/WARRIOR: Artists, they tend to ramble, neglect the moment. I am passion, the libido. I am the anarchy of lust, the romantic and the lover. I am also the warrior, the perfect line which never wavers.

HARMONY/BALANCE: I am that which binds all the others together. I am harmony, wisdom, balance.

PICARD: Remarkable. And so these—

[Riva steps forward with an angry expression on his face.]

SCHOLAR/ARTIST: Speak to me!

PICARD: What?

SCHOLAR/ARTIST: Speak directly to me.

PICARD: The uniqueness of this presentation provoked this inadvertent breach in protocol. No insult was intended.

SCHOLAR/ARTIST: Then none is perceived.

INCOMING MESSAGE:
When an interpreter is assisting, speak to the directly to the person
and not the interpreter.
With his chorus, Riva is not disabled.
Communication can be achieved by means other than the spoken word.

While meeting the warring factions, Riva's chorus is killed and he nearly abandons his role as mediator. Data quickly learns Riva's sign language so that he can work as Riva's interpreter on the Enterprise. I guess Troi isn't much use because she is busy flirting with Riva. In the end, Riva decides to "turn his disadvantage into an advantage" by teaching both sides how to communicate with him using sign language while they negotiate a peace.

INCOMING MESSAGE:
Deafness is not a disability,
but a communication difference.

In our century, the Deaf community became somewhat divided regarding the use of a device invented in the 1970s called a *cochlear implant*. Some people in the Deaf community consider themselves to speak a different language rather than impaired. As the technology improves, the acceptance of the device appears to be improving as well.

I interviewed Lelia Rose Foreman, a *Star Trek* fan, about her recent cochlear implant experience. Lelia admits she was resistant about getting the implant because she still had some hearing in her left ear. Her audiologist told her that he could preserve her residual hearing in that ear. She told me that for the first few weeks after the surgery she had considerable nerve pain. She was given hearing lessons on a DVD and was disappointed that she couldn't make out the differences between the sounds. About four weeks later, she was able to hear her car's turn signal. A few days after that she heard a clock tick. From her description, the best part of her experience is being able to talk to her husband "without struggling over every word." Lelia never learned sign language and felt left out of social situations in her younger days. She said that when she watched "Loud As A Whisper" she enjoyed watching the signing in the episode. She pointed out that it was difficult to understand why three people would give up their own lives to be Riva's chorus.

"Sensors Are Off-line" (Visual Impairments)

Based on the number of characters and episodes, the most common disability in the galaxy in the future will be vision impairments. The World Health Organization 2010 report "The estimated number of people visually impaired in the world is 285 million, 39 million blind and 246 million having low vision; 65 % of people visually impaired and 82% of all blind are 50 years and older."

On *Star Trek* there were four Starfleet officers (Kirk, Spock, La Forge, and Tuvok), two non-credited crew members (a transporter assistant and an unnamed lieutenant), two alien species (the Vorta and the Aenar) and one Federation Ambassador (Dr. Miranda Jones) who had vision impairments.

Like other Humans (including this one), Kirk's vision didn't deteriorate until the famous captain was older. In "Star Trek II: The Wrath of Khan" (1982), Dr. McCoy presents Kirk with the gift of a pair of glasses on his birthday.

> KIRK: Oh—Bones, this is—charming. [Looking at the 18th century eyeglasses.]
> McCoy: For most patients of your age, I generally administer Retinax Five—
> KIRK: —I'm allergic to Retinax Five. [Puts on the glasses and looks at a page in a book.]

From the scene it's possible to assume that Kirk has *presbyopia* which is a condition associated with age where the eye exhibits a progressively diminished ability to focus on near objects.

INCOMING MESSAGE:
In the future medications will be used to cure vision impairments.
In the future few people will wear glasses.
The future won't hold a cure for the effects of aging on the body.

Only two other crewmen have been seen wearing glasses: the transporter assistant in "The Menagerie" (1966, TOS; 1:11 & 12) and a lieutenant in "The Terratin Incident" (1973, TAS; 1:11). Although glasses are the most common way to correct vision impairments, contact lenses and surgical interventions are also available in this century. The inclusion of glasses on three members of Starfleet may mean either that there is less vanity in the 23rd century (which would explain some of the clothes), or in the future glasses will be more comfortable than mine are now.

Although Weyoun states that the Vorta don't have good eyesight in "Favor The Bold" (1997, DS9; 6:5), they don't wear glasses or undergo any kind of surgical correction. Nor does their poor sight prevent them from being formidable Federation adversaries. Therefore, their eyesight wouldn't be considered a disability unless they stopped religiously following the orders of the Founders, left the Dominion, and aspired to an occupation where keen eyesight is required.

INCOMING MESSAGE:
Weak eyesight is not a disability under most circumstances.

The most severe form of vision impairment is blindness. As I described in chapter one, blindness was in fact a job qualification for the Federation ambassador Dr. Miranda Jones in "Is There In Truth No Beauty?" (1968, TOS; 3:7). Jones hides her blindness by wearing a bejeweled mesh (sensory net) over her dress because she can sense pity in others when they become aware of her inability to see.

RED ALERT!
It's necessary to hide a disability in order to avoid the pity of others.

INCOMING MESSAGE:
A disability may provide some people with an advantage under certain circumstances.

In "The Aenar" (2005, ENT; 4:14) Captain Archer visits Shran's icy homeworld in the hope of finding out who's piloting an attacking drone. Using information about the brainwave patterns of the "telepresence" operating the drone, Dr. Phlox determines that the closest match is the Andorians. Shran confirms his findings.

SHRAN: I just received a transmission. Our scientists identified the brain wave pattern.
ARCHER: And?

SHRAN: It's from my world, but it's not from any Andorian you'd know. It's Aenar. They're a kind of subspecies. Blind ice-dwellers. For most of our history, they were considered a myth, stories we told our children, but fifty years ago, they were discovered living in the Northern Wastes. They're extremely secretive. I can count on one hand the number of Andorians who've seen one face-to-face.

When Archer meets the Aenar it is clear they're not only telepathic aliens, they're also pacifists and highly ethical humanoids. They do not enter an individual's thoughts without permission. Although the Aenar are blind, they wouldn't be considered disabled except by a medical model definition of disability because they're able to function in their environment without limitation.

INCOMING MESSAGE:
Differences in abilities don't mean the difference is a disability.
Telepathy is cool.

In "Operation: Annihilate!" (1967, TOS; 1:29), Mr. Spock goes blind in an experimental treatment designed to kill aliens who have infected him and the colonists on Deneva. The alien creatures look similar to single-cell neurons, but are the size of Frisbees. Spock goes back to the planet and captures one of the creatures so McCoy can find a means to kill the parasite without killing the hosts: Spock, Kirk's sister-in-law, Kirk's nephew, and the rest of the colony. No pressure here.

Spock suggests that light may provide the lethal treatment because as they arrive, one of the colonists takes a shuttle into the sun. Shortly before the craft enters the sun's gravity well, he exclaims he's free from the pain and control evoked by the alien. McCoy agrees that Spock, who's already infected, is the logical choice to be his lab rat. After Dr. McCoy floods Spock with high intensity bright light, Spock leaves the experimental chamber free from the pain yet totally blind. As he walks out of the light chamber, Spock bumps into the table in front of him. Shortly afterwards the lab tests on the creature are given to Dr. McCoy.

McCoy: I threw the total spectrum of light at the creature. It wasn't necessary. I didn't stop to think that only one kind of light might've killed it.

SPOCK: Interesting. Just as dogs are sensitive to certain sounds which humans cannot hear, these creatures evidently are sensitive to light which we cannot see.
KIRK: Are you telling me that Spock need not have been blinded?
MCCOY: I didn't need to throw the blinding white light at all, Jim. Spock, I—
SPOCK: Doctor it was my selection as well. It is done.

Apparently Klingons aren't the only aliens with physiological redundancy, as Spock demonstrates by his miraculous recovery from total blindness.

MCCOY: The blindness was temporary, Jim. There's something about his optical nerves which aren't the same as a human's.
SPOCK: An hereditary trait, Captain. The brightness of the Vulcan sun has caused the development of an inner eyelid, which acts as a shield against high-intensity light. Totally instinctive, Doctor. We tend to ignore it, as you ignore your own appendix.
KIRK: Mr. Spock. Regaining eyesight would be an emotional experience for most. You, I presume, felt nothing?
SPOCK: Quite the contrary, Captain. I had a very strong reaction. My first sight was the face of Dr. McCoy bending over me. [The looks on their faces are price-less.]

RED ALERT!
McCoy and Kirk feel pity for Spock when he becomes blind.

Spock isn't the only Vulcan to become blind. In "The Year of Hell, Part II" (1997, VOY; 4:9), Tuvok is blinded in a Jefferies tube accident when a torpedo detonates in front of him. He refuses to let Seven assist him with shaving, but allows her to escort him for his customary security rounds. Before they can begin, Voyager is attacked and Tuvok orders Seven to go to Deflector Control and bring the new shields online. Tuvok then feels his way to the bridge, and takes his position at Tactical Control. With a single command, Tuvok continues as the chief of Voyager's security.

TUVOK: Computer, activate tactile interface.

INCOMING MESSAGE:
Assistive technology will allow people who have
become injured to remain in their chosen careers.

Twenty years after the pitiful examples of Dr. Jones and Mr. Spock, different messages about blindness are presented on *Star Trek: The Next Generation*. At the beginning of the series, Lieutenant Geordi La Forge is both blind and the ship's pilot. In the series premiere, "Encounter at Farpoint" (1987, TNG; 1:1), La Forge tells Dr. Crusher about his blindness and the pain he experiences from using the VISOR which allows him to *see*.

CRUSHER: Naturally I've heard of your case. The VISOR appliance you wear—
LA FORGE [finishing her sentence]: —Is a remarkable piece of bio-electronic engineering by which I quote: see much of the EM spectrum ranging from simple heat and infrared through radio waves—et cetera, et cetera—and forgive me if I've said and listened to this a thousand times before— [La Forge laughs.]
CRUSHER: You've been blind all your life?
LA FORGE: Ah hum. I was born this way.
CRUSHER: And you've felt pain all the years that you've used this? [She indicates the VISOR.]
LA FORGE: They say it's because I use my natural sensors in different ways.
CRUSHER: Well, I see two choices. The first is painkillers—
LA FORGE: Which would affect how this works. [He indicates the VISOR.]
CRUSHER: Ah hum.
LA FORGE: No. Choice number two?
CRUSHER: Exploratory surgery. Desensitize the brain areas troubling you—
LA FORGE: Same difference. No, thank you, Doctor.
CRUSHER: I understand.
LA FORGE: See you. [Geordi leaves sickbay.]

Unlike Dr. Miranda Jones, Lieutenant La Forge uses an assistive technology device, which doesn't disguise his vision impairment. La Forge appears to have accepted his blindness and the pain associated with wearing his VISOR. (At the same time I can't help but wonder why he didn't choose a bejeweled mesh like Dr. Jones did—to avoid the pain.)

In many respects, since La Forge can *see* with his VISOR, he isn't visually impaired as long as he's wearing it. It appears to me that this scene removes the focus from Geordi's vision impairment, and places it instead on the discomfort he experiences while using his VISOR.

However, La Forge's acceptance of his blindness is brought into question in "The Naked Now" (1987, TNG; 1:3), when La Forge becomes infected with a virus that acts like alcohol intoxication. He tells Tasha Yar about his desire to see naturally.

LA FORGE: Help me to see. Like you do.
YAR: But you already see better than I can.
LA FORGE: I see more. But more isn't better.
[He takes off his VISOR.]
YAR: Geordi, please put—
LA FORGE: I want to see in shallow, dim, beautiful human ways.

There are two possible ways to interpret this scene. Either La Forge isn't always as accepting of his vision impairment as he appears, or it was the *virus* talking. In my interview with Higley I learned that part of La Forge's character was that he accepted his blindness without question.

INCOMING MESSAGE:
People who have accepted their disability still want to feel accepted like everyone else.
In the future people won't need to hide vision impairments.

In "Heart of Glory" (1988, TNG; 1:20), a device called a Visual Acuity Transmitter links Geordi's VISOR to the main viewer which allows Captain Picard to see what La Forge sees, the way he sees it.

PICARD: How can you make head or tail of it?
LA FORGE: I select what I want and then disregard the rest.
PICARD: But how is that possible?
LA FORGE: Well, how, in a noisy room, can you select one specific voice or sound?

PICARD: Of course, something you learn.

LA FORGE: Exactly. It's something I have learned. Does that make it more clear?

PICARD: Look over at Data. There's an aura around Data.

LA FORGE: Well, of course. He's an android.

PICARD: You say that as if you think that's what we all see.

LA FORGE: Don't you?

INCOMING MESSAGE:

Using assistive technology doesn't necessarily restore the person
to functioning in exactly the same manner as everyone else.
There's a learning curve to adapting to assistive technology.

When La Forge meets the Deaf mediator, Riva, in "Loud As A Whisper" (1989, TNG; 2:5), it becomes clear that the blind chief of engineering and the Deaf mediator have much in common.

HARMONY/BALANCE: What is that you're wearing?

LA FORGE: A VISOR. It interprets the electromagnetic spectrum and then carries the readings to my brain.

HARMONY/BALANCE: And without it, can you see?

LA FORGE: Without it I'm as blind as a stump.

HARMONY/BALANCE: Then your VISOR serves the same function as my Chorus, which interprets my thoughts and translates them into sound?

LA FORGE: Yes.

SCHOLAR/ARTIST: And you don't resent it?

LA FORGE: The VISOR or being blind?

SCHOLAR/ARTIST: Either.

LA FORGE: No, since they're both part of me, and I really like who I am, there's no reason for me to resent either one.

La Forge with his VISOR and Riva with his chorus aren't disabled because they're not impaired in their work or personal lives. They simply use other means to see and hear.

INCOMING MESSAGE:

Assistive technology allows people with disabilities to
perform "as if" they were not otherwise impaired.

Later, while having his implants examined by Dr. Pulaski, La Forge is given some new options.

PULASKI: It's possible to install optical devices which look like normal eyes, and would still give you about the same visual range as the VISOR.

LA FORGE: Done? [Referring to Dr. Pulaski's examination.] You say almost. How much reduction?

PULASKI: Twenty percent. There is another option. I can attempt to regenerate your optic nerve, and, with the help of the replicator, fashion normal eyes. You would see like everyone else.

LA FORGE: Wait a minute. I was told that was impossible.

PULASKI: I've done it twice, in situations somewhat similar to yours. Geordi, it would eliminate the constant pain you are under. Why are you hesitating?

LA FORGE: Well, when I came to see you, it was to talk about modifying this [he taps his VISOR.] And now you're saying it could be possible for me to have normal vision?

PULASKI: Yes.

LA FORGE: I don't know. I'd be giving up a lot.

PULASKI: There's something else you must know. This is a one shot. If you decide to change your mind, there's no going back. And there are risks. I can offer choices, not guarantees.

LA FORGE: Well, this is a lot to think about. I'll get back to you, Doctor. Thank you.

INCOMING MESSAGE:

La Forge is comfortable with who he is which includes wearing his VISOR.
Sometimes assistive technology provides extra or different abilities
that people may be reluctant to give up even if they returned to normal.

By the time Commander La Forge meets "The Father of Warp Speed" in "Star Trek: First Contact" (1996), his VISOR has been replaced by fully functional cybernetic eyes. When the Enterprise goes to observe the Ba'ku on their planet in "Star Trek: Insurrection" (1998), the fictional "metaphasic radiation" has rejuvenating powers that allows La Forge to see normally for the first time.

PICARD: Geordi?

LA FORGE: Captain—As it turned out there wasn't anything wrong with my implants at all. There was something right—with my eyes—when Dr. Crusher removed the ocular connections, she found that the cells around my optic nerves had—

PICARD: —started to regenerate.

LA FORGE: It may not last and—if it doesn't—I just wanted—before we go, I— You know, I've never seen a sunrise—At least not the way you see them.

INCOMING MESSAGE:

When his vision is restored without medical intervention,
La Forge enjoys seeing the world with Human eyes.

The effects of the *metaphasic radiation* wear off after leaving the planet and La Forge has cybernetic eyes the next time we see him in "Star Trek: Nemesis" (2002).

INCOMING MESSAGE:

No discussion about La Forge's sight or assistive technology means
he's just the chief of engineering, not "the blind" chief of engineering.

Ten years after Geordi La Forge demonstrated that a blind man could pilot the Enterprise and become the ship's chief of engineering, the association between blindness and pity is resurrected in "When It Rains..." (1999, DS9; 7:21). Kai Winn, the self-righteous villain, describes to Gul Dukat the charity of Bajorans toward people who are blind in highly prejudicial terms. Dukat has been blinded by trying to sneak a peek at the holy text known as the Kosst Amojan.

WINN: You'll find the Bajoran people are very kind. A blind beggar will elicit their sympathies, I'm certain. And with any luck, you'll earn enough to eat and perhaps even enough for shelter each night.

Since my biases against Kai Winn are obvious, I'll leave it to others to determine if the Kai is denigrating the Bajoran people for marginalizing people with disabilities, or if she thinks all people who are blind are automatically going to be beggars and should be treated with pity.

INCOMING MESSAGE:

Even religious people can express negative attitudes towards people with disabilities.

Recent developments in assistive technology for the visually impaired have been quite remarkable. According to a 2013 report by Allison Barrie, artificial eyes have been created which, like a VISOR, use an implanted camera and computer to convert the world into electronic signals that enable the brain to see. Barrie reports that according to the *British Journal of Ophthalmology* twenty-one blind patients were able to see well enough to locate and identify objects as well as read short words.

For people with severe low vision, NASA has developed a device called a *Joint Optical Reflective Display*, or JORDY, named after Commander Geordi La Forge. The device enables a person to magnify objects by a factor of fifty, and allows the user to change contrast, brightness, and display modes, customizing the device to enhance their residual vision condition. However, the most promising research, has been published in the *Proceedings of the National Academy of Sciences* and described in *Medical News Today* (2013), where researchers reported that they successfully restored full vision to blind mice using cells transplanted into their eyes.

According to the report:

> The cells reformed the entire light-sensitive layer of the retina, rather like replacing the film in a camera. The researchers believe their cell transplantation therapy might be applied to treat blindness resulting from the progressive condition retinitis pigmentosa.

Considering these recent advancements, it would appear science may eliminate blindness even before we're traveling at warp speeds. When Gene Roddenberry put the VISOR on Geordi La Forge, he made a bold statement. In the future, disabilities won't need to be hidden because there will be less stigma associated with individual differences. La Forge's VISOR reminded the audience in every episode that this competent, good-looking, Starfleet officer also happened to be blind.

Chapter 9
"Make It So!"

TUCKER: ...I don't think I'm going to be much help over here. I'm having a little more trouble adjusting than I thought I would.
"Unexpected" (2001, ENT: 1:4)

Adjustment to Disability

In the *Star Trek* universe, regular crewmen usually recover from their injuries or medical crisis by the end of the episode. Guest stars aren't always as lucky. Extras have high mortality rates—especially if they wear a red shirt on the original series. Off-screen, quick recoveries for injuries or illnesses are rarer than blonde Romulans. Some never completely recover, but instead must find a way to adapt to a disability. The process of learning to cope can often be emotionally arduous, as various episodes demonstrate.

Adjustment to disability refers to the psychological acceptance of new limitations. *Adaptation*, on the other hand, describes how the person compensates for their loss of abilities. The adaptation may be through assistive technology, assistance with the activity, or simply learning to do tasks differently. To be clear, in this chapter I'm talking about acceptance of acquired disabilities. People who are born with disabilities don't adjust; they begin life with a physical or mental difference and grow up learning to do things differently. While they may feel the same stigma, they usually don't report the same sense of loss experienced by people who acquire a disability through injury or chronic illness.

"Red Alert! Battle Stations" (Emotional Reactions to Disability)

When engaging the enemy, starships, like Humans, have various methods to defend themselves. The ships can launch torpedoes, fire phasers, raise shields, take evasive maneuvers, or get out of harm's way at warp factor ten. Emotional reactions to a disability can be similar to a ship's defenses in that there are a variety of responses, some of which work better than others. Some emotional reactions to disability can put a person at further risk for additional social and mental health problems. When someone becomes disabled they may react with anger or depression, isolate themselves, and deprive themselves of the support of their social network. The more isolated the person becomes, the more angry and depressed they may also become. Remember you have to lower your shields to beam anyone onto your ship.

"Weapons Offline" (Grief)

When Captain Picard was captured by the Borg in "Best of Both Worlds, Part I" (1990, TNG; 3:26), his resistance proved futile as he was turned into "Locutus of Borg"—the mouthpiece of the cybernetic monster collective. As Locutus, Picard helplessly watched the Borg destroy most of the Federation's fleet at Wolf 359. After Locutus was rescued by Data and Worf in "Best of Both Worlds, Part II" (1990, TNG; 4:1), Locutus' cybernetic implants were removed and he returned to being Captain Picard. In "Family" (1990, TNG; 4:2), the effects of his Borg assimilation were consistent with the symptoms of post-traumatic Stress Disorder (PTSD).

PICARD: Your help has been invaluable during my recovery, but—look—I'm better. The injuries are healing.

TROI: Those you can see in the mirror.

PICARD: The nightmares have ended. All I need now is a little time to myself.

TROI: I agree. In fact, I'm delighted you're going. It's just that the choice of where you're going could stand some scrutiny.

PICARD: If you wish to believe that my going home is a direct result of being held captive by the Borg, be my guest.

TROI: Is that what you believe?

PICARD: I hate it when you do that—

TROI: Captain, you do need time. You cannot achieve complete recovery so quickly. And it's perfectly normal, after what you've been through, to spend a great deal of time trying to find yourself again.

Picard's visit home is far from smooth. He considers leaving Starfleet and working on Earth due to his emotional turmoil. After exchanging a few punches and rolling in the mud with his brother, Robert, Picard expresses how broken his spirit has become and the depth of his grief. In addition to the trauma of becoming Borg, Picard lost his sense of self.

PICARD: You don't know, Robert. You don't know. They took everything I was. They used me to kill and to destroy, and I couldn't stop them. I should have been able to stop them! I tried. I tried so hard, but I wasn't strong enough. I wasn't good enough. I should have been able to stop them. I should! I should!
ROBERT: So, my brother is a human being after all. This is going to be with you a long time, Jean-Luc. A long time. You have to learn to live with it. You have a simple choice now. Live with it below the sea with Louis, or above the clouds with the Enterprise.

Robert helps Picard accept that the grief isn't going to fade quickly—Picard must make room for it in his life. Realistically, it takes longer than one or two episodes for grief to begin to subside. A normal reaction to loss is to feel sad. The pain of that sadness can sometimes impel a person to try to escape rather than deal with their disability.

When Christopher Reeve was thrown from his horse, his acting career ended. His body was transformed from that of a strong leading man to a man with quadriplegia who needed a machine to breathe. His identity also changed from movie star to former movie star to founder of a research organization that supports finding a cure for spinal cord injuries. Reeve's acceptance and adjustment to his disability took time; they weren't accomplished in the span of a television episode.

Acceptance of the loss is a necessary part of the grieving process as a person adjusts to a new disability. Mud is optional.

"Fire Torpedoes" (Fear and Anxiety)

Fear and anxiety are normal responses to a perceived threat of loss. The potential to lose function, love, independence, or security can create reactions of fear and anxiety because what will be lost is not always immediately known. At times, the paralyzing effects of these emotions can be more disabling than a high-energy force field.

In "Miri" (1966, TOS; 1:8), when the away team beams onto an Earth-like planet, they become infected with a virus that causes rapid aging, disfigurement, and death within seven days. Ensign Rand is overcome with anxiety about losing her attractiveness. Since Rand has less than one week to live, this woman obviously has some problems with her priorities.

> RAND: I'm upset, so upset. Back on the ship, I used to try to get you to look at my legs. Captain, look at my legs. [They are covered in bluish blotches.]
> KIRK [holds her]: We're all frightened.

When a person acquires a disability, it's important to help them regain a sense of control over their life. Ensign Rand doesn't provide a good example because rather than assisting the others in finding the cure, she gets kidnapped by a gang of 300-year-old children. Another good example of how women were viewed in the 1960s, and another good reason to avoid red uniforms.

When B'Elanna Torres has her Klingon DNA removed by the Vidiians in "Faces" (1995, VOY; 1:14), she has difficulty adjusting to her new emotional experiences. Without her Klingon half, she experiences Human-quality fear for the first time.

> PARIS: B'Elanna, I'm no doctor, but I have to believe that whatever they did to you has seriously depleted your strength. There's nothing you could have done.
> TORRES: No—that's not it—I think that when they extracted my Klingon DNA, they turned me into some kind of a coward.

Unlike Ensign Rand, Torres focuses her fear on developing a plan to escape from her captors and rescue her crewmates. While Torres assumes that the loss of her Klingon DNA is the reason she's now fearful, her fear may actually originate from how her altered appearance affects how she views herself. When a disability is visible to others, the person with the disability may feel that their previous identity has been taken from them. In the end, Torres makes peace with her Klingon heritage—at least until she gets pregnant several seasons later.

"Shields Up" (Anger)

Counselor Deanna Troi suddenly loses her empathic abilities in "The Loss" (1990; TNG; 4:10). Without her empathic Betazoid powers Troi suffers a tremendous sense of loss, and goes through several emotional reactions including:

Denial...

> CRUSHER: Deanna, it's no different than one of us suddenly going blind.
> TROI: You don't have to tell me, Beverly. I understand the psychology.
> CRUSHER: You may understand it but you've never had to live with it.
> TROI: I may be perfectly fine by tomorrow.

Fear...

> RIKER: I don't have a psychology degree, but if you'd like to talk?
> TROI: You know what the worst part of this is? And I've seen it happen to so many patients.
> RIKER: What?
> TROI: The way other people change. How they start to treat you differently. They walk on eggshells around you. Sometimes they avoid you altogether. Sometimes they become overbearing, reach out a helping hand to the blind woman.
> RIKER: I'm sorry if I—
> TROI: I will not be treated that way!
> RIKER: Hey! Imzadi—
> TROI: Oh, please.
> RIKER: Deanna, I've never seen you quite so scared.
> TROI: I'm fine. If I get better, I get better. If I don't, I'll adapt. Life goes on.

And *Anger* with a capital "A"—first at Dr. Crusher—

TROI: How do you people live like this?

CRUSHER: We get by pretty well, actually. And so will you, in time.

TROI: You have no idea. No idea what this is like. How can you know what it's like to lose something you never had?

CRUSHER: I don't claim to.

TROI: And yet you're telling me I'm supposed to get used to it.

—and then at Captain Picard.

TROI: It's time I accept the truth, Captain, and resign as ship's counselor.

PICARD: Resign?

TROI: I can no longer fulfill my obligations. What other option is there?

PICARD: Deanna, I've been fortunate to have access to your Betazoid abilities. Most starship captains have to be content with a human counselor. Empathic awareness is not a requirement of your position.

TROI: It is for me.

PICARD: I'm sure that after a while you'll be able to adjust. They say when one loses a sense, the other senses become stronger to compensate. A blind man develops better hearing.

TROI: With all due respect, Captain, you don't know what you're talking about. That is a common belief with no scientific basis, no doubt created by normal people who felt uncomfortable around the disabled. I am disabled, and I'm telling you I cannot perform my duties.

PICARD: There was a teacher of mine at the Academy who had been confined to a wheelchair since birth. She was a woman—

TROI: Captain, spare me the inspirational anecdote and just accept my resignation.

While it's obvious that Captain Picard means well, he does what many people do when faced with a friend who has become disabled: he tries to cheer her up rather than affirm her sense of loss. One of the reasons peer counseling is effective for various disabilities, is that talking with someone who has been through a similar experience can help break through feelings of isolation or the "No-One-Knows-How-I-Feel" problem.

A significant misstep is the objectionable term "confined to a wheelchair" used in the dialogue. This term is offensive because wheelchairs are mobility devices. There's nothing confining about them—it's physical barriers that limit access that are the problem. Not the wheelchairs.

In my experience, anger is the most common reaction to disability. The anger may be directed internally, at oneself, because the person may feel partially responsible. Or the individual may direct their anger at others because they resent their new dependency. People often become frustrated by how others treat them, such as offering assistance on tasks they can still perform independently. Different treatment is a constant reminder that others no longer see them as the same person they once were.

At the onset of a disability, it's unreasonable to expect the person to be reasonable. Emotional reactions most often overwhelm logical thinking. Anger can serve to protect the individual from grief or fear just as the shields protect the Enterprise from enemy weapons.

"I'm Picking Up A Distress Signal" (Depression)

After the Founders strip Odo of his shape-shifting abilities, the chief of security on Deep Space Nine has trouble adjusting to life as a solid. In "Apocalypse Rising" (1996, DS9; 5:1), Sisko empathizes with Odo's sadness, but at the same time reminds the constable that he can still do his job.

> SISKO: …Odo, I know this has been a difficult time for you. That you never would've chosen to become a solid. But what's done is done. Brooding isn't going to change anything, and shirking your responsibilities isn't going to make you feel better about yourself.
> ODO: No, I don't suppose it will.
> SISKO: Then I suggest you get back in there and do your job.

When grief continues for a prolonged period, it's possible that the person can develop depression, which differs from grief in that the sadness is accompanied by other physical symptoms.

Sleep disturbance, changes in appetite, difficulty concentrating, and withdrawing from activities can all signal depression. The emotional components of depression include feelings of helplessness, hopelessness, discouragement, worthlessness, dejection, and apathy. Furthermore, it's unrealistic to expect someone to experience only one episode of grief while adjusting to a disability. The feelings of sadness related to loss may often re-emerge throughout the person's life.

Although Quark isn't qualified to diagnose depression in Odo (apparently Ferengi bartenders, like their Human counterparts, often act as pseudo-psychologists), he's observant and realizes that Odo is more than simply sad. Quark feels miserable over his inability to help his sparring partner overcome his sense of loss.

SISKO: I'm looking for Odo.
QUARK: Oh, Captain, we all have our failures, and he's mine. Ever since he lost his shape-shifting abilities—I haven't been able to get a smile out of him.
SISKO: Where is he?
QUARK: I'm telling you, Captain, that's one depressed ex-changeling. He's upstairs at his usual table. Just follow the black cloud.

Contagion depression is common among the family and friends of someone with a disability. Unfortunately, the effects of a disability can also cause distress for the person's entire social network. It's important that loved ones also receive support as they deal with their own emotional reactions, their new roles, and the limitations and personality changes in their family member or friend. Too often family and friends will feel guilty for their own emotional reactions to the disability and attempt to bury their feelings because they think their feelings are less important. They may also feel helpless as they try to support their loved one and watch him or her struggle. Adjusting to a disability isn't something you can do for another person. Depression can therefore affect both the person with the disability as well as their social network.

Odo's ability to maintain his pre-injury role as Deep Space Nine's constable is one of the factors that contribute to his eventual positive adjustment to his new limitation. This occurs in large part because his previous social support network—his relationships with his coworkers—remains the same. Fortunately for Odo, his disability doesn't last the entire fifth season. Humans are rarely so lucky.

Evasive Maneuvers (Coping Strategies)

Emotional reactions to disability occur *within* the person, although evidence of the reactions can be found in the person's behaviors. Coping strategies are a constellation of actions that people perform to manage, tolerate, or reduce their stress. Since acquiring a disability is stressful, there are several more common behaviors associated with adjusting to a disability.

"Engage Cloaking Mechanism" (Denial)

One of the most common reactions to stresses, including those brought on by a disability, is to deny the situation exists. Denial is no more effective at coping with a disability than phasers are at stopping a Borg. When T'Pol receives assistance to repress a traumatic memory in "The Seventh" (2002, ENT; 2:7) she uses a coping skill similar to denial and the consequences are equally problematic.

The episode begins when the Vulcan High Command orders T'Pol to complete a mission she'd been assigned to while she worked for the Ministry of Security. This previous assignment was to capture an undercover Vulcan agent who had infiltrated criminal factions of Agaron society and then failed to return to the ministry after Agaron formed an alliance with the Vulcans. The agent, Menos, had become a smuggler of synthetic biotoxins, a criminal but highly lucrative activity. The Vulcan High Command has now located Menos and sends T'Pol to arrest him.

Once T'Pol apprehends Menos, she explains to Captain Archer that in her previous attempt to capture him, she killed one of his associates, a man named Jossen. T'Pol's emotions, especially her guilt over killing Jossen, cause her to doubt the evidence against Menos as the repressed memory re-surfaces.

T'POL: Have you heard of the Fullara?

ARCHER: No.

T'POL: It's an obsolete Vulcan ritual where the memory of an event is repressed along with the emotions associated with it.

ARCHER: And you had this—

T'POL: —Fullara.

ARCHER: —This Fullara ritual performed?

T'POL: When I returned to Vulcan, I was unsettled. I resigned my position with the Ministry and sought guidance at the Sanctuary of P'Jem. For months, one of the Elders worked with me to control the guilt, to restrain the despair of having taken a life, but the feelings remained.

ARCHER: Why would you feel guilty if this Jossen was about to fire at you?

T'POL: I suppose I was never certain what his intentions were. The Elder had no choice but to perform the ritual. When I left the Sanctuary I didn't remember anything about Jossen or the Fullara.

T'Pol's inability to continue to repress the memories and the emotions they evoke forces her to deal with them rather than deny them. Because of her experience with Humans on the Enterprise, she has witnessed new coping strategies which she can attempt to use as she copes with her past.

ARCHER: ...Dealing with these memories it's not going to be easy for you, is it?

T'POL: No, it's not.

ARCHER: If you feel you need a leave of absence—

T'POL: That won't be necessary. I was much younger then.

ARCHER: You've also spent a lot of time around humans lately.

T'POL: You 'do' have a way of putting questionable actions behind you.

ARCHER: When you don't have the ability to repress emotions, you learn to deal with them and move on...

In some ways, refusing Captain Archer's offer of a leave of absence may be considered another expression of denial because T'Pol may be denying herself the healing qualities of time.

Denial in recently diagnosed individuals often takes the form of refusing medical treatment. Martok, the Klingon general who later becomes Worf's friend, was forced to fight Jem'Hadar in hand-to-hand combat while in prison in "By Inferno's Light" (1997, DS9; 5:15). During one of these combat training exercises, a Jem'Hadar injures Martok resulting in the loss of his left eye. After Worf, Bashir, Garak, and Martok are rescued from the prison, Martok continues to practice for battle in holosuites on Deep Space Nine. So if everyone can turn off the safety protocols; why bother having them?

Martok refuses medical treatment in "Soldiers of the Empire" (1997, DS9; 5:21). By refusing medical treatment, he denies the injury to his eye is a disability.

> BASHIR: Turning off the holosuite safety protocols during a battle simulation is at best dubious. For a man with only one eye it's positively idiotic. Now, if you would consider ocular—
> MARTOK: I do not want an artificial eye!
> BASHIR: Then you must accept the fact that you have a disability and stop acting like—
> MARTOK: There are limits as to how far I will indulge you, Doctor.

Both T'Pol and Martok use denial to cope with their disabilities. They also illustrate that there are cultural considerations in adjusting to a disability. For a Klingon warrior such as Martok, his denial of being impaired is culturally related. Neither Worf nor Martok is prepared to be a considered a *Klingon with disability*. The Vulcan culture places a high value on their ability to repress emotions and rely on logic. This is why T'Pol's struggle over her feelings of guilt is a culturally defined disability as well. Given the Vulcans' reverence for science, I wonder what the Vulcan equivalent to the ICD-10 would be and how it would label her condition.

Denial can be a strategy for those close to the person with a disability as well. When Seven's cortical node malfunctions and efforts to find a replacement fail, Seven confronts Janeway about the captain's denial of Seven's impending death in "Imperfection" (2000, VOY; 7:2).

> SEVEN: You refuse to acknowledge the severity of my condition, just as I did at first.
> JANEWAY: Are you giving up?
> SEVEN: I'm merely accepting reality.
> [Dialogue Omitted]
> SEVEN: ...I want you to know that the failure has been mine, not yours.
> JANEWAY: You haven't failed, Seven. You've exceeded my expectations. You've become an individual, an extraordinary individual. If I'm having trouble accepting your condition it's only because I don't want to lose a friend.

Icheb, one of the former drone children rescued by Voyager and mentored by Seven, refuses to accept Seven's death as inevitable. He offers to have The Doctor transplant his cortical node into Seven. However, The Doctor and the rest of the *we've never heard of transplants* committee reject Icheb's plan, so he takes matters into his own alcove and deactivates the relays to his cortical node. After The Doctor transplants Icheb's cortical node into Seven, both Icheb and Seven recover. Icheb teaches Seven that she's not the only former Borg drone resisting dependency on others.

ICHEB: You think I need to learn to rely on other people?

SEVEN: Yes.

ICHEB: What about you? You've refused to rely on a single member of this crew. You hid your condition from the rest of us, you deactivated The Doctor, and now you're rejecting my help. You're the one who needs to rely on others. Isn't that what people on this ship do? They help each other?

JANEWAY: Whenever we can.

ICHEB: If the Captain were dying you'd risk your life to save her, wouldn't you? And when you respond to a distress call you're risking the life of everyone on this ship to respond to the aid of strangers.

JANEWAY: He's right.

SEVEN: Captain, he's just a child.

JANEWAY: I don't think he is. Not anymore.

One of the difficulties of coping with a disability can be the increased dependency on others. Balancing the need to rely on others with regaining independence can be more difficult that attempting to align the targeting scanners. Icheb, however, appears to score a direct hit.

"Reverse Engines" (Regression)

Regression is a coping strategy wherein a person reverts to an earlier stage of development. The person may appear to be acting childlike or childish. He or she may become passive and dependent on others. Heightened emotionality or mood swings are common as well. Regression towards a younger developmental stage may serve to help someone with a disability gain a renewed sense of safety as others take care of them.

Nog's leg was amputated due to injuries in battle while on an away mission in "The Siege of AR-558" (1998, DS9; 7:8). In "It's Only A Paper Moon" (1998, DS9; 7:10) Nog returns to Deep Space Nine for medical leave after receiving an artificial leg.

Nog moves into the holosuite and begins living with Vic Fontaine, a holosuite character in a nightclub program. I refer to this as his *Lieutenant Barclay Maneuver*. However, Nog is doing more than escaping into a holosuite fantasy. He's regressing to a time in his life before he was a member of Starfleet. Regressing into a time when he was simply a Ferengi and had fewer responsibilities allows Nog to heal from his emotional wounds. The senior officers confer, agreeing to allow Nog to remain in the holosuite, and to employ the assistance of Fontaine. Apparently, in addition to Ferengi bartenders, holosuite characters can also be pseudo-psychologists as well.

> EZRI: ...But I think Nog might be subconsciously trying to seek out his own form of therapy.
> JAKE: I'm sorry, but moving into a holosuite isn't my idea of therapy.
> EZRI: Okay, it sounds a little odd.
> QUARK: It sounds ridiculous.
> BASHIR: Not really—I'm inclined to agree with Ezri on this one. The mind has a strong natural instinct for survival. Now, for whatever reason, Nog's mind has chosen to take shelter in the world of Vic Fontaine.
> EZRI: I think we should wait and see how this plays out.
> SISKO: Then someone should talk to Vic, make him aware of Nog's emotional and physical condition.
> EZRI: I'll do it.

When Nog begins making plans to build a new casino, Ezri reminds Fontaine that he's part of a holosuite program and all their plans are fantasies. Fontaine decides the time has come to help Nog return to his life and obligations in Starfleet. At an unexpected moment, Fontaine both thanks Nog for keeping his program running and boots him out into the real world.

> VIC: It's incredible. Since you've been here, I've slept in a bed every night, gone to work every day, had time to read the paper, play cards with the boys.

I've had a life. And I have to tell you, it's a precious thing. I had no idea how much it means to just live. Now I'm going to return the favor and give you your life back.

NOG: But I don't want that life anymore, Vic. I'm perfectly happy here.

VIC: What here? There is no here. Don't you get it? This is nowhere. It's an illusion and so am I. In fact, the only thing in this entire program that is not an illusion is you.

NOG: Okay. You're right. But I'm not ready to go back yet. I need more time. So let's just sleep on this and talk about it tomorrow—

VIC: Kid, I hate to do this to you, but you're not giving me any choice. Computer—

NOG: No—don't—

VIC: —End program.

Children often engage in fantasy during their play, it's a natural part of normal Human development. While adults still engage in play and fantasy, such as when I attend *Star Trek* conventions, we do it for a limited amount of time. Likewise, Nog's regression into the holosuite program is only therapeutic for a short period. After Chief O'Brien reveals to Nog that Vic controls his own holosuite program, Vic returns for another attempt at helping Nog understand why it's important to get back to his life.

VIC: You stay here, you're going to die. Not all at once, but little by little. Eventually you'll become as hollow as I am.

NOG: You don't seem hollow to me.

VIC: Compared to you, I'm hollow as a snare drum. Look, kid, I don't know what's going to happen to you out there. All I can tell you is that you've got to play the cards life deals you. Sometimes you win, sometimes you lose, but at least you're in the game.

At the onset of a disability, feelings of mortality can be overwhelming. Typically a person will become more dependent out of medical necessity, just like Nog's dependence on the cane while he adjusted to his artificial leg. However, dependency that's not (or is no longer) medically necessary can impair a person's long-term adjustment to their disability.

When Nog continues to use the cane even though he no longer physically needs it, the cane becomes a symbol of his resistance to accepting his disability and his uncertainty about the future. When the time comes to move from medically necessary dependency to adjusting to disability, the process can be unpredictable at times, much like entering a holosuite program with a self-aware character.

I asked David Mack, co-author of "It's Only A Paper Moon" about the messages concerning disability that were intended in this episode. He said:

> I don't know that we had a message about disability. The core of the story, in my opinion, is really about the dissonance between self-image and how others perceive us. Nog's true impediment is not his leg; in the episode it is stated that his cybernetic prosthetic is functioning perfectly, and that Nog should not feel any pain from it. He is not genuinely disabled, in a physical sense. He has been psychologically wounded.

Mack provided the following paragraph from the final version of the story outlines which identifies the crux of Nog's trouble as he explains to Vic why he wants to hide in the holosuite.

> Nog doesn't want to be called a hero. Maybe he was a hero, that one time, but that was when deep down, like most young people, he thought he was invulnerable, immortal—he didn't think he could really get hurt. Now he knows he can, and he's terrified to go out the door and back to the real world, because now everyone expects so much of him. Before they thought he was just a green rookie Ferengi, they didn't expect anything; now they think he's a hero. It's too much for him. He doesn't want to fail to live up to everyone's new expectations. Not Vic's, not Sisko's, nobody's.

Mack went on to say:

> I think part of what drove me to zero in on this shift in Nog's thinking was my own reaction after surviving a serious car accident many years earlier, in July of 1990. Before that night, I hadn't really thought of myself as mortal or vulnerable. I

was still hanging on to youthful illusions. But then the car in which I was riding as a passenger was struck broadside by a pickup truck driven by a drunk 18-year-old...I had come within inches of being paralyzed. After that night, I never again took my life or health for granted.

I asked him to tell me about the feedback from the fans about the episode:

As far as feedback from fans regarding "It's Only a Paper Moon," it has been almost unanimously positive. I have received heartfelt e-mails from soldiers serving overseas in combat zones, or aboard ships, who have seen the episode and felt that it rang true for them. I've been proud to share many of those messages with my co-writers, John Ordover and Ron Moore. I've also heard from others who have struggled from PTSD, or with the arduous challenges of physical and occupational therapy, after they have seen the episode. It is deeply gratifying to me to know that something I wrote so many years ago continues to resonate with people, and that it so frequently gives them even a small measure of hope or clarity.

Even though Nog struggles with his adjustment, eventually he leaves the holosuite and goes back to Starfleet.

"Re-route Auxiliary Power to the Engines" (Compensation)

Compensation refers to a coping strategy that counteracts the feelings of loss a person experiences by developing a new skill. This coping skill can be either negative or positive depending on how the behavior is used. Q demonstrates a positive aspect of compensation in "Déjà Q" (1990, TNG; 3:13), even though Q is far from being a positive role model.

After Q is divested of his omnipotent powers by the Q-Continuum, he experiences a loss. Admittedly, he loses a *superpower*, but for Q it is a disability because he has lost his previous ability to control his environment and his appearance. It is only as Q begins to experience life as a Human that he begins to understand the significance of his loss.

Q: It was a mistake. I never should have picked human. I knew it the minute I said it. To think of the future in this shell.

Forced to cover myself with fabric because of some outdated human morality. To say nothing of being too hot or too cold, growing feeble with age, losing my hair, catching a disease, being ticklish, sneezing, having an itch, a pimple, bad breath. Having to bathe.

[Dialogue Omitted]

Q: ...Truthfully, Jean-Luc, I have been entirely preoccupied by a most frightening experience of my own. A couple of hours ago, I, realizing, that my body was no longer functioning properly. I felt weak. I could no longer stand. The life was oozing out of me. I lost consciousness.

PICARD: You fell asleep.

Q: Terrifying. How can you stand it day after day?

PICARD: You get used to it.

Q finds very little sympathy among the Enterprise crew. His previous behavior of disrupting the crew's lives hasn't been forgotten. As Q is forced to find a way to deal with his new limitations, he uses the crisis at hand and offers Captain Picard assistance. Q taps into his knowledge and experience with his supernatural powers (outside of tormenting other beings). In other words, Q must compensate for his lost ability since he's retained all of his arrogant personality.

Q: Jean-Luc, wait! [Walks into the forcefield.] This is getting on my nerves, now that I have them. You have a moon in a deteriorating orbit. I've known moons through the universe. Big ones, small ones. I'm an expert. I could help you with this one, if you let me out of here.

PICARD: Q, there are millions of lives at risk. If you have the power to—

Q: —I don't have any powers. But I have the knowledge, locked up in this puny brain. You cannot afford to not take that advantage, can you?

At the same time, compensation can take negative forms as well. Compensating for the loss with self-destructive behaviors can isolate an individual even beyond his or her perception of being *undesirable* or *less than* because of the disability.

Q: Picard thinks I can't cut it on his starship. I can do anything his little trained minions can do.

DATA: I do not perceive your skills to be in doubt, Q. The Captain is more concerned with your ability to interact successfully with his little trained minions.

[Dialogue Omitted]

DATA: Human interpersonal relationships are more complex. Your experiences may not have adequately prepared you.

Q: I'm not interested in human interpersonal relationships. I just want to prove to Picard that I'm indispensable.

Data provides excellent counsel to Q. Q has a history of obnoxious behaviors towards the crew, but his disability now requires him to foster interpersonal relationships, and not further *alienate* those around him. (I couldn't resist.)

Q: It is a joke. A joke on me. The joke of the universe. The king who would be man. As I learn more and more what it is to be human, I am more and more convinced that I would never make a good one. I don't have what it takes. Without my powers, I'm frightened of everything. I'm a coward, and I'm miserable, and I can't go on this way.

For better or worse, depending on your perspective, Q has his Q-powers returned when he performs an act of selflessness to save the Enterprise. Compensation as a coping skill is generally limited to adults because they have the knowledge and life experiences necessary to compensate for their disability. (Well, while the overall maturity of Q may be in question—he's tall enough to be considered an adult.)

Compensation is usually less common as a coping skill for younger people because they have more limited life experience. Although, I could argue that Wesley Crusher keeps saving the Enterprise to compensate for his disability: being a know-it-all teenager.

"Full Impulse Engines" (Rationalization)

As a coping strategy, rationalization occurs when people find socially acceptable reasons to justify their behavior or try to excuse themselves for not reaching goals or not accomplishing tasks. While exploring a black hole, the entire crew of the NX-01 Enterprise begins to exhibit symptoms similar to *obsessive-compulsive disorder* (OCD) because of their exposure to radiation. Only T'Pol is unaffected ("Singularity", 2002, ENT; 2:9).

> T'POL: ...It wasn't long before I realized the odd behavior wasn't limited to Commander Tucker. In fact, everyone I encountered was acting strangely, growing consumed with matters that seemed trivial at best. I also discovered that although I appeared to be immune, the captain was not.

Everyone has a rationalization for their obsessive behavior, and their OCD symptoms can be considered disabilities, since the entire ship is about to be destroyed. But to a person with obsessive compulsive disorder, their preoccupations make sense. For example, Tucker becomes preoccupied with fixing the captain's chair on the bridge. T'Pol confronts him about his odd behavior he explains that it's completely rational.

> TUCKER: I know you don't think this chair is important, but you're wrong. What's the most critical component on this ship? The main computer? The warp reactor? Uh-uh, it's the crew. And the most important member of the crew is the captain. He makes life and death decisions every day and the last thing he needs to be thinking in a critical situation is, 'Gee, I wish this chair wasn't such a pain in the ass.'

Ironically, the only way to save the crew from their OCD is to go through the trinary star system emitting the radiation. In order to get past rationalization, the individual with the disability must recognize that this coping strategy is a form of avoidance. Even if the person can justify his or her actions, it's not the same thing as accepting new limitations or the loss of previous abilities.

In order to get the Enterprise out of danger, T'Pol plots the trajectory and announces course corrections as Captain Archer pilots the ship. Sometimes getting beyond rationalization is best accomplished with the help of someone you can trust. I just wonder if Porthos was immune from the effects of the radiation like T'Pol. Or was the cute beagle sitting around Archer's quarters obsessing about cheese?

"Engage the Tractor Beam" (Diversion of Feelings)

One of the most constructive of all coping strategies is the diversion of unacceptable feelings or ideas into socially acceptable behaviors. In "Realm of Fear" (1992, TNG; 6:2), Lieutenant Barclay's hidden transporter phobia is revealed.

> BARCLAY: Actually, this isn't the first time I've been apprehensive. Every single time that I tried to do it, I had a certain feeling. I guess you could call it mortal terror.
>
> TROI: Why have you kept it a secret?
>
> BARCLAY: Why? Because my career in Starfleet would be over—that's why.
>
> TROI: I doubt that—
>
> BARCLAY: I've always managed to avoid it somehow. You wouldn't believe how many hours that I've logged in shuttlecraft. I mean, the idea of being deconstructed, molecule-by-molecule. It's more than I can stand. Even when I was a child, I always had a dreadful fear that if ever I was dematerialized that I would never come back again whole. I know it sounds crazy, but—

In an attempt to overcome his phobia, Barclay decides to transport over to the science vessel. On the Yosemite, he joins the away team who are trying to solve the mysterious disappearance of the crew. Although Barclay is still fearful of transporters, he replaces his sense of doom with determination not to be limited by his disability.

When Barclay transports back to the Enterprise, he sees a strange creature in the energy stream. The creature moves toward him and bites his arm. Barclay does what many people with hypochondria and transporter phobia would do (well, other people with hypochondria anyway), he engages in a little extracurricular research. Adding to his already anxious state, Barclay becomes convinced that he has developed "transporter psychosis."

Rather than giving in and allowing his anxiety to impair his functioning on the Enterprise, Barclay uses *diversion* and puts his energy into investigating anomalies in the transporter logs, and consulting with Chief O'Brien. The mystery is solved, and four of the science vessel's crewmen are rescued.

Barclay's fear of transporters could have been a career-ending disability because transporting around the galaxy is the socially acceptable way to travel in Starfleet. Barclay even bonds a little with Chief O'Brien when O'Brien tells Barclay about how he previously overcame his own spider phobia. Which leads to the question: Will Barclay develop arachnophobia after being introduced to O'Brien's pet tarantula, Christina?

The more limitations a disability imposes on a person, the more they may feel they're under attack. Acquiring a disability is much like experiencing the loss of a loved one. The emotional reactions of grief, anger, depression, fear and anxiety are similar. The emotional reactions and the coping skills a person with a disability employs are as individual as a Starfleet security code. At times, the first step in adjusting to a disability is determined by where one wants to go. Without a destination, it's impossible to chart a course. As the Enterprise seeks out new life and new civilizations, the helm is given a direction or destination, a speed at which they will travel, and then Captain Picard gives the order to "make it so." If only adapting to a disability were as easy.

"I Like My Species The Way It Is" (Assistive Technology)

Technology becomes *assistive technology* when it's used to compensate for an impairment due to a disability. On *Star Trek: The Next Generation* the most frequently seen assistive technology is the VISOR worn by La Forge. However, Data often changes the speed of the computer displays to fit his android rate of absorbing information, so it's not difficult to imagine a person with a reading disability slowing down the same computer, or using a voice output. There are several pieces of technology that might be useful to someone with a disability. Changing the computer display as well as the voice interface with the computer are only two examples of accommodations that would be helpful to people with different types of disabilities.

Part of the process of adjustment to a disability may require the person to learn how to use assistive technology, which may add to feelings of being different or not whole. In an environment like the Enterprise, where everyone is playing with high-tech toys, the stigma is significantly reduced. At the same time, Klingons seem to enjoy fighting with Bat'leth as much as with disruptors, maybe even more. Worf's resistance to the motion-assist bands after his injury in "Ethics" (1992, TNG; 5:16) is a good example of how assistive technology must be culturally sensitive and not increase stigma.

In the brilliantly written "The Measure of a Man" (1989, TNG; 2:9), a hearing is convened regarding whether Data is a Starfleet officer or toaster. Because Data is an android, he has been told he is not allowed to resign from Starfleet in order to avoid an experiment which could very well cost him his life.

> DATA: Sir, Lieutenant La Forge's eyes are far superior to human biological eyes. True? Then why are not all human officers required to have their eyes replaced with cybernetic implants? [Picard looks away.] I see. It is precisely because I am not human.

I can't imagine a future when assistive technology would be desired over our organic body, but that isn't to say it's impossible. While I have no desire to join the Borg collective, please don't take away my reading glasses.

Chapter 10
"Infinite Diversity in Infinite Combinations"

PICARD: The Tamarian was willing to risk all of us just for the hope of communication, connection. Now the door is open between our peoples. That commitment
meant more to him than his own life—
"Darmok" (1991, TNG; 5:2).

Communication Disorders, Autism, and Asperger's Syndrome

While seeking out new life and new civilizations, communicating with new life is central
to the life of Starfleet members. Communication is central to all relationships. On *Star
Trek*, communication can involve anything from subspace to telepathic. Humans must
resort to non-telepathic forms of communication such as words, music, Morse code, sign
language, facial expression, and others. Humans experience occasional communication
failures, such as *disfluency*. When the communication failure is more pervasive, we say the
person has a *communication disorder*. People with autism spectrum disorders experience
some of the most severe disabilities when it comes to communication failures. But not
every communication disorder is a result of autism or Asperger's, as I will describe later in
this chapter. While autism is associated with inherent communication differences,
communication disorders can exist independently of autism spectrum disorders.

"Communications Channels Are Down" (Communication Disorders)

The first diagnosed communication disorder shown was on "Babel" (1993, DS9; 1:4) when a virus brings on a form of *aphasia*, first affecting a perpetually overworked Chief O'Brien.

> KIRA: Chief?
> O'BRIEN: How can I help you, Major?
> KIRA: You're the one who could use a little help.
> O'BRIEN: Oh, no, I'm fine, really.
> KIRA: I suppose this isn't a good time to tell you that number three turbolift has broken down again. Joking, Chief.
> O'BRIEN: Major, larks true pepper.
> KIRA: What?
> O'BRIEN: Let birds go further loose maybe. Shout easy play.
> KIRA: Chief, you're not making any sense.
> O'BRIEN: Round the turbulent quick. Well, close the reverse harbor. Ankle try sound. Reset gleaming. Dinner to bug.
> KIRA: Chief, wait.
> O'BRIEN: When?
> KIRA: Chief!

Dr. Bashir explains aphasia to Kira after examining the chief.

> KIRA: What's wrong with him?
> BASHIR: He appears to be suffering from a form of aphasia. It's a perceptual dysfunction in which aural and visual stimuli are incorrectly processed by the brain. His actual thinking hasn't been affected, but he's incapable of expressing himself or understanding others.
> O'BRIEN: Victory strike limits frosted wake. Simple hesitation!

According to the ICD–10, O'Brien would be diagnosed with *global aphasia* where the person can't speak, understand speech, read, or write. The other three types of aphasia are *expressive aphasia*—the person knows what's being said to them, but they are unable to make themselves understood in return. In *receptive aphasia* the person can hear the voice or see the print, but is unable to make sense of the words. An example of receptive aphasia actually appears on "And The Children Shall Lead" (1968, TOS; 3:4) when Kirk gives an order to one of the guards on the bridge, but the guard only hears gibberish. And finally, in *anomic aphasia* the person has trouble using the correct word for objects, places, or events. Generally aphasia is caused by a stroke or other brain injury rather than produced by a Cardassian virus hiding in a food replicator.

The nonsensical conglomeration of words is also similar to *schizophasia* which is also known as *word salad*. In "Statistical Probabilities" (1998, DS9; 6:9), as the four patients listen to Damar's speech, Jack displays word salad patterns. His expressions are only intelligible because of the contributions of Lauren and Patrick who know him well.

JACK: Methought I heard a voice cry, Sleep no more! Damar does murder sleep!
PATRICK: He's killed someone.
LAUREN: Someone close to him.
O'BRIEN: How could they know that?

Jack's strange manner of expressing himself would be attributed to his psychiatric disability if this was anywhere but Deep Space Nine.

Communications disorders are rare on *Star Trek*, but disfluency errors plague everyone from starship captains to Ferengi. In "Hollow Pursuits" (1990, TNG; 3:21) Captain Picard suffers a "slip of the tongue" calling Mr. Barclay "Mr. Broccoli" which Data accurately explains is a common pronunciation error.

DATA: Metathesis is one of the most common of pronunciation errors, sir. A reversal of vowel and consonant, Barc to Broc.

Most disfluency errors take the form of stuttering, as Mr. Broccoli, I mean, Mr. Barclay does on several occasions. Here is an example from "Hollow Pursuits."

BARCLAY: Yes. It—it wasn't a maintenance problem. [Duffy looks disapprovingly around the room] Every—everything checked out. I'm—I'm going to check for a surge in the transfer coils—

WESLEY: —Oh, a coil surge wouldn't have resulted in field dissipation.

BARCLAY: I—I—I realize that—

LA FORGE: But we shouldn't ignore the possibilities, Wes.

WESLEY: You ought to check the flow capacitor. A breakdown of that could have caused a chain collapse of the antigrav fields [Wesley brings up something on a display console].

BARCLAY: I—I was going to— [Barclay turns off the display]

LA FORGE: Good. Okay. Then let's take a look at that realignment procedure. Gentlemen.

This dialogue demonstrates stuttering, which is one of many speech errors considered disfluency. With stuttering, the flow of speech is broken by repetitions. Barclay also demonstrates some of the usual facial and body movements when he starts to speak, opens his mouth, but doesn't say anything. According to Professor Higley, that scene was nearly cut:

> They almost ditched Captain Picard's slip of the tongue on the grounds that the Captain would never be so lacking in control. That was a silly notion that unfairly curbed interesting character development and I'm glad they rethought it. When Picard calls Barclay "Mr. Broccoli" after all that moralizing it was one of the funniest moments on *Star Trek*.

Stressful situations, such as running late into an engineering briefing, can contribute to the degree of stuttering. Barclay stutters more than most, but Rom, Neelix, and The Doctor also occasionally have trouble getting their words out when under pressure.

Seven teaches "The Void" (2001, VOY; 7:14) alien, named Fantome by The Doctor, to communicate without speech when she learns he enjoys music.

[Opera music is playing in sickbay.]

SEVEN: How is he?

THE DOCTOR: Much better. He seemed to relax when he heard me humming an aria from Rigoletto, so I had the computer play the full orchestral version. Fantome seems to be a music lover.

SEVEN: Fantome?

THE DOCTOR: After the Phantom of the Opera, a tormented character who is soothed by music.

[Dialogue Omitted]

THE DOCTOR: I wish we could find a way to communicate with him. I suspect he'd have a lot to tell us. [Seven stops the music that's playing.] We were enjoying that.

SEVEN: Exactly. He may not be able to speak, but he can hear. [Seven holds up items while creating high and low tones, then puts them down and plays the tones. Fantome picks up the item relating to the tone.]

THE DOCTOR: He understands.

SEVEN: So it would seem.

The communication skills of the alien grow at light speed. Pretty soon The Doctor starts acting as the translator for his musical tones. I would have thought the Universal Translator could have taken over.

TUVOK: How's your patient?

THE DOCTOR: Technically, he's not a patient anymore, but it's taken me this long to coax him out of sickbay. He's quite shy. [The Doctor plays notes on a PADD) I'm telling him not to worry, that you're the one who keeps us all safe. [Fantome plays notes on a PADD.] He says thank you.

TUVOK: An ingenious method of communication.

THE DOCTOR: It began with a few simple words, but now we're capable of rudimentary conversation.

Soon Fantome is joined with his fellow Void aliens and they all communicate using PADDs to create musical tones. Janeway witnesses what she thinks is a concert.

JANEWAY: Lovely piece. Did they compose it or did you?

THE DOCTOR: They did, though strictly speaking, it's not a composition. It's more of a conversation.

JANEWAY: I'm impressed.

THE DOCTOR: I wish I could take credit but it was Fantome who taught the others in a fraction of the time it took him to learn. They're a highly intelligent species.

SEVEN: The language is already developing its own grammar and syntax.

JANEWAY: That suggests they have a language of their own.

THE DOCTOR: It could be telepathic, but they seem just as comfortable communicating with music now.

Although I could argue that Seven and The Doctor violated the Prime Directive by providing Fantome with the PADD to communicate which may influence the natural evolution of his species, I won't. First, Seven isn't a member of Starfleet. The Doctor is either a member of Starfleet or a program Starfleet owns. More important, however, is that a patient needs to be able to communicate with the physician. This fact was recognized in 1981 when Medicare began funding the first speech generating devices. Communication is a necessity for everyone; facilitating communication is a necessity for people with a disability. Alternative devices such as the PADD or Stephen Hawking's communication board are but two examples. Captain Pike in the original series has a low-budget communication device that only generates a monotone signal and restricts him to *yes* or *no* answers. I'm glad Starfleet's budget has improved.

As I'll illustrate in the next section, autism spectrum disorders are characterized by global deficits in communication which encompasses even more dramatic impairments than disfluency problems or using technology to speak.

Autism

Humans can feel like aliens even here on Earth. People with autism spectrum disorders keenly feel a sense of being different in a world full of, what people with autism call, *neurotypicals*. *Star Trek* provides many fans with autism spectrum disorders a sense of being understood, role models, and a reduction in isolation by including aliens and an android who are also different from everyone else around them. The diversity of Humans living alongside aliens allows for an entertaining commentary on social interactions. Awkward, funny, even dangerous at times, misunderstandings are as common as temporal anomalies on *Star Trek*. My discussion of autism is limited to the milder forms of the disorder, largely because there are no examples on *Star Trek* of the more severe forms.

According to the ICD–10 autism occurs before the child reaches three years of age. Autism is characterized by abnormal functioning in all three areas of social behavior: reciprocal interaction, communication, and behaviors that are repetitive and restricted. So far we haven't had a *Star Trek* character who's openly defined as having autism in the same way that Geordi La Forge is blind without his VISOR. However, we see several characters with autistic behaviors which allows me to illustrate autism traits.

Socio-Emotional Cues

People with autism don't seem to respond to other people's emotions and appear to lack empathy. They often lack the ability or understanding required to adapt their own behavior according to the social context. They have difficulty paying attention to social signals which is most often seen by a lack of socio-emotional reciprocity. This communication deficit is most evident in the general lack of "figures of speech" in their conversation and their tendency to take words literally. An example of the kind of misunderstandings that can occur can be seen in the conversation between Jenna and Data during the episode "In Theory" (1991, TNG; 4:25), where Data explores having a romantic relationship with a shipmate, Jenna D'Sora. D'Sora brings Data a gift before their dinner date.

DATA: Enter.

[Jenna is carrying a sculpture]

D'SORA: I know it's a little unexpected.

DATA: You are correct. I did not anticipate your arrival until nineteen hundred hours.

D'SORA: I couldn't wait. I wanted you to have this.

DATA: You have often expressed dissatisfaction with the Spartan nature of my quarters. Is this an attempt at embellishment?

D'SORA: The cat's out of the bag.

DATA: Spot? [Data looks around for his cat, Spot.]

D'SORA: No, I mean you've caught me in the act. I'm just trying to brighten things up around here. It's Tyrinean. What do you think?

DATA: Its line is both fluid and formal, yet retains an unpremeditated quality. The tactility of its surface embellishment is evocative of the neo-primitive period in Tyrinean blade carving.

D'SORA: I hadn't thought of it that way. I'm sorry. Don't let me interrupt.

DATA: As you wish. [Data returns to his painting.]

D'SORA: Data?

DATA: Yes?

D'SORA: The Book of Love, chapter four, paragraph seventeen: When your girlfriend arrives with a gift, stop whatever it is you're doing, and give her your undivided attention.

DATA: I should not have resumed my painting?

D'SORA: No.

DATA: Despite your suggestion that I continue?

D'SORA: Exactly.

DATA: I have much to learn.

As this example illustrates, Data frequently misunderstands figures of speech because he tends to take words literally. He has a difficult time understanding the nuances of conversation in addition to the subtleties of social cues.

Communication

Communication for a child with autism is usually devoid of a social usage of language which can be seen in the lack of make-believe and social imitative play. There's no flexibility in their language expression so they won't vary their vocabulary to reflect nuances of meaning from similar words. They may sound deadpan due to the lack of variation in the cadence of their speech, lack of emphasis on key words, or missing gestures and expression that provide context and aid meaning in their spoken communications.

To some people, a child with autism may sound like a computer or an android. In "The Offspring" (1990, TNG; 3:16), Data creates another android, Lal. Getting settled into Data's quarters, their conversation provides a good example of this stilted type of conversation:

[Data leads Lal into his quarters.]

DATA: This is home, Lal.

LAL: Home. Place of residence. Social unit formed by a family living together.

DATA: Yes. We are a family, Lal. [Data looks around the room and points to a chair.] Chair. To sit in. [Data demonstrates siting in the chair, and then gets up to allow Lal to sit in the chair.] Sit. [Lal approaches the chair and sits down.] Good. [Data points to a painting on the wall behind the chair where Lal is sitting.] Painting.

LAL: Painting. Colors produced on a surface by applying a pigment.

Although Lal can define the items and words, this isn't a normal conversation. Because of her unconventional (and autistic-like) behavior, Lal has difficulty finding an accepting peer group—as many children with autism often experience. The teacher, Ms. Ballard, explains to Data the limitations of having Lal at school with the children.

BALLARD: She achieved a very high score on a test of academic achievement.

DATA: A perfect score?

BALLARD: Yes, which is why we started her out with the older children. But Lal couldn't understand the nuances of how they related to each other.

DATA: I see.

BALLARD: We decided the best thing to do would be to put her with younger children.

DATA: That would seem to be reasonable.

BALLARD: It isn't working out that way.

[She shows him the classroom. Lal is standing by the wall while the children are around a table together.]

BALLARD: The children were afraid of her.

Lal does better when working for Guinan in Ten-Forward and observing the crew's interactions.

[A couple by the far wall are gazing into each other's eyes and holding hands.]

GUINAN: You see?

LAL: What are they doing?

GUINAN: It's called flirting.

LAL: They seem to be communicating telepathically.

GUINAN: They're both thinking the same thing, if that's what you mean.

LAL: Guinan, is the joining of hands a symbolic act for humans?

GUINAN: It shows affection. Humans like to touch each other. They start with the hands, and go from there.

LAL: He's biting that female—

GUINAN: No, he's not biting. They're pressing lips. It's called kissing.

LAL: Why are they leaving?

GUINAN: Lal, there are some things your father's just going to have to explain to you when he thinks you're ready.

As Guinan points out, the context of a behavior is crucial to the understanding. People with autism spectrum disorders often have a difficult time taking the context into account.

Repetitive Behaviors

Autism is also associated with a narrow range of interests and a need for routine and structure in their daily lives, which can appear rigid to others. Participation in leisure activities is often done on a scheduled basis. Someone with autism may have a preoccupation with certain interests such as dates, routes, or timetables. Disrupting their routine is often met with resistance or outright anger. Their lack of spontaneity and creativity often results in difficulty with unorganized leisure time.

Although not autistic, Scotty often appears to have both a narrow range of interest as well as difficulty with leisure time. Both are portrayed in "The Trouble With Tribbles" (1968, TOS; 2:15). Kirk observes Scotty looking at a monitor in the recreation room on the Enterprise.

KIRK: Another technical journal, Scotty?

SCOTT: Aye.

KIRK: Don't you ever relax?

SCOTT: I am relaxing.

Later, after a bar fight breaks out on Space Station K-7, Scotty admits to throwing the first punch. Scotty had been sent to the space station in order to keep the other Starfleet officers out of trouble with those Klingon thugs. Captain Kirk has no choice but to include him in the disciplinary proceedings.

KIRK: All right, Scotty. Dismissed. [Scotty looks a little sheepish.] Scotty, you're restricted to quarters until further notice.
SCOTT: Yes, sir. [A large grin spreads across his face.] Thank you, sir. That'll give me a chance to catch up on my technical journals.

I could even argue that the repeated greeting by The Borg, "Resistance is futile. You will be assimilated" is an example of a repetitive behavior often seen in autism.

Asperger's Syndrome

The similarities between Asperger's syndrome and autism are analogous to the shared heritage between Vulcans and Romulans. Asperger's syndrome is considered part of autism spectrum disorders, with at least three primary differences between autism and Asperger's syndrome. First, people with autism, including high functioning autism, also have general communication delays, not achieving milestones for spoken communication at the same time as their peers. Second, people with Asperger's syndrome generally score above average on intelligence tests, while this isn't true of those with autism with the exception of high-functioning autism. Finally, people with Asperger's syndrome generally have larger vocabularies than those with autism or even their same-aged neurologically-typical peers. This is true even though people with Asperger's syndrome often (but not always) lack an understanding of non-verbal cues and humor. These communication impairments can adversely affect the person's social skills as well.

Some of the characters identified as having Asperger's-like characteristics are: Mr. Spock, Data, Barclay, Tuvok, Seven of Nine, and T'Pol. Spock, Tuvok and T'Pol share a Vulcan heritage providing the stoic aliens with some commonalities in their behaviors. Vulcans are far from Klingon party animals. However, Spock doesn't fit the criteria for Asperger's syndrome and neither do Tuvok or T'Pol for the same reasons: communication is neither delayed nor impaired; recreational activities are not limited, and disruption in routine is normally tolerated. Apparently it is mere coincidence that some of Barclay's behavior appear to be similar to Asperger's syndrome. Higley, who invented Mr. Barclay, stated that she was not even aware of the term *Asperger's syndrome* when she wrote "Hollow Pursuits."

Spock understands others without difficulty. In "The Enemy Within" (1966, TOS; 1:6), Spock provides insights on the effects of splitting Kirk into two selves (savage Kirk and gentle Kirk) during the transporter accident. Not only does Spock clearly empathize with the captain's experience, he helps Dr. McCoy understand why Spock acts the way he does.

> SPOCK: Being split in two halves is no theory with me, Doctor. I have a human half, you see, as well as an alien half, submerged, constantly at war with each other. Personal experience, Doctor. I survive it because my intelligence wins over both, makes them live together. Your intelligence would enable you to survive as well.

Spock is half Human and half Vulcan, and both halves have emotions. One of the myths about people with Asperger's is that they lack emotions or sympathy. While Captain Kirk frequently makes command decisions based on his intuition, Spock's decisions are predominantly based on logic rather than feelings. Logic is more accessible and easier to master for both Vulcans and people with Asperger's syndrome.

Not only does Mr. Spock have little difficulty understanding others, most of the Enterprise crew understands him with little difficulty as well (with the exception of Dr. McCoy's weekly anti-Vulcan cracks).

Spock has no trouble with humor, sarcasm, or non-verbal cues. In the "The Galileo Seven" (1967, TOS; 1:17) Mr. Spock is in charge of an away mission when the shuttle crashes on a planet and the away team's attempt at a rendezvous with the Enterprise has little chance of success due to the damage the craft has sustained. At the last minute, the crew is saved as the Enterprise beams them to safety, the shuttlecraft breaking up around them. On the bridge there's speculation regarding the basis for Spock's actions.

> KIRK: There's really something I don't understand about all of this. Maybe you can explain it to me. Logically, of course. When you jettisoned the fuel and

ignited it, you knew there was virtually no chance of it being seen, yet you did it anyhow. That would seem to me to be an act of desperation.

SPOCK: Quite correct, Captain.

KIRK: Now we all know, and I'm sure the doctor will agree with me, that desperation is a highly emotional state of mind. How does your well-known logic explain that?

SPOCK: Quite simply, Captain. I examined the problem from all angles, and it was plainly hopeless. Logic informed me that under the circumstances, the only possible action would have to be one of desperation. Logical decision. Logically arrived at.

KIRK: I see. You mean you reasoned that it was time for an emotional outburst.

SPOCK: Well, I wouldn't put it in exactly those terms, Captain, but those are essentially the facts.

KIRK: You're not going to admit that for the first time in your life, you committed a purely human emotional act?

SPOCK: No, sir.

KIRK: Mr. Spock, you're a stubborn man.

SPOCK: Yes, sir.

Spock's agreement with the captain demonstrates a sense of humor. This is one example of many funny and sarcastic retorts by Mr. Spock. Many people with Asperger's syndrome may have trouble appreciating some humor because they have a tendency to understand words literally. At the same time, that doesn't mean they can't comprehend jokes. They may, however, have a different opinion as to how funny something is which may cause them to laugh harder, or not as much, as their peers.

Vulcans have more leisure interests than most people with Asperger's syndrome. Mr. Spock plays a Vulcan musical instrument, three-dimensional chess, and meditates. At the same time, Spock doesn't appear to enjoy unstructured leisure time as he explains in the episode "Shore Leave" (1966, TOS; 1:16):

KIRK: Mr. Spock, we're beaming down the starboard section first. Which section would you like to go with?

SPOCK: Not necessary in my case, Captain. On my planet, to rest is to rest, to cease using energy. To me, it is quite illogical to run up and down on green grass using energy instead of saving it.

A different perspective on how Spock's emotions are misunderstood is portrayed in "Star Trek Into Darkness" (2013). As the shuttle is approaching Kronos in a dangerous undercover mission, Uhura takes the opportunity to confront Spock about risking his life in the volcano. Uhura feels Spock wasn't concerned about the effects his death would have on her.

UHURA: ...You didn't feel anything. You didn't care. [Pause] And I'm not the only one who's upset with you. The captain is too.
KIRK: No, no, no—don't drag me into to this. [To Spock] She is right.
SPOCK: Your suggestion that I do not care about dying is incorrect. A sentient being's optimal chance at maximizing their utility is a long and prosperous life. [Uhura and I are both rolling our eyes.]
UHURA: Great.
KIRK: Not exactly a love song, Spock.
SPOCK: You misunderstand. It is true I chose not to feel anything upon realizing my own life was ending. As Admiral Pike was dying I joined with his consciousness and experienced what he felt at the moment of his passing. Anger. Confusion. Loneliness. Fear. I had experienced those feelings before; multiplied exponentially on the day my planet was destroyed. Such a feeling is something I choose never to experience again. Nyota, you mistake my choice not to feel as a reflection of my not caring. Well, I assure you the truth is precisely the opposite.

While the make up fight is cut short by a rude Klingon ship firing on the shuttle, the dialogue illustrates how even when discussing emotions, Vulcans sound detached. Likewise, people with Asperger's syndrome can have similar disconnects between the subject matter and their expression of their feelings.

Vulcans' logical approach to life doesn't mean Vulcans are the equivalent of an Asperger's syndrome species. Spock, Tuvok, and T'Pol don't have Asperger's syndrome, even though they're less emotional than their Human crewmates. Unlike people with autism spectrum disorders, Vulcans consciously choose to be less emotional.

According to an interview Leonard Nimoy gave to *The Jewish Chronicle* (2013), "His [Spock's] dilemma is a human dilemma. Particularly for young people. Teenagers really understand what Spock is dealing with, which is finding the proper balance between logic and emotion."

A person with Asperger's syndrome might not detect sadness based solely on someone's body language, or sarcasm from the other person's tone of voice. But, when emotions are communicated more directly, people with Asperger's syndrome are much more likely than their peers to feel sympathy for others even if they struggle to express it.

Just because someone is Vulcan or has Asperger's syndrome doesn't mean they don't have the same desire for friendships. Vulcans prefer logic over emotionality, but they also make good friends. Spock is friends with Captain Kirk and Dr. McCoy. Tuvok is friends with Captain Janeway and—eventually—Neelix. T'Pol has a relationship with Commander Tucker and develops affection for Captain Archer in an alternate timeline. People with Asperger's syndrome have more struggles in expressing their feelings than their peers, but they're capable of making good friends when those around them understand this difficulty. Data provides a good example.

At the "25th Anniversary Star Trek: The Next Generation Reunion" in Calgary, Canada (2012), Brent Spiner commented that, over the years, he has often been told by fans with Asperger's syndrome that they related to him because Data's struggles to fit in were similar to their own. In discussing Data, I'll limit the analysis to Data prior to his "emotion-chip" experiences.

In "Data's Day" (1991, TNG; 4:11) Data tells Commander Maddox that understanding his crewmates provides several challenges:

> DATA: I found it difficult to maintain friendships, since human emotions are often puzzling to me. Eventually, I developed a program enabling me to predict human emotional responses to specific actions.

When Data's head is discovered in a cave under San Francisco, the crew has trouble dealing with what they perceive to be Data's future death in "Time's Arrow, Part I" (1992, TNG; 5:26):

TROI: Have you ever heard Data define friendship?

RIKER: No.

TROI: How did he put it? [Troi mimics Data's android voice.] "As I experience certain sensory input patterns, my mental pathways become accustomed to them. The inputs eventually are anticipated and even missed when absent."

RIKER: So what's the point?

TROI: He's used to us, and we're used to him. It's like finding out someone you love has a terminal illness and— [The turbolift arrives, the doors open and Data walks in.]

RIKER: Data.

DATA: [Data nods at Troi.] Counselor. [Data nods at Riker.] Commander. [Riker and Troi look uncomfortable and do not continue their conversation.]

DATA: Would either of you mind if I made a personal inquiry?

TROI: Personal inquiry? No, go right ahead.

DATA: I am perceiving an apparent change in the way others behave toward me. For example, people abruptly end conversations when I appear, just as you did when the turbolift doors opened. Is that an accurate observation?

RIKER: Not at all—

TROI: [At the same time] —Yes.

RIKER: Yes.

TROI: You're right, Data. And it's not a very nice thing to do.

RIKER: It's just that our mental pathways have become accustomed to your sensory input patterns.

DATA: I understand. I am also fond of you, Commander. And you as well, Counselor.

Even though Data, by his own admission, struggles with interpersonal relationships, it's clear in this scene that Data understands and is understood by his friends.

At the same time, Data often fails to recognize non-verbal cues, such as the facial expressions of others that indicate he should stop talking. In the series premiere, "Encounter at Farpoint" (1987, TNG; 1:1), the crew attempts, and fails, to help Data know when to stop explaining. Like people with Asperger's syndrome, Data is slow to pick up their non-verbal communication through facial expressions.

DATA: Inquiry. The word snoop?

PICARD: Data, how can you be programmed as a virtual encyclopedia of human information without knowing a simple word like snoop?

DATA: Possibility, a kind of human behavior I was not designed to emulate.

PICARD: It means to spy, to sneak.

DATA: Ah! To seek covertly, to go stealthily, to slink, slither

PICARD: Exactly, yes. [Picard glares at Data, but Data goes on.]

DATA: Glide, creep, skulk, pussyfoot, gumshoe. [By now both La Forge and Riker are shooting Data "shut up" looks.]

Data learns to take the tone of voice of his shipmates into account when trying to understand them, as in "Data's Day" (1991 TNG; 4:1).

DATA: The tone of Commander Riker's voice makes me suspect that he is not serious about finding Ambassador T'Pel charming. My experience suggests that in fact he may mean the exact opposite of what he says. Irony is a form of expression I have not yet been able to master.

Irony is a difficult form of expression to understand. Data's admission that he has yet to master irony doesn't negate his ability to perceive it. Irony, metaphors and similes are difficult for people with Asperger's to comprehend or produce.

Unlike people with Asperger's, however, Data has multiple interests and a broad range of hobbies. Data paints in "1101001" (1988, TNG; 1:14), plays Sherlock Holmes on the holodeck in "Elementary, Dear Data" (1988, TNG; 2:3), plays a violin in "Sarek" (1990, TNG; 3:23), recites his "Ode to Spot" poem in "Schisms" (1992, TNG; 6:5), and frequently plays poker with his fellow bridge officers ("The Measure of a Man" 1989, TNG; 2:9, among others).

While it's clear that Data wouldn't be diagnosed with Asperger's syndrome, at times his behavior is similar to the behaviors of people with Asperger's syndrome. Fans with Asperger's syndrome identify with Data because of the deliberate effort needed to fit in with their peers. Data must create a new subroutine or ask for guidance when people don't behave as he expects them to. Many people with Asperger's syndrome likewise need coaching in social interactions because they aren't able to absorb the information from simply experiencing the interactions.

One of the first similarities that people with Asperger's syndrome have with Data is their desire to have friendships and even romantic attachments—despite the difficulties they present.

> DATA: There are still many human emotions I do not fully comprehend— anger—hatred—revenge. But I am not mystified by the desire to be loved or the need for friendship. These are things I do understand.
> "Data's Day" (1991 TNG; 4:1)

Many *Star Trek* fans with Asperger's syndrome have similar desires as other fans. They want to have friends, fall in love, and above all–be understood by others. Since people with Asperger's syndrome have impairments in accurately reading the emotional reactions of others, as well as being able to anticipate them, they're often mistaken for being emotionless. However, people with Asperger's syndrome, unlike pre-emotion-chip Data, do have emotions.

Even before Data implanted the emotion chip into his positronic brain, he wouldn't have qualified for a diagnosis of Asperger's syndrome. Yet Data's struggles to be like everyone else on board the Enterprise resonate with *Star Trek* fans who have autism spectrum disorders.

There is one *Star Trek* character who displays more traits that are similar to people with autism spectrum disorders than any of the others: Seven of Nine, Tertiary Adjunct of Unimatrix Zero-One.

Seven of Nine

Born Human, Annika Hansen was assimilated by the Borg when she was only six years old. When she joined the crew on Voyager, Seven's struggles to embrace her humanity were more about social interactions than the remaining Borg implants in her head and hands.

Seven struggled with simple behaviors such as talking with her crewmates; allowing for the inefficiency of those around her, as well as walking around in a skin-tight metallic leotard. Actually, she did that last one the best.

Initially, Seven's difficulty in fitting in with the rest of the Voyager crew is mutual because the crew isn't sure they want her on board. Seven did, after all, try to betray them to the Borg. Much like children with autism, Seven's efforts to fit in with the crew aren't consistent; at times she appears not to value the outcome.

Seven states she has no difficulty with humor and understands the reservations others may have about her presence on the ship in "Revulsion" (1997, VOY; 4:5).

KIM: Seven?

SEVEN: I am here. Am I to work with you?

KIM: Oh, hi! Yes, I thought we'd start in Jefferies tube thirty two b, enhance the astrometric sensors, if that's okay with you. Unless this is a bad time. Maybe I can come back later.

SEVEN: Ensign Kim, you seem apprehensive.

KIM: No, not at all.

SEVEN: The last time we worked together I struck you at the base of your skull and attempted to contact the Collective.

KIM: These things happen.

SEVEN: I assure you, it will not happen again.

KIM: That's good to know.

SEVEN: I've designed new navigational sensors. Some of the alphanumerics are Borg.

KIM: No problem. I always wanted to learn Borg.

SEVEN: That is difficult to believe.

KIM: I was kidding. It was a joke. You know, humor.

SEVEN: I understand the concept of humor. It may not be apparent, but I am often amused by human behavior.

Seven's deadpan manner of expressing herself is characteristic of someone with an autism spectrum disorder. So is Seven's inability to relax and enjoy free time. Reminiscent of Scotty reading technical journals in his free time, Seven describes studying the Starfleet database in her off-duty time.

KIM: So, what do you do for fun down in cargo bay two?

SEVEN: Fun.

KIM: You know. Relaxation, entertainment, during your off hours.

SEVEN: I regenerate in my alcove. I study the Starfleet database, and I contemplate my existence.

KIM: That's a lot of time by yourself.

Seven's attempts to practice her conversation skills in a holodeck simulation with Lieutenant Torres and Ensign Kim in "One" (1998, VOY; 4:25) is an excellent portrayal of her difficulty with understanding the give-and-take of Human conversation, and her less than complete belief in the necessity of the effort involved.

SEVEN: Ensign Kim, what is your place of origin?

KIM: You mean, where am I from? Well, I was born in South Carolina, but I grew up in— [Seven interrupts, talking over Ensign Kim as she directs a question at Lieutenant Torres.]

SEVEN: Lieutenant Torres, explain why you became a member of the Maquis.

TORRES: It was through Chakotay. I met him. Well, actually, he saved my life— [Seven interrupts again, and turns towards Ensign Kim.]

SEVEN: List the sports you play.

KIM: I've dabbled in quite a few. Tennis, Pareses Squares, but my favorite is volleyball, it's— [Seven interrupts, and turns towards Torres again.]

SEVEN: Specify the foods you find enjoyable.

TORRES: Seven, what is this?

SEVEN: Describe the nature of your sexual relationship with Lieutenant Paris.

TORRES: Okay, that's it— [Torres throws her napkin on her plate, and looks at Seven, her expression angry.]

THE DOCTOR: Computer, freeze program. Would you care to explain what you're doing?

SEVEN: I'm doing exactly what you instructed me to do.

THE DOCTOR: I hardly think so. I created this program to help you become more comfortable in social situations, not to practice alienating people.

[Dialogue Omitted]

THE DOCTOR: That doesn't mean subjecting them to an interrogation. You have to let them answer, listen to what they say, ask another question on the same subject. Take your time. Shall we try again?

SEVEN: I believe I am overdue for my weekly medical maintenance. We should go.

THE DOCTOR: Seven, you've never volunteered for a check-up before.

SEVEN: It is preferable to remaining here.

Not only does the dialogue provide a good example of the lack of give-and-take in the conversation, Seven doesn't take into account the public nature of the mess hall environment when she asks Torres about sex with Paris. Also, Seven remains standing while Torres and Kim are sitting. Seven doesn't understand the non-verbal messages she's sending with her body language. This scene accurately depicts what it can be like for someone with autism to be taught social skills directly. Teaching social skills by means of computer simulations is one of the new approaches used with people who have Asperger's syndrome and autism spectrum disorders. Using the holodeck made it possible for Seven to royally screw-up the lesson and not get her pretty face rearranged by the Klingon engineer.

The naïve Ensign Kim isn't the only Voyager crew member who attempts to teach Seven how to relax during her free time. Janeway invites Seven to her Leonardo da Vinci studio on the holodeck in "The Raven" (1997, VOY; 4:6).

SEVEN: This activity is truly unproductive. The end result has no use. No necessary task has been accomplished. Time has been expended—nothing more.

JANEWAY: That depends on how you look at it, doesn't it? I find sculpting helps me unwind, relax.

SEVEN: The concept of relaxation is difficult for me to understand. As a Borg, my time was spent working at a specific task. When it was completed, I was assigned another. It was efficient.

Until she takes up cooking, Seven does little in terms of recreation. (For someone who had to be taught how to eat, cooking is an ironic hobby for the woman who looks like she never eats.) While Seven provides ample examples of communication styles and behaviors of someone with autism, not everyone will easily relate to her character. Her aggressive communication style creates problems for others, especially young Harry Kim in "Revulsion" (1997, VOY; 4:5). Seven joins Kim in the mess hall and looks over some data regarding reconfiguring astrometric projectors. When Kim attempts to engage Seven in small talk, she outs him for flirting with her.

SEVEN: I may be new to individuality, but I am not ignorant of human behavior. I've noticed your attempts to engage me in idle conversation, and I see the way your pupils dilate when you look at my body. [Seven moves closer to where Kim is sitting.]

KIM: I don't know what you're talking about. [Kim's tone of voice reflects obvious embarrassment.]

SEVEN: Obviously you've suggested a visit to the holodeck in the hopes of creating a romantic mood. Are you in love with me, Ensign?

KIM: Well, no.

SEVEN: Then you wish to copulate?

KIM: No! I mean, I, I don't know what I mean. [Kim's voice reflects his confusion, not only in his own desires, but in how Seven is being so direct.]

SEVEN: All of these elaborate rituals of deception. I didn't realize becoming human again would be such a challenge. Sexuality is particularly complex. As Borg we had no need for seduction, no time for single cell fertilization. We saw a species we wanted and we assimilated it. [Kim looks physically uncomfortable as Seven speaks.] Nevertheless, I am willing to explore my humanity. [Seven puts down the PADD.] Take off your clothes.

KIM: Ah, Seven. [Kim stands up and looks as though he's ready to back away.]

SEVEN: Don't be alarmed. I won't hurt you.

KIM: Look—this is a little sudden. I was just trying to. Part of the team, you know? Maybe we should just quit for now. [Kim picks up the PADD and forces a smile.]

SEVEN: All right. Let me know when you wish to resume our work. [Seven leaves the mess hall and Kim breathes multiple sighs of relief.]

I have watched this scene several times and it's so well played that I'm never completely sure whether Seven was being direct, or trying to intimidate the naïve Ensign Kim. The ambiguity in this situation isn't much different from what many people with autism feel in equally confusing interactions. Generally speaking, those with autism will take conversations literally because they're not able to understand the nonverbal cues or tone of voice cues of the other.

Bill, a *Star Trek* fan with high functioning autism, said in our interview that he didn't relate to Seven because she was a woman. Seven has the advantage of having same-gender role models, Janeway and Torres, as well as a male tutor in the form of The Doctor. In working with others with autism, Bill has seen where females with autism related to Seven's struggles. Bill talked about how having a social skills role model of a different gender can lead to social problems because many of the unwritten rules of behavior continue to be different for males and females.

Not everyone with autism has difficulty relating to someone of a different gender. Gavin, a *Star Trek* fan from Australia, relates to Seven (as well as Data and The Doctor) because he "had a similar journey to them, developing my inner self, my individuality, and my creativity." He went on to say, "Like the characters mentioned, I'm underestimated because I'm different."

In "Prey" (1998, VOY; 4:16), The Doctor provides more than just medical care to Seven in helping her fit in with the crew.

THE DOCTOR: I know it's awkward. For me it was even painful, but you'll find the rewards are well worth the effort.

SEVEN: Rewards?

THE DOCTOR: The ability to put others at ease, make them feel more comfortable around you. You're a lot like me when I was first activated. If I'd had a mentor things would have gone a lot more smoothly. I'm willing to share my wisdom but, if you're not interested, fine, I'll stick to your physiological maintenance.

SEVEN: I will examine your data.

THE DOCTOR: Oh, good! Pay special attention to exercise seventeen, Bridge Banter for Beginners.

SEVEN: Have a pleasant day.

Seven's social skill lessons never go smoothly. She appears more candid when interacting with The Doctor and Captain Janeway than anyone else at this point. Seven offers this observation to The Doctor, who tries to teach her how to date in "Someone To Watch Over Me" (1999, VOY; 5:21).

SEVEN: I wish to terminate our social lessons.
THE DOCTOR: Just because you didn't achieve perfection your first time out, doesn't mean you should give up.
SEVEN: Dating is a poor means of interaction. There is far more efficiency in the way you and I communicate. We say what we mean, simply and directly.
THE DOCTOR: You and I do have a rapport, but we're colleagues. We're not pursuing romance.
SEVEN: No.
THE DOCTOR: I'm certain you'll be able to master these basic skills in short order.
SEVEN: My first date was certainly short.
THE DOCTOR: Was that a joke?
SEVEN: Lesson Six, beguiling banter.

Communication is central in understanding children with autism. Todd, a *Star Trek* fan from Australia, is the father of four children. Three of his children are "on the spectrum." He told me about how meaningful it would be to have a Universal Translator for his children. He described it for me:

You've got a group of people going through the universe and no matter where they go they can instantly understand anything anyone says, and I think you can sort of imagine from looking at it from an autism point of view how much, how magical something like that would seem. That no matter where you go. It doesn't matter what you do. You can understand what people are saying.

While parents learn to understand their children with autism because of their familiarity with the child's experience, teachers aren't always aware of these experiences.

For a parent with children on the autism spectrum a Universal Translator would help the teachers understand the children in a school setting. And it would work the other way too. The child with autism would be able to understand the instructions they were being given, as well as have the teachers understand the meanings of responses from the child. Todd stated that one of his twin boys talks in a manner similar to The Children of Tama on "Darmok" (1991, TNG; 5:2). "Darmok" ventures into an area of communication known as *psycholinguistics*. Psycholinguistics is the study of the mental aspects of language and speech which involves the meanings of words, sentences and conversation.

The episode makes the point that simply understanding another person's words doesn't necessarily guarantee that the meaning will be understood as well. In other words, true communication is more than just understanding the words spoken; it involves what the words mean in that specific context.

As Captain Picard, stranded on the planet's surface, tries to work out with Captain Dathon the meaning of Dathon's expressions, Counselor Troi and Data explain to the crew the problems with Tamarian communication.

DATA: The Tamarian ego structure does not seem to allow what we normally think of as self-identity. Their ability to abstract is highly unusual. They seem to communicate through narrative imagery by reference to the individuals and places which appear in their mytho-historical accounts.

TROI: It's as if I were to say to you, "Juliet on her balcony."

CRUSHER: An image of romance.

TROI: Exactly. Imagery is everything to the Tamarians. It embodies their emotional states, their very thought processes. It's how they communicate, and it's how they think.

RIKER: If we know how they think, shouldn't we be able to get something across to them?

DATA: No, sir. The situation is analogous to understanding the grammar of a language but none of the vocabulary.

CRUSHER: If I didn't know who Juliet was or what she was doing on that balcony, the image alone wouldn't have any meaning.

TROI: That's correct. For instance, we know that Darmok was a great hero, a hunter, and that Tanagra was an island, but that's it. Without the details, there's no understanding.

Todd related how his son would also speak in similes saying, "…'Dora the Explorer goes on a picnic' or 'the princess in the forest' and it's all that idea that 'I'm too little to do that, or I don't understand' but if you didn't know him well enough, you would just see the randomness of it and not put it together as to what he was communicating."

Picard learns enough to talk to the Tamarians after Dathon dies on the planet. Back on the bridge of the Enterprise, he delivers Dathon's journal to the Tamarians and is given a gift of Dathon's dagger. Without watching the entire episode, it would be impossible to understand this dialogue, even with the additional cues of changes in tone of voice and physical gestures which add to our understanding of the exchange.

PICARD: Hail the Tamarian ship. [Picard enters the bridge with a Kirk-styled ripped shirt.]

WORF: Aye, Captain.

TAMARIAN [On viewscreen]: Zinda! His face black, his eyes red. [Tone of voice indicates his is angry.]

PICARD: Temarc! The river Temarc in winter. [Picard's tone is assertive.]

TAMARIAN: Darmok?

PICARD: And Jalad. At Tanagra. Darmok and Jalad on the ocean. [This last line delivered softer than the previous expressions.]

TAMARIAN [On viewscreen]: Sokath, his eyes open! [There is a "finally they understand" quality to this line.]

PICARD: The beast at Tanagra. Uzani, his army. Shaka when the walls fell. [It is clear from Picard's tone of voice and the behavior of the Tamarians on the other ship, that the Tamarians have been told their captain has died.]

[Picard holds up Dathon's journal, and the Tamarians beam it away.]

TAMARIAN [On viewscreen]: Picard and Dathon at El-Adrel. [The Tamarian puts down the journal, as if it has been named.] Mirab, with sails unfurled. [The Tamarians stand in a formal manner.]

PICARD [Holds out the dagger]: Temba, his arms open.

TAMARIAN [On viewscreen]: Temba at rest.

PICARD: Thank you. [Picard puts the dagger down.]

DATA: Power has been restored, sir.

[The Tamarian nods at someone off screen and the transmission ends.]

RIKER: New friends, Captain?

PICARD: I can't say, Number One. But at least they're not new enemies.

Autism spectrum disorders aren't well understood. The most common therapy is *Applied Behavioral Analysis.* This therapy uses reinforcement to teach children with autism how to live adaptively in their environment. Various behaviors that might come naturally to neurotypical children, such as making eye contact, are reinforced by the behavior analyst. In this manner, social skills, communication skills, and coping skills are taught to those with autism.

It's easy to assume that people with disabilities, which are not visually apparent, will pass as non-disabled—but that's not the case. People with autism and communication disorders appear different during social interactions, but the source of this difference isn't readily apparent or understood. As a result, people often treated them with less compassion than those whose disability is observable. Technology has provided little assistance for the people described in this chapter, and medical science continues to struggle with the causes and treatments for these disorders. However, *Star Trek* has played an important role in the lives of fans with autism, Asperger's syndrome, and other communication disorders. Indeed, the role models on the shows provide special messages of hope for these fans.

Chapter 11
"Dismissed"

JANEWAY: Dismissed. That's a Starfleet expression for 'get out.'
"The Cloud" (1995; VOY; 1:5)

Stigma, Cognitive Disabilities, and Body Image

Stigma

In "The Sons of Mogh" (1996, DS9; 4:14) Worf's brother, Kurn, describes the humiliation he's suffered owing to Worf's allegiance to the Federation.

KURN: For you, it's done. You and your comfortable Federation life, your glorious Starfleet career. But not for me. Our family had a seat on the High Council. We were feared by our enemies, respected by our friends. It was even said that if Gowron died the leadership of the Council might be passed to someone from the House of Mogh. Then you chose to side with the Federation against the Empire. Gowron took our ships, our land, our seat on the Council, everything.

WORF: Kurn, I know this has been difficult for you.

KURN: What do you know? Did you watch as Gowron's men seized our land and stripped our family of its name? Did you have to endure the humiliation of being ejected from the High Council in front of the Emperor himself? No.

You chose to stay here, safe, comfortable, secure. You have everything you want and I have nothing, not even my honor. But you can give that back to me.

Social stigma is the extreme disapproval of a person or group based on perceived characteristics that differentiate them from other members of a society. Too often, such attitudes result in unfair treatment. On *Star Trek*, social stigma was more often attributed to aliens rather than to our enlightened members of Starfleet. Klingons, like Romulans, have a strict warrior culture with an emphasis on physical strength.

In "The Enemy" (1989, TNG; 3:7) La Forge is marooned with a Romulan, Centurion Bochra. The two adversaries crash land on a Federation planet. Bochra explains how Romulans view people born with disabilities.

LA FORGE:... What's the matter?

BOCHRA: Nothing.

LA FORGE: Wrong. Your heart rate just shot way up. [He taps his VISOR.] It translates a wide range of radiation into neural impulses. Allows me to see.

BOCHRA: Without it, you're blind?

LA FORGE: Yes.

BOCHRA: How did this happen?

LA FORGE: I was born that way.

BOCHRA: And your parents let you live?

LA FORGE: What kind of question is that? Of course they let me live.

BOCHRA: No wonder your race is weak. You waste time and resources on defective children.

INCOMING MESSAGE:
Some people believe it's better to be dead than have a disability.

The radiation on the planet interferes with both the VISOR and the men's nervous systems. Unable to use his VISOR, La Forge is functionally blind and Bochra must work with him to signal the Enterprise and be rescued.

BOCHRA: We have the sensor device you are carrying.

LA FORGE: Tricorder? It's not set up to detect neutrinos.

BOCHRA: Your eye device does. Connect them.

LA FORGE: That's crazy. They don't speak the same language. Besides, I'd never be able to get an accurate sampling. Wait a second. Wait, I wouldn't need an accurate sampling, just need a pointer. A neutrino Geiger counter. No, it's still not possible.

BOCHRA: You cannot do it?

LA FORGE: Under normal circumstances, maybe. Here, no way.

BOCHRA: Why?

LA FORGE: Because I can't see. Adapting the neural output pods of the VISOR is tricky work. It can't be done by touch.

BOCHRA: Then I will be your eyes.

INCOMING MESSAGE:
Abilities are more important than disabilities.
When people work together, good things can happen.

Much of the dialogue from "The Enemy" accurately portrays the problem of social stigma and its relationship to disability. How people with disabilities are treated depends on their culture. *Star Trek* has brought to the screen several episodes that deal with the stigma of disability, even if in passing. The concept of stigma is universal; it is, however, socially constructed.

Degra, a Xindi-Primate scientist, experiences an instant dislike for Commander Dolim, a Reptilian. Degra relates the story to Captain Archer in "The Council" (2004, ENT; 3:22):

DEGRA: Which brings us to the Reptilians, and Commander Dolim. There's a story about him. I don't know if it's true, I'd like to believe it isn't. His daughter gave birth to a son. He had a deformity in his right arm, not life-threatening, but enough to preclude his ever joining the military. Commander Dolim had his own grandson poisoned.

ARCHER: From what I've seen that's not hard to believe.

DEGRA: As I said, it may be just a story, but as a father it's always in the back of my mind whenever I have dealings with him.

INCOMING MESSAGE:
Children should be valued for what they can do,
not devalued for what they can't do.

The idea that a grandfather would poison his own grandson is so repulsive to Western society it's easy to dislike not only Dolim, but to view Reptilians as a group of villains. At the same time, cruel behavior isn't limited to aliens as Data explains to his android daughter, Lal in "The Offspring" (1990, TNG; 3:16):

LAL: Father, what is the significance of laughter?

DATA: It is a human physiological response to humor.

LAL: Then judging from their laughter, the children at school found my remarks humorous. So without understanding humor, I have somehow mastered it.

DATA: [As they enter the turbolift] Deck fifteen. [Data looks at Lal.] Lal.

LAL: Yes, Father?

DATA: The children were not laughing with you, they were laughing at you.

LAL: Explain.

DATA: One is meant kindly, the other is not.

LAL: Why would they wish to be unkind?

DATA: Because you are different. Differences sometimes scare people. I have learned that some of them use humor to hide their fear.

LAL: I do not want to be different.

Data's observation regarding the use of humor by Humans is on target. While there are plenty examples of stigma on *Star Trek*, there are no examples of people with *mental retardation* or "intellectual disability" as it is now called. According to the research, people with intellectual disability due to genetic factors such as Down syndrome (formerly called "Down's syndrome") don't experience as much stigma as those with psychiatric disabilities or obesity. At the same time, people with milder intellectual disabilities, such as learning disabilities or mild brain injuries, are often treated with skepticism because they look normal. While intellectual disability occurs during childhood, *cognitive impairments* can be acquired from illness, stroke, trauma, or as part of aging. Intelligence and cognitive ability are used interchangeably on *Star Trek* even though they are not the same. And while there are no alien species with mental retardation on *Star Trek*, there are examples that allow me to illustrate some types of cognitive disabilities. Similar to autism, cognitive impairment is largely detected through social interactions.

Cognitive Disabilities

The personalities of the doctors on *Star Trek* were like a box of Troi's assorted chocolates. From the cantankerous Dr. McCoy to the sweet Dr. Crusher. From the confrontational Dr. Pulaski to the philosophical Dr. Phlox. From the sarcastic, romantic, narcissistic, and opera-singing Emergency Medical Hologram to the playful, part time spy, and genetically engineered Dr. Bashir. But they all had one thing in common—their ability to perform amazing medicine.

In "Star Trek IV: The Voyage Home" (1986), while smuggling Chekov out of Mercy Hospital, Dr. McCoy gives a woman a pill, apparently ending her need for kidney dialysis. Dr. Pulaski offers to replace Captain Picard's artificial heart. On *Star Trek: Voyager*, The Doctor provides both medical care and teaches interpersonal relationships. Dr. Phlox cures lung cancer. Dr. Bashir keeps Vedek Bareil alive with artificial organs and implants. But the one area that continues to challenge the superdocs of the future is the brain.

When the brain is involved, there are limits to what even a Starfleet doctor can do as Dr. Bashir states in "Life Support" (1995, DS9; 3:13).

> BASHIR: ...There's still a great deal about the way the brain operates we don't understand. One of my professors at medical school used to say that the brain had a spark of life that can't be replicated. If we begin to replace parts of Bareil's brain with artificial implants, that spark may be lost.

The idea that the brain is the body part where personhood resides is made clear in "What Are Little Girls Made Of?" (1966, TOS; 1:8). In this episode, Nurse Christine Chapel finds her long lost love, Dr. Roger Korby, on a planet where he has been building androids. Chapel soon discovers he's not the same man she was engaged to marry. Korby tries to convince everyone about the importance of his work by building an android that looks exactly like Captain Kirk (simultaneously offering William Shatner the opportunity to show off his manly physique). The android is such a perfect copy, even Chapel can't tell the difference between the captain and android Kirks.

Korby explains to Kirk that creating a duplicate isn't the extent of his new technology:

KORBY: ...What you saw was only a machine, only half of what I could've accomplished. Do you understand? By continuing the process I could've transferred you—your very consciousness into that android. Your soul, if you wish. All of you. In android form, a human being can have practical immortality. Can you understand what I'm offering mankind?

KIRK: Programming. Different word, but the same old promises made by Genghis Khan, Julius Caesar, Hitler, Ferris, Maltuvis.

KORBY: Can you understand that a human converted to an android can be programmed for the better? Can you imagine how life could be improved if we could do away with jealousy, greed, hate?

KIRK: It can also be improved by eliminating love, tenderness, sentiment. The other side of the coin, Doctor.

KORBY: No one need ever die again. No disease. No deformities. Why, even fear can be programmed away, replaced with joy. I'm offering you a practical heaven. A new paradise, and all I need is your help.

KIRK: All you wanted before was my understanding.

KORBY: I need transportation to a planet colony with proper raw materials. I'm sure there are several good possibilities among your next stops. No diversion from your route. I want no suspicions aroused. I'll begin producing androids carefully. Selectively.

KIRK: Yes, yes. No one need know—only to frighten uninformed minds.

KORBY: They must be strongly infiltrated into society before the android existence is revealed. I want no wave of hysteria to destroy what is good and right. You with me, Captain?

INCOMING MESSAGE:
Humans can't be programmed like machines.
Humans fear anyone who's different.

RED ALERT!
Unlike Humans, machines are perfect.

Later, Korby reveals that he had transferred his own existence to an android body.

KORBY: It's still me, Christine. Roger. I'm in here. You can't imagine how it was. I was frozen, dying. My legs were gone. I was—I had only my brain between life and death. This can be repaired [showing his skin tear which has revealed the electronics below the skin] easier than another man can set a broken finger. I'm still the same as I was before, Christine, perhaps even better.

INCOMING MESSAGE:
The desire to avoid pain and death is strong in Humans.

The commentary on Humans and intelligence is central to the character of Lieutenant Commander Data on *Star Trek: The Next Generation*. From the show's premiere in "Encounter at Farpoint" (1987, TNG; 1:1), Data provides more examples of what makes Humans Human than anyone else on board.

RIKER: But, your file says that you're an—
DATA: Machine, Correct, sir. Does that trouble you?
RIKER: To be honest, yes, a little.
DATA: Understood, sir. Prejudice is very human.
RIKER: Now that does trouble me. Do you consider yourself superior to us?
DATA: I am superior, sir, in many ways. But I would gladly give it up to be human.

INCOMING MESSAGE:
Being an android is not the same as being perfect.

According to the ICD-10, mental retardation is a condition characterized by impairments in cognitive, language, motor, and social abilities. These abilities are considered to contribute to overall intelligence. There is a general tendency for all these skills to develop during childhood to a similar level in each individual, although there is a wide range of what is considered normal development. When development falls outside that range, the child is considered mentally retarded—in the US the term "developmentally delayed" is more commonly used, but the criteria are the same.

Memory and Learning

Learning is heavily dependent on memory. Without the ability to remember instructions and previous experience, learning cannot take place. In "Twilight" (2003, ENT; 3:8) Captain Archer can no longer form long-term memories due to an infection of outer space parasites. Unable to remember for more than a few hours, Archer wakes up each day with no memory of the infection, or how his first officer became his caregiver. However, Archer is aware that due to his lack of memory he must have been a burden on T'Pol for the last twelve years.

> ARCHER: It was a little disturbing. From my perspective, I saw most of those people just a few hours ago. It couldn't have been easy for you, telling me the same story over and over again for twelve years.
> T'POL: I don't always tell it in detail.
> ARCHER: I hope I've told you before, but, I'm very grateful for everything you've done for me. If this works…

Mike Sussman, the script writer of "Twilight," stated "Archer not remembering anything was really the basic idea for the show. The central notion was that someone with Alzheimer's disease, in some ways, could be thought of as a time-traveler" (November 07, 2003 - TrekToday). (Apparently wiping a memory is easier for the superdoc than restoring one, a procedure that has repeatedly saved several careers when violations of the Prime Directive are involved.)

Many characters experience short-term amnesia: "The Paradise Syndrome," (1968; TOS; 3:3) and "Conundrum," (1992, TNG; 5:14); and full amnesia in "Sons of Mogh," (1996, DS9; 4:14). In "Dagger of the Mind," (1966, TOS; 1:10) and "Retrospect" (1998,

VOY; 4:17), false memories rather than memory loss are the subject matter. Amnesia typically involves *retrograde* memory loss in which the individual forgets the past. Captain Archer's inability to form new memories as opposed to losing old ones is called *anterograde* amnesia.

Severe memory loss, such as that on "Twilight," is rare, but it does happen. In 1985, Cambridge University graduate and choir master of the London Sinfonietta, Clive Wearing, lost his memory and his ability to form new long-term memories when a herpes simplex virus caused severe inflammation of his brain. After he recovered, he couldn't remember his past, nor could he remember anything after seven seconds. The relationship with his wife, who he did remember, had become strained over the years. But like Archer and T'Pol, their relationship survived. Once again, the story was one of acceptance and compassion.

Not all learning impairments are related to a deficit in memory. Many of the most famous scientists in our history have had disabilities separate from memory impairments. In one of my favorite scenes, Data plays poker with holographic representations of Einstein, Hawking, and Newton ("Descent Part 1", 1993; TNG; 6:26).

> EINSTEIN: Perhaps we should return to the game. Let's see, where were we? Yes, you raised Mr. Data four, which means that the bet is, er, seven to me?
> NEWTON: The bet is ten! Can't you do simple arithmetic? I don't even know why I'm here in the first place. What is the point of playing this ridiculous game?
> DATA: When I play poker with my shipmates, it often appears to be a useful forum for exploring the different facets of humanity. I was curious to see how three of history's greatest minds would interact in this setting. So far, it has proved most illuminating.

Although these men of science are known for their contributions, it's also important to remember that all three people had or have different disabilities. Einstein had a learning disability involving simple math computations. Hawking has amyotrophic lateral sclerosis. Some historians believe that Newton had a personality disorder owing to his premature birth and subsequent neglect during infancy.

Language

Too often, we judge a person's intelligence by the way they speak. Accents, vocabulary, and even the speed at which a person talks, are often processed by our own brains in a way that leads to an evaluation of the mental abilities of others—accurate or not.

When the Enterprise responds to a distress signal, these prejudices are central to the "Samaritan Snare" (1989, TNG; 2:17).

RIKER: Do you need help?

GREBNEDLOG [On viewscreen]: We are Pakleds. Our ship is the Mondor. It is broken.

Worf cautions against sending La Forge over to the Mondor to complete repairs. However, Riker allows the chubby bulldog appearance and simple vocabulary of the Pakleds to guide his decision.

RIKER: Do you have anything else on them?

DATA: They are a relatively benign species.

RIKER: Don't they seem a little slow?

DATA: They may merely have poorly developed language skills.

INCOMING MESSAGE:

Simple words can make the same points as a multi-syllable vocabulary.

Ever the alpha male, Riker also dismisses the warnings of the ship's counselor.

TROI: Commander? Lieutenant La Forge is on an alien ship?

RIKER: Yes. We're rendering assistance to some curious throwbacks.

DATA: How they ever mastered the rudiments of space travel is a genuine curiosity.

TROI: Commander. Those aliens—what they feel is not helplessness. Lieutenant La Forge is in great danger! He's in danger. Great danger.

The Pakleds threaten to harm La Forge if the Enterprise doesn't turn over their computer library. The technology of the Pakleds is a hodgepodge of devices from other worlds—an indication that this subterfuge of theirs has worked on others in the past as well.

TROI: It's all deception. Nothing the Pakleds have said or done has been sincere.

DATA: Intensified scan shows their guidance system to be perfectly intact, as is their power generator.

RIKER: Then what was Geordi repairing?

DATA: Apparently, the putative malfunctions were carefully programmed into their ship's computer.

RIKER: I didn't think the Pakleds had that kind of technology.

DATA: They seem to have made some technological leaps forward, Commander.

RIKER: Why would they go through the charade of needing our help?

TROI: For the sole purpose of making Lieutenant La Forge their prisoner.

Whether or not the Pakled captain may be as intelligent as the Humans isn't certain. He certainly isn't a fool. He confronts Riker on his arrogance.

GREBNEDLOG [On viewscreen]: You think we are not smart.

RIKER: I think you need to continue to develop.

GREBNEDLOG [On viewscreen]: We are smart.

RIKER: Prove it. Return our man to us.

GREBNEDLOG [On viewscreen]: You want him?

RIKER: Yes, damn it.

GREBNEDLOG [On viewscreen]: Good. We want all computer information from your ship. Now.

INCOMING MESSAGE:
Don't judge someone's intelligence by
their appearance or manner of speaking.

While trying to devise a plan to free La Forge, Riker attempts to understand the motivations of the Pakleds.

> TROI: They are unwilling to wait for the timely evolution of their species' intellectual capacity. They want instant knowledge, instant power and gratification.
> PULASKI: The more they get, the more they want.
> RIKER: And the more aggressive and dangerous they become. I think it's time we set some limits.

In the end, Riker tricks the Pakleds into lowering their shields, which allows the Enterprise to beam La Forge back to the Enterprise. "Samaritan Snare" provides a realistic portrayal of how our society treats people who are considered cognitively impaired. While the Pakleds have language impairments in terms of their restricted and simple vocabulary, they wouldn't be considered mentally retarded by current standards. In the end, it's Riker who looks foolish as he misjudges the manipulative ability of the Pakleds.

Problem Solving

Humans aren't the only species who treat those with less intelligence as inferior. Neelix confronts Voyager's Vulcan security officer about his demeaning behavior in "Rise" (1997, VOY; 3:19).

> NEELIX: I don't know. I've got a funny feeling about this.
> TUVOK: I'm not interested in your funny feeling.
> NEELIX: You're not listening to what I'm saying. Delirious or not, he said he needed whatever's up there. What if it's something that can help us?
> TUVOK: I will not debate this with you. Please pilot the craft and remain silent.
> NEELIX: You're going to listen to me!
> TUVOK: You are becoming emotionally distraught. There is little point in furthering this discussion.
> NEELIX: I'll tell you who's being emotional. You! You hide it beneath that Vulcan calm but truth is, you're filled with contempt and sarcasm, and I'm tired of being the target of all your hostility.

TUVOK: You are mistaken.

LILLIAS: No, he's not. I can see it every time you talk to Neelix. You're dismissive and condescending.

TUVOK: You are projecting your own emotional bias onto my actions. I have no feelings towards Mr. Neelix.

NEELIX: That's right! That's exactly what I'm talking about! You have no feelings for me, but you have feelings against me. For three years you've ridiculed me and made it obvious to everyone that you have no respect for me, and I've tolerated it. You know why? You know why? Because you are smarter than I am, Tuvok, and more logical, stronger, superior in almost every way, and I admire you. But you don't have any instincts, have any gut feelings, and you don't really understand people. But non-Vulcans have feelings and they have to listen to them. I've got to listen to mine, and right now they're telling me we need to get up on that roof and find out what The Doctor was talking about.

INCOMING MESSAGE:
Don't dismiss the experience of others even if you think
they are less intelligent than you.
Don't piss off the Talaxian.

In the end, Neelix's intuition is proven correct. Even more important, it is Neelix's experience with the orbital tether that provides a means of escaping and being rescued. To Tuvok's credit, he listens to Neelix and climbs onto the roof to find the evidence they need.

The ability to use *intuition* effectively is an area of growing scientific interest. Researchers from Boston College, George Mason University, and Rice University have demonstrated that at times intuition may be as equally effective as an analytical approach in decision-making.

> "It turns out intuition isn't always bad and there are conditions where it is a good way to make the right decision," said co-author Michael Pratt, the O'Connor Family Professor of Management and Organization at Boston College's Carroll School of Management. "What we found demystifies a

lot of the information out there that says intuition isn't as effective as if you sat down and walked through an analytical approach."

Problem solving is one form of intelligence. People who have difficulties with problem solving can be taught methods of compensating using a variety of strategies, and new ones are being added all the time. One of the most common ways that problems are solved on *Star Trek* is for the senior officers to meet and brainstorm approaches. Everyone contributes their unique skills and perspectives on the crisis of the day.

Concentration

Long before Attention Deficit Hyperactivity Disorder became as common in schools as holodeck injuries are on *Star Trek*, attention or concentration was considered necessary while on "Shore Leave" (1966, TOS; 1:16). On this unnamed, lush planet, allowing your mind to wander could result in coming face-to-face with the thing you were just thinking about, as Mr. Spock explains.

SPOCK: Which supports a theory I've been formulating.
KIRK: That we're all meeting people and things that we happen to be thinking about at the moment.
SPOCK: Yes. Somehow our thoughts are read, these things are quickly manufactured and provided for us.
KIRK: Dangerous if we happen to be thinking about—
SPOCK: Yes. We must all control our thoughts.
KIRK: Difficult.

INCOMING MESSAGE:
Controlling your own thoughts takes effort.

The planet was created as an amusement park for the caretaker's race to enjoy. The planet's technology allowed for the creation of people and things based on the daydreams of its customers.

CARETAKER: This entire planet was constructed for our race of people to come and play.

SULU: Play? As advanced as you obviously are, and you still play?

KIRK: Yes, play, Mr. Sulu. The more complex the mind—the greater the need for the simplicity of play.

CARETAKER: Exactly, Captain. How very perceptive of you.

KIRK: But that still doesn't explain the death of my ship's surgeon.

MCCOY: Possibly because no one has died, Jim. [McCoy strolls in with a Vegas show girl on each arm. The women appear to be wearing what looks like pastel colored Tribbles.] I was taken below the surface for some rather remarkable repairs. It's amazing. They've got a factory complex down there you wouldn't believe. They can build or do anything immediately.

INCOMING MESSAGE:

Even mental giants need to get silly once in a while.

It's not only permissible, but restorative, to be distracted while on vacation. However, when distraction or the inability to concentrate interferes with work, it becomes a form of cognitive disability. People with attention deficit disorders (estimated to be 10% of the population) are often considered less intelligent because of their inability to concentrate, tangential thinking, and lack of impulse control. However, many people with these disorders are actually above average in intelligence, just like the aliens on the "Shore Leave" planet. In the U.S., attention deficit disorders are generally treated with stimulants and behavioral therapy in school-age children. However, it's important that all sources of inattention be considered before deciding on a treatment. Sleep disorders, anxiety, and other possible causes of inattention should be considered before concluding that medication is the best option.

Visual Comprehension

Lal has trouble with visual comprehension in "The Offspring" (1990, TNG; 3:16), which Data describes in his science log.

DATA: Second officer's science log, supplemental.

[Lal and Data are in Ten-Forward. He hands her a drink.]

Training in social skills at the most elementary level has begun.

[Lal takes a drink, but lets the liquid dribble out of her mouth.]

Lal is progressing very slowly but is not deterred by early setbacks.

[Data, Lal, and Wesley are playing catch in Data's quarters.]

While motor coordination has improved twelve percent, reflexes still need to develop.

[Wesley throws the ball to Lal and it bounces off her shoulder. Lal looks at Data and puts her hand up to catch the ball. Data forces a smile at her.]

Visual comprehension is especially difficult for Lal.

[Lal is looking at the computer screen, a map and text are displayed.]

Translating her vast data banks into recognizable applications may improve with additional transfers. She is also learning to supplement her innate android behavior with simulated human responses.

[Data points at his face and blinks. Lal imitates his blinking herself.]

And it is interesting to note that as I observe Lal learning about her world, I share in her experience, almost as though I am learning things over again.

[Lal and Data are back in Ten Forward, Lal is enjoying eating from a bowl and drinking from the glass without spilling. Data points to her mouth, but Lal stops him and wipes her mouth on the napkin from her lap. Data smiles.]

Although Lal is an android, my point is that all the cognitive abilities are mentioned, if in passing, on *Star Trek*. The lack of examples of mental retardation could be interpreted to mean that, in the future, these cognitive disabilities will no longer occur.

Dyslexia is a real-life example of how important visual comprehension is to reading and being considered intelligent. This specific learning disability manifests primarily as a difficulty with written language, particularly with reading and spelling. Both Whoopi Goldberg (the actress who played Guinan) and John de Lancie (the actor who played Q) on *Star Trek: The Next Generation*, struggled with dyslexia as children.

Goldberg said in an interview on the Academy of Achievement's website, Goldberg said, "When I was a kid they didn't call it dyslexia. They called it—you know—you were slow, or you were retarded, or whatever." Goldberg credits a man who worked to help her learn to read and her mother for believing in her intelligence. It's apparent Goldberg overcame her dyslexia because in addition to her screen work, she has authored children's books and a collection of humorous essays.

Whether it's Captain Picard reading Shakespeare or Wesley Crusher studying for Starfleet Academy, reading is important to the development of intelligence. Even with all of the computers on board the Enterprise, people still engage in a lot of reading from what look like eReaders as well as old-fashioned printed books.

In "The Nth Degree" (1991, TNG; 4:19), the future of treatment for cognitive disabilities is portrayed. Barclay becomes a super-genius after an encounter with an alien probe.

> CRUSHER: Incredible! The production of neurotransmitters in your brain has jumped by over five hundred percent. Pre and postsynaptic membranes have increased permeability to match it. I couldn't even guess at your IQ level now.
> BARCLAY: Probably somewhere between twelve hundred and fourteen fifty.
> CRUSHER: But that isn't all. The corpus callosum, the connecting bridge between both sides of the brain, it is so active now that the hemispheres are essentially behaving as one.
> LA FORGE: So, it's not just raw intelligence we're talking about here.
> CRUSHER: No. Creativity—resourcefulness—inspiration—imagination—they've all been enhanced. Lieutenant, you could very well be the most advanced human being who has ever lived.

To say Barclay's intelligence goes to his head is an understatement. While attempting to repair the Argus Array, a remote subspace telescope at the edge of Federation space, the repair work goes awry. Barclay attempts to save the day and the array by connecting his brain to the ship's computer using a workstation of his own design on the holodeck. Having someone take over the Enterprise should be nothing new to Captain Picard by this time, yet he acts as though he's more than a little miffed at Barclay.

> BARCLAY [OC]: I'm sorry, Captain, I was only trying to help. Our computer was too slow to compensate for the overload on the Array. So I created an interface that communicated my thoughts directly to the central processing unit.

RIKER: Exactly what does that mean?

BARCLAY [OC]: My body is as you see it here, but much of my higher brain functions and memory have been transferred to the starboard computer core.

PICARD: Mr. Barclay, remove yourself from the computer system. Leave the holodeck.

BARCLAY [OC]: I'm afraid I can't, sir.

PICARD: Why not?

BARCLAY [OC]: My primary cerebral functions are now operating almost entirely from within the computer. They have expanded to such a degree that it would be impossible to return to the confines of my human brain. Any attempt to do so would mean my death.

It turns out that Barclay is able to disconnect himself from the computer after hurling the Enterprise to the center of the galaxy to meet the Cytherian race. The Cytherians explore the galaxy much like Starfleet, but rather than waste resources on ships to go out into the cosmos, they drag aliens to their home by enhancing and then controlling a person's brain.

The science of creating an interface between a Human brain and a computer is called *Intelligence Amplification* or IA. With intelligence amplification, the starting point is a Human brain which receives the implant. The *brain chip* allows for memories to be restored if the person had a stroke or other brain injury. Research reported in *The Journal of Neural Engineering* reported that a brain implant sharpened decision making and restored lost mental capacity in monkeys. The so-called *brain prosthesis* could eventually help people with damage from dementia, strokes, or other brain injuries. Although we are several years away from the widespread application of this neuroscience, it has already sparked some ethical debates about restoration versus augmentation in Humans. Depending on the source, Human trials could begin in 2030 to 2080, which is a pretty wide spread.

"When Is A Vulcan Not A Vulcan"? (Brain Injury)

Tuvok gets blasted by an alien weapon and displays the classic symptoms of a traumatic brain injury in "Riddles" (1999, VOY; 6:6). Not only does the injury affect Tuvok's cognitive, memory, and logic centers, he also loses his sense of self. Neelix becomes determined to help Tuvok recover from the injury.

> THE DOCTOR: There have been rare cases in which comatose patients responded to external stimuli—aromas—touch—voices.
> NEELIX: So, you're saying that if I stay here and, and try to talk to Tuvok, I might be able to provoke some sort of response?
> THE DOCTOR: If anyone can provoke Tuvok, Mr. Neelix, it's you.

Neelix provides a form of rehabilitation therapy by talking to Tuvok, walking him around the familiar parts of the ship, reintroducing him to his quarters, and engaging him in a game of *kal-toh*.

> NEELIX: You're an extraordinary fellow, Tuvok.
> TUVOK: I was an extraordinary fellow.
> NEELIX: You're still the same person.
> TUVOK: Then why do I no longer work on the Bridge?
> NEELIX: We talked about that. You had an accident.
> TUVOK: And now I'm not smart enough.
> NEELIX: Tuvok, you've just got to be patient. Look how much progress you've made already.
> TUVOK: He could dismantle a photonic warhead in less than thirty seconds. I can't even play kal-toh.
> NEELIX: It's going to take time, but you'll re-learn all those things.
> TUVOK: How do you know that?
> NEELIX: Well, because The Doctor—
> TUVOK: The Doctor? The Doctor doesn't know how to make me better, does he?
> NEELIX; Well, not yet, but—
> TUVOK: I'll never be him again.
> NEELIX: You don't know that. The Vulcan mind—
> TUVOK: I'm not a Vulcan. Not anymore!

Tuvok displays emotional instability, personality changes, and depression. All classic symptoms of traumatic brain injury. Neelix's efforts to help Tuvok are nothing short of heroic. While Neelix ponders Tuvok's declaration that he's no longer Vulcan, Seven enters the mess hall and offers Neelix another perspective regarding Tuvok's rehabilitation.

NEELIX: All right. When is a Vulcan no longer a Vulcan?

SEVEN: When his genetic code is sufficiently altered.

NEELIX: No, I was speaking metaphorically.

SEVEN: In that case, a person is no longer Vulcan when he has lost his logic.

NEELIX: Right! And how does he get it back?

SEVEN: He must be taught.

NEELIX: Exactly. But what if he's brain damaged and emotionally unstable? How does he learn?

SEVEN: It may be impossible for him to learn what you're trying to teach.

NEELIX: Well, thanks for the pep talk.

SEVEN: I was merely suggesting that you adapt to the circumstances.

NEELIX: What circumstances? Are you saying that the Tuvok I know is gone, that I should stop trying to help him?

SEVEN: When I was separated from the Collective I, too, was damaged. I was no longer connected to the hive mind. I lost many abilities that I had acquired as a drone, but I adapted.

NEELIX: Because Captain Janeway didn't give up on you. She kept trying to help you.

SEVEN: But not by restoring me to what I'd been, by helping me discover what I could become.

By the end of the show, Tuvok's traumatic brain injury is cured. Although Tuvok no longer hangs out with Neelix, their relationship appears stronger after the ordeal. Ironically, it's Neelix who convinces Tuvok to have the procedure that counters the effects of the alien weapon because Neelix knows Voyager needs its tactical officer. So, despite this inspiring dialogue, Tuvok is restored rather than actualized.

Revisiting "The Void"

In "The Void" (2001, VOY; 7:14), the native race wasn't accepted by aliens from outside that part of flypaper space.

BOSAAL: What's that parasite doing aboard your ship?

JANEWAY: I beg your pardon?

BOSAAL: They're vermin.

THE DOCTOR: I don't know who you are, sir, but your choice of words is offensive.

BOSAAL: What is offensive is the way they slip aboard during transport, hide in conduits, steal food, spread disease.

THE DOCTOR: Fantome is perfectly healthy, and unlike some people in this Void he hasn't stolen anything.

BOSAAL: If my sensors could detect where they are on my ship I'd exterminate them. I suggest you do the same.

INCOMING MESSAGE:
Aliens can be as prejudiced as Humans.
Different lifestyles aren't necessarily dangerous to others.

These Void aliens didn't communicate with those around them until they were given PADDs to create a musical language. Both script writers, James Kahn and Raf Green, are musicians. In our interview, Kahn said the idea that music is a language and something that comes deeply from the heart was an underlying thematic element in the episode. Kahn also describes the Void aliens as being treated like ship rats in addition to being viewed as simpletons and worthless. He said it was nice to end the episode with the Voyager crew being saved by these aliens' cleverness and their ability to do whatever it was they did.

The source of the stigma suffered by the Void aliens isn't entirely clear, but they're unmistakably considered outcasts. Research has shown that stigma due to disability is significantly associated with the type of disability. With one significant exception–people with disabilities which are visually apparent, generally experience less stigma than people with invisible disabilities. The significant exception to this generalization pertains to obesity.

When a person is obese, prejudice often takes the form of a *blame the victim* mentality. When the excessive weight reaches the point where one is considered to have morbid obesity, their weight becomes a disability. Sadly, prejudice against people with obesity may be the only acceptable form of bias against people with disabilities in our society. This is largely due to the belief that the disability is within the person's control.

"Pink-skins" and Body Image

In outer space skin comes in various colors, with and without ridges, and sometimes with spots on the face and body. Andorians have blue skin with antennae on the tops of their heads. On *Star Trek: Enterprise*, the Andorian regimental commander, Shran, refers to Captain Archer as a "pink-skin" in a tone that doesn't indicate it is a term of endearment. The Andorians' blind cousins, the Aenar, have nearly white skin. Orions have green skin. Romulans and Vulcans have pointy ears, slanted eyebrows, and what appears to be a genetically inherited hairstyle. Bajorans have small ridges on their noses; Klingons have large ridges on their foreheads (usually.) Trill hosts (usually) have spots from head to toe. The list goes on. Humans aren't always considered by aliens to be aesthetically pleasing.

Stigma is associated, not only with disability, but also with a person's behavior and appearance. Even though physical appearance isn't considered a disability, it can be a source of additional prejudice and discrimination. According to research, sixty-five percent of what we communicate to others is done through visual messages. Facial expressions, body language, gestures, and clothing are some of the visual messages we send. But those are also contingent on a person's overall appearance. Do they look like an athlete, Starfleet officer, or couch potato? Cognitive disabilities and differences are usually discovered through interactions—in contrast to physical disabilities, which are apparent due to assistive technology such as a wheelchair or a VISOR.

In "Devil In the Dark" (1967, TOS; 1:26), the Horta considers Humans as repulsive in appearance as the miners find the Horta. Kirk and Spock are mutated into water-breathing creatures in "The Ambergris Element" (1973, TAS; 1:12). Spock is aware how a physically different appearance can be stigmatizing and can even generate fear in others.

SPOCK: It is quite possible, Captain, that they find us grotesque and ugly. And many people fear beings different from themselves.

INCOMING MESSAGES:
Standards of beauty are culturally based.

Humans aren't visually pleasing to the aliens on Velera Three in "Home Soil" (1998, TNG; 1:17).

> DATA: The Universal Translator is coming on line, sir.
> ALIEN: Ugly, ugly giant bags of mostly water.
> PICARD: Bags of mostly water?
> DATA: An accurate description of humans, sir. You are over ninety per cent water surrounded by a flexible container.

INCOMING MESSAGE:
Beauty is in the eye of the alien.

Body image is important to self-concept and involves not only the person's mental image of their body with regards to appearance, but also sexuality and fitness. And it changes over time as a person matures and their social roles change. Research has shown that the media's influence on a person's body image can lead to eating disorders as people, especially teenagers and young adults, attempt to mold their bodies into impossible thinness to emulate what they see in magazines and on television.

Overweight actors rarely appear on any screen, and the cast of *Star Trek* is no exception. William Shatner, the heroic Captain James Tiberius Kirk of the starship Enterprise, may have defeated the Gorn on the planet provided by the Metrons, but he had a much more difficult time fighting the battle of the bulge. Herb Solow and Bob Justman recall in their book, "Inside Star Trek: The Real Story" how Shatner would work out strenuously and diet in order to begin each season thin and trim. However, as the season went on, his mid-section would expand, causing the bottom of his tunic to become estranged from the top of his pants. Apparently the gym seen on "Charlie X" (1966, TOS; 1:3) was no longer available by the time he fought the Klingons in "Errand of Mercy" (1967, TOS; 1:27).

Even though Shatner might not have fit Hollywood's definition of slender in the 1960s, he wouldn't be considered overweight in comparison to non-actors in that era.

Unfortunately, owing to the effects of television cameras, research has shown that an actor can appear much heavier than when they are seen off-camera.

The Hollywood obsession with weight and its bias towards exceptionally thin woman is apparent in the women who were selected to play on *Star Trek* as well. Kate Mulgrew wore a size 4 and Jolene Blalock a size 2. Even though Starfleet officers were constantly dodging phaser fire, moving faster than the speed of light didn't excuse them from needing to exercise during their time off. Counselor Troi, for example, participates in a Klingon led Tai-Chi class in "Man of The People" (1992, TNG; 6:3) and exercises while gossiping with Dr. Crusher in "Sub Rosa" (1994, TNG; 7:14). Much to Worf's surprise, Jadzia Dax has created a Klingon exercise program on the Deep Space Nine holosuite.

When we judge a person's physique, we do it by comparison. Unfortunately, people with cognitive disabilities have been associated with the less than svelte aliens who have appeared on the show, such as the Pakleds in "Samaritan Snare" (1989, TNG; 2:17). The Tellarites in "Journey To Babel" (1967, TOS; 2:10) are depicted as argumentative pigs. The stout Phlox of the Hierarchy isn't smart enough to separate The Doctor's daydreams from reality in "Tinker, Tenor, Doctor, Spy" (1999, VOY; 6:4). In "Night" (1998, VOY; 5:1) the radioactive waste haulers and polluters, the Malons, are not only insensitive to their intergalactic neighbors, but they also have a somewhat swinish appearance as well. Another important difference is that we only see rotund *male* aliens.

The incidence of obesity among people with disabilities, including cognitive disabilities, is 69% higher than among those without disabilities. People often assume that if someone is overweight, they have a cognitive disability. The other negative assumptions about obesity such as laziness, gluttony, or lack of self-discipline, increase the stigma toward those who are both cognitively disabled and significantly overweight. *Star Trek* reflection of the current stigma associated with body shape may have inadvertently perpetuated negative stereotypes regarding the emphasis on a slender physique rather than a healthy lifestyle and physical fitness.

Even without jumping to the conclusion that a person is intellectually inferior, Humans don't always accept the appearance of aliens who are less humanoid than their shipmates. For example, in "Manhunt" (1989, TNG; 2:19), Commander Riker asks Wesley Crusher about aliens who appear more fishlike than humanoid.

RIKER: So what did you think of the Antedeans, Wesley?

WESLEY: They are rather strange-looking, Commander.

DATA: Judging a being by its physical appearance is the last major human prejudice, Wesley.

PICARD: Your point is well taken, Mr. Data. I'm sure that to the Antedeans, we are equally unattractive.

INCOMING MESSAGE:

One shouldn't judge another by their appearance.

Riker's question to Wesley sets up the situation and Data should be scolding Number One rather than the boy. Appearance, separate from weight, can be a source of stigma and prejudice.

In "Sanctuary" (1993, DS9; 2:10), a group of alien refugees called the Skrreeans arrive at Deep Space Nine believing that Bajor is their *Kentanna*, a planet they were destined to re-settle. Quark reveals his own prejudicial opinion of the aliens based on their appearance.

QUARK: Oh, come on, Odo. You know these Skrreeans are nothing but trouble. They're all over the station, looking and touching, never buying anything. And they flake.

ODO: I didn't notice.

QUARK: Come to my place. You'll see little pieces of Skrreean skin all over the bar and the floor. It's disgusting.

ODO: They won't be here long.

QUARK: I hope not. They're driving my paying customers away. If they stay here too long I'll be out of business.

INCOMING MESSAGE:

Skin conditions are highly stigmatized (even by Ferengi with big ears.)

Apparently it is well known that Humans judge others by their appearance. Balok looks like a young child in "Corbomite Maneuver" (1966, TOS; 1:11) so he uses a puppet to project a menacing appearance to Captain Kirk.

KIRK: Commander, that puppet.
BALOK: My alter ego, so to speak. In your culture, he would be Mr. Hyde to my Jekyll. You must admit he's effective. You would never have been frightened by me. And I thought my distress signal quite clever. It was a pleasure testing you.

Disabilities or medical conditions that affect an individual's appearance will generally also affect their body image. For Humans, body image influences not only social relationships, but also psychological characteristics, behavior, and perceptions of the world. Nowhere is this point more vibrant than in "Lifesigns" (1996, VOY; 2:19).

The Voyager crew rescues a dying Vidiian physician, Dr. Denara Pel, who is returning from Fina Prime after treating an outbreak of the phage. In order to save her life, The Doctor puts her body in stasis, but interacts with her mind through a holographic interface resembling what Dr. Pel would look like if she were healthy.

THE DOCTOR: It's quite simple, really. I used the undamaged chromosomes in your cerebellum to recreate your original DNA code, and then programmed the computer to project a holographic template based on that genome.

INCOMING MESSAGE:
Our DNA determines our appearance.

Since Pel is also a physician, The Doctor believes she can assist him in treating her condition. He begins by taking her medical history.

PEL: I was first diagnosed with the phage when I was seven.
THE DOCTOR: And when did you begin receiving replacement tissue?
PEL: About that same time. At first, it was hard to get used to the changes, but it happened so often that after a while I, I almost stopped noticing. I never, I never

thought I'd see myself again. Thank you. This is the most extraordinary thing anyone has ever done for me.

[Scenes and Dialogue Omitted]

PEL: I guess I'm just not used to so much attention. Where I come from, when you're as sick as I am, people, healthy people stay away from you. I guess I forgot for a second that I don't look like that anymore. [She indicates her physical body on the bio-bed.]

After Pel and The Doctor spend a little leisure time on the holodeck, The Doctor confesses to The Doctor's assistant, Kes, about his romantic attraction to his patient (violating the ethics of nonmaleficence and fidelity.) When Kes talks to Pel about The Doctor's attraction, Pel has difficulty.

KES: One thing you're not very good at is accepting a compliment. The next time someone has something nice to say about you, maybe you should just take them at their word and feel good about yourself.

PEL: It's not easy to feel good about yourself when you're used to living your life like that. [Again, she indicates her physical body.]

INCOMING MESSAGE:
People with scars or other disfiguring conditions may have trouble accepting
that someone can be attracted to them.
People tend to judge themselves based on how they think others see them.

Pel attempts to kill her physical body by injecting herself with nytoxinol. Fearing an attempted murder, The Doctor is about to call security when Pel admits she poisoned herself because she does not want to be returned to her diseased body. Pel tries to explain to The Doctor how isolating her life is due to the ravages of the phage.

PEL: What it's like to be a nine-year-old child, and suddenly your best friend doesn't want to come to your house anymore. And when you ask your mother why, why won't Mala come and play with me anymore? And she tells you it's because, it's because the other children are afraid of you. Listen to me. Before I met you, I was just a disease. But now, everything's different. When people look at me, they don't see a disease anymore. They see a woman. A woman you made. A woman you love. A woman you're not afraid to touch.

THE DOCTOR: Denara, I was never afraid to touch you.

PEL: Why? Because you're a doctor?

THE DOCTOR: Because I love you.

PEL: You say that now. But if I go through with the transfer...

THE DOCTOR: If you go through with the transfer.

PEL: I will be sick again, and ugly.

THE DOCTOR: Denara, you're not ugly. You're simply ill.

PEL: Oh, please. Stop patronizing me! I know how people see me.

THE DOCTOR: Denara, do you think if you go back into your own body, I'll feel different about you?

PEL: Won't you?

THE DOCTOR: Listen to me. Nothing could ever change the way I feel about you. Not a few scars, not some diseased skin. Nothing.

PEL: You have given me the most extraordinary gift that anyone has ever given me. You, you brought me to this ship where no one is sick and people are friendly. You've made me healthy and beautiful. I don't want to go back to the way things were.

THE DOCTOR: You said before you knew me that you were just a disease. Well, before you, I was just a projection of photons held together by force fields. A computerized physician doing a job, doing it exceptionally well, of course, but still it was just a profession, not a life. But now that you are here and my programming has adapted, I'm not just working anymore. I'm living, learning what it means to be with someone, to love someone. I don't think I can go back to the way things were, either. Denara, please; don't die.

In the end, Dr. Pel is reintegrated into her body and she meets The Doctor on the holodeck, where he touches her diseased skin gently, with love.

INCOMING MESSAGE:

People can sense when others look at them with judgment.
You should never be afraid to touch or hug a person with a disability.

"Lifesigns" conveys powerful messages about the need to look beyond physical appearance in order to end prejudice against people who look different.

Physical appearances are also important to the two different depictions of Captain Pike. In "The Menagerie" (1966, TOS; 1:12 and 1:13) Pike had facial burns in addition to using a wheelchair and communication device. The physical appearance of Pike at Spock's court-martial added to his disabled appearance, while hiding the fact that a different actor was used in the court-martial scenes than in "The Cage" (TOS; The Original Pilot) scenes. Pike (1966) clearly couldn't captain a starship. However, at the end of "Star Trek" (2009), Pike appears in a wheelchair, but the chair is minimalistic by comparison, and he has no facial disfigurement. In other words, Pike doesn't look as disabled. Indeed, Pike is given command of the Enterprise back in "Star Trek Into Darkness" (2013) after Kirk violates the Prime Directive. Well, some things didn't change in the reboot.

Physical differences can bother actors as well as characters. James Montgomery Doohan played Montgomery "Scotty" Scott on *Star Trek*. Mr. Doohan served in the Royal Canadian Artillery during World War II and was hit by six rounds, one of which resulted in the amputation of his middle finger on the right hand. According to Doohan's autobiography, "Beam Me Up Scotty" he became adept at hiding his injured hand to the point even directors didn't realize he was missing the digit. Due to his skill at compensating for his missing finger, his right hand can only be spotted in a few *Star Trek* episodes, and only if you know exactly when and where to look.

INCOMING MESSAGE:

Even war heroes are expected to have perfect bodies.

Reducing stigma that results from individual differences is one of the many positive messages on *Star Trek*. At the same time, the actors on *Star Trek* are often victims of our society's obsession with *the body beautiful*. Episodes such as "Lifesigns" depict the Vulcan ideal of, "Infinite Diversity in Infinite Combinations."

While physical fitness is by definition healthy, attempts to have a model thin body is not. It is my desire that *Star Trek* fans, including fans with disabilities, are comfortable with the diversity of their body shapes and sizes.

Chapter 12
"Live Long and Prosper"

KIRK: How we deal with death is at least as important as how we deal with life.
"Star Trek II: The Wrath of Khan" (1982)

Aging, Quality of Life, and Suicide

Aging

Since people with disabilities have, on average, shorter life spans than others, it is relevant to explore the *Star Trek* messages about aging and death. Included in this discussion will be two related topics: quality of life and suicide. Quality of life is relevant to both topics because with aging and impairments a question arises as to where the line can be drawn between living and simply prolonging existence. Suicide, and especially physician-assisted suicide, is a possible escape from an existence riddled with pain and suffering. There are multiple attempts on *Star Trek* to avoid aging or extend life span; however, they have a one hundred percent failure rate. Yet on *Star Trek*, even death isn't without its funnier moments.

Manmade attempts to prolong life have met with disaster such as in "Miri" (1966, TOS; 1:9) when an experiment goes wrong and results in the rapid death of people after they become mature adults.

In "The Deadly Years" (1967, TOS; 2:12) a passing comet puts an aging whammy on the Gamma Hydra Four colony.

KIRK: Captain's log, stardate 3478.2. On a routine mission to re-supply the experimental colony at Gamma Hydra Four, we discovered a most unusual phenomenon. Of the six members of the colony, none of whom were over thirty, we found four had died and two were dying of old age.

The landing party suffers a host of infirmities associated with growing old.

KIRK: Captain's log, stardate 3579.4. The Enterprise personnel who beamed down to the planet's surface, Dr. McCoy, Engineer Scott, Mr. Spock, Lieutenant Galway, and myself are all showing definite signs of aging. Only Ensign Chekov appears to be normal.

In expedient *Star Trek* style, stereotypical aliments of age are reported by the crew.

Hearing

GALWAY: I know this is going to sound foolish, but I seem to be having a little trouble hearing.
McCoy: It's probably nothing important.
GALWAY: I never had trouble before.

Mental abilities

SPOCK: [Looking about the same as usual] Based on what Dr. McCoy gave me, I estimate that physically we each have less than a week to live. Also, since our mental faculties are aging faster than our bodies, we will be little better than mental vegetables in considerably lesser time.
KIRK: Total senility?
SPOCK: Yes, Captain. In a very short time.

Eyesight, Concentration, and Body Temperature Regulation

SPOCK [Sitting up]: I must differ with you, Doctor. I'm having difficulty concentrating, which is most disturbing, my eyesight appears to be failing, and the normal temperature of the ship seems to me to be increasingly cold.

Changes In Physical Appearance

KIRK: Bones, I believe you're getting gray.

Arthritis

MCCOY: What's your problem, Jim?
KIRK: Shoulder. Just a twinge. Probably muscular strain.
[Dialogue omitted]
[McCoy scans Kirk's arm, then takes hold of a finger. Kirk pulls back in pain.]
MCCOY: Jim, I think we'd better run a complete physical on you.
KIRK: Why? Just muscular strain, isn't it?
MCCOY: No, Jim. It's advanced arthritis, and it's spreading.
KIRK: That's impossible.

Kirk's physical and mental decline becomes so pervasive that Commodore Stocker holds a hearing to determine whether the captain is fit for duty. The hearing illustrates one of the most dreaded aspects of aging: being viewed as less than capable.

SPOCK: Your inability to remember having given commands, reading and signing important orders and then forgetting them, your physical analysis as compiled by our own chief surgeon. All these things would appear to be irrefutable proof of failing physical and mental conditions.
KIRK: So I'm a little confused. Who wouldn't be at a time like this? My ship's in trouble, my senior officers are ill. And this nonsense about a competency hearing is enough to mix up any man. Trying to relieve a captain of his command is, well—that's—that's—Spock, I wouldn't have believed it of you. Go ahead.

Ask me questions. I'll show you what I'm capable of. There's nothing wrong with my memory. Go ahead! Ask me anything! We're in orbit around Gamma Hydra Two, right? Anyhow, it doesn't matter. There's a lot more to running a starship than answering a lot of fool questions. A lot more. Go ahead. Ask me questions.

In the nick of time, Bones discovers the treatment. And in the nick of time Kirk takes his rightful place in the captain's chair. And in the nick of time the Enterprise is saved from attacks by the Romulans, using Kirk's "Corbomite Maneuver" again. Timing is everything in the Neutral Zone.

Fountains of Youth

In "The Omega Glory" (1968, TOS; 2:23) Captain Tracey violates more Starfleet regulations than a member of the Maquis when he finds himself on a planet where people live long, healthy lives.

TRACEY: ...No native to this planet has ever had any trace of any kind of disease. How long would a man live if all disease were erased, Jim? Wu. [Wu enters.] Tell Captain Kirk your age.

WU: Age? I have seen forty-two years of the red bird. My eldest brother—

TRACEY: Their year of the red bird comes once every eleven years, which he's seen forty-two times. Multiply it. Wu is four hundred and sixty two years old. His father is well over a thousand. Interested, Jim?

KIRK: McCoy could verify all that.

TRACEY: He will if you order it. We must have a doctor researching this. Are you grasping all it means? This immunizing agent here, once we've found it, is a fountain of youth. Virtual immortality, or as much as any man will ever want.

INCOMING MESSAGE:
People want to live for hundreds of years.

In genuine Star Trek irony, the planet is not a fountain of youth. People on the planet live longer because it's natural for them to have long lives. A person's life span is strongly linked to their genetics. And there's more *Star Trek* irony the following season in "The

Mark of Gideon" (1969, TOS; 3:16), where it's the lack of disease which leads to overpopulation, suffering, and the kidnapping of Captain Kirk.

> KIRK: Your report to the Federation was a tissue of lies. You described environmental, physical, cultural conditions that would make Gideon a paradise.
>
> HODIN: And so it was! A long, long time ago what we described was true! The atmosphere on Gideon has always been germfree. And the people flourished in their physical and spiritual perfection. Eventually, even the life span increased. Death became almost unknown to us. It occurred only when the body could no longer regenerate itself, and that happens now only to the very old.
>
> KIRK: Those are conditions most people would envy.
>
> HODIN: But Gideon did not find it enviable. The birth rate continued to rise, and the population grew, until now Gideon is encased in a living mass who can find no rest, no peace, no joy.

For reasons not explained in the episode, death by disease introduced through Kirk's blood doesn't violate the sanctity of life that prevents the people on Gideon from practicing birth control. Eye of the beholder and all that I guess.

In "Star Trek: Insurrection" (1998) another fountain-of-youth planet is discovered along with another customary madman. Gal'na of the Son'a dupes Starfleet's Admiral Matthew Dougherty into attempting to relocate the colony of about six hundred Ba'ku. Data discovers their plan and a battle of wits and wills ensues. Picard and the rest of the magnificent seven attempt to hide the Ba'ku from the Son'a and prevent the madmen from stealing the paradise.

Worf is the first of the Enterprise crew to experience the planet's rejuvenating powers. Unfortunately, this comes in the form of a glowing Klingon-sized zit called a Gorch. One of the problems with those fountains of youth is that you don't always get to pick and choose which aspects of youth are regenerated. At least Picard's mambo dancing in his quarters isn't seen by the rest of the crew, but it does get him thinking. He beams down to the Ba'ku village and visits the leaders, Sojef and Anij.

> [Picard knocks on a door and Anij opens it.]
> PICARD: How old are you?

[Inside the home, Sojef, Anij and two young Ba'ku, Artim and Tournel, are sitting in a large room.]

SOJEF: We came here from a solar system on the verge of self-annihilation—where technology had created weapons that threatened to destroy all life. A small group of us set off to find a new home—a home that would be isolated from the threats of other worlds—that was three hundred and nine years ago.

PICARD: And you haven't aged a day since then?

SOJEF: Actually, I was a good deal older when we arrived—in terms of my physical condition.

ANIJ: There's an unusual metaphasic radiation coming from the planet's rings. It continuously regenerates our genetic structure. You must have noticed the effects by now. [Artim offers Picard a mug.]

PICARD: We've just begun to— [To Atrim] I suppose you're seventy-five.

ARTIM: No. I'm twelve.

TOURNEL: The metaphasic radiation won't begin to affect him until he reaches maturity.

PICARD: To most offlanders, what you have here would be more valuable than—gold-pressed latinum—I'm afraid that's the reason that someone may be trying to take your world away from you.

INCOMING MESSAGE:

People don't want to physically deteriorate as they age.

The movie provides some insights into what it would be like if our life spans were longer, while at the same time commenting that a longer life with physical deterioration isn't desirable.

[Picard pauses to inspect some beautifully handcrafted quilts.]

PICARD: Apprenticing for thirty years—[They keep walking.]—Did your people's mental discipline develop here?

ANIJ: More questions. Always the explorer—If you stay long enough that'll change.

PICARD: Will it?

ANIJ: You stop reviewing what happened yesterday—stop planning for tomorrow—Let me ask you a question—Have you ever experienced a perfect moment in time?

PICARD: A perfect moment?

ANIJ: When time seemed to stop—and you could almost live in that moment.

INCOMING MESSAGE:
With age comes wisdom.

Picard confronts the Admiral about the immorality of his behavior-attempting to relocate the Ba'Ku without their knowledge or consent. Then, the dashing Captain Picard becomes even more dashing as he dons civilian clothes and goes down to the shuttle bay where he's met by most of the senior staff—who also happen to be wearing civilian clothes.

DATA: I feel obliged to point out that the environmental anomalies may have stimulated certain rebellious instincts common to youth which could affect everyone's judgment—Except mine, of course.

CRUSHER: Okay, Data, what do you think we should do?

DATA: Saddle up. Lock and load.

In addition to the youthful impulsiveness that some of the crew is experiencing, Troi and Crusher also noticed physical changes in their bodies.

TROI: And have you noticed how your boobs have started to firm up?

CRUSHER: Not that we care about such things in this day and age.

TROI: Uh huh.

INCOMING MESSAGE:
Even in the future, Human bodies will succumb to effects of gravity.

Other effects on the crew include Geordi's eyes regenerating to the point where he is able to see without his implants. Riker and Troi become frisky with each other.

Data converses with Artim about what it's like to be a child, and metaphorically, about being young.

DATA: Perhaps it would surprise you to know that I have often tried to imagine what it would be like to be a child.

ARTIM: Really?

DATA: Really.

ARTIM: For one thing, your legs are shorter than everyone else's.

DATA: But they are in a constant state of growth. Do you find it difficult to adapt?

ARTIM: Adapt?

DATA: A child's specifications are never the same from one moment to the next. It is a wonder that you do not—trip over your own feet.

ARTIM: Sometimes I do.

DATA: My legs are exactly eighty-seven point two centimeters in length. They were eighty-seven point two centimeters the day I was created. They will be eighty-seven point two centimeters the day I go off line. My operation depends on specifications that do not change. I will never know the experience of—growing up or—tripping over my own feet.

ARTIM: But you've never had adults telling you what to do all the time—or bedtimes—or having to eat food you don't like.

DATA: I would gladly accept the requirement of a bedtime in exchange for knowing what it is like to be a child.

ARTIM: Do machines ever play?

DATA: Yes, I play the violin—and my chess routines are quite advanced.

ARTIM: No, I mean, have you ever just played—for fun?

DATA: Androids do not have fun.

ARTIM: Look, if you want know what it's like to be a child, you need to learn to play.

INCOMING MESSAGE:
People should put aside time every day to play in order to keep feeling young.

"Star Trek: Insurrection" provides a commentary on how long life could be enjoyed if Humans remained physically healthy. The movie is a contrast to the episode "The Deadly Years," which portrays the current disadvantages of prolonged life spans without correcting the problems of physical decline associated with age. Dr. Pulaski also encounters declines as she ages rapidly in "Unnatural Selection" (1989, TNG; 2:7). Long life isn't always enjoyable, especially for people with serious medical conditions or disabilities. Quality of life is important to everyone.

Captain Dunsel and Quality of Life

One philosophical question that *Star Trek* poses but does not answer is *What kind of life is worth living?* This question often arises when someone acquires a disability at birth, through injury, or as part of a chronic illness. It's too easy to conclude *I wouldn't want to live like that* in reference to another person's situation. Indeed, the term *quality of life* is not well defined. For some people, it means maximizing independence. For others, it refers to continuing to live even though there may be significant dependence on others for care. For still others, quality of life is part of the meaning of death. It's impossible to know which aspects provide meaning to another person's life.

The first original series pilot began with this question. And even before the Talosians capture Captain Pike and put him in "The Cage" he ponders his life choices with the ship's physician, Dr. Boyce:

> PIKE: The point is this isn't the only life available. There's a whole galaxy of things to choose from.
> BOYCE: Not for you. A man either lives life as it happens to him, meets it head-on, and licks it, or he turns his back on it and starts to wither away.
> PIKE: Now you're beginning to talk like a doctor, bartender.
> BOYCE: Take your choice. We both get the same two kinds of customers. The living and the dying.

INCOMING MESSAGE:
Living a life that isn't fulfilling is as bad as being dead.

Eventually, the Talosians get a clue and realize that death isn't the worst thing for Humans to experience.

MAGISTRATE: We had not believed this possible. The customs and history of your race show a unique hatred of captivity. Even when it's pleasant and benevolent, you prefer death. This makes you too violent and dangerous a species for our needs.

INCOMING MESSAGE:
There are things which cause more suffering than death.

In "The Ultimate Computer" (1968, TOS; 2:24), the Enterprise is ordered by another annoying Wesley, Commodore Wesley, to participate in scientific experiments with the famous Dr. Daystrom. During the first practice exercise, the M-5 computer demonstrates it can do the work of an entire crew, including the captain.

WESLEY [On viewscreen.]: Our compliments to the M-5 unit, and regards to Captain Dunsel. Wesley out.
McCOY: Dunsel? Who the blazes is Captain Dunsel? What does it mean, Jim? [Kirk leaves the bridge.] Spock? What does it mean?
SPOCK: Dunsel, Doctor, it is a term used by midshipmen at Starfleet Academy. It refers to a part which serves no useful purpose.

INCOMING MESSSAGE:
When a person is no longer valued for their knowledge and skills,
they can feel a diminished quality of life.
McCoy must have been absent from Starfleet Academy
the day Captain Dunsel was discussed.

Later, it becomes clear that Dr. Daystrom built the M-5 in an effort to prevent himself from becoming Dr. Dunsel.

KIRK: Genius is an understatement. At the age of twenty-four, he made the duotronic breakthrough that won him the Nobel and Zee-Magnees prizes.

McCOY: In his early twenties, Jim. That's over a quarter of a century ago.

KIRK: Isn't that enough for one lifetime?

McCOY: Maybe that's the trouble. Where do you go from up? You publish articles. You give lectures. Then spend your life trying to recapture past glory.

INCOMING MESSAGE:

Quality of life depends on continued challenges and achievements.

Captain Kirk begins to see the catastrophe on the horizon when M-5 goes out of its way to destroy an ore ship. The threat is no longer about Kirk's job when M-5 fires on the Lexington and destroys the Excalibur, killing all crewmembers on board. As Dr. Daystrom talks to M-5 in an effort to prevent the computer from destroying the other five ships, he has trouble separating himself from his creation.

DAYSTROM: We will survive. Nothing can hurt you. I gave you that. You are great. I am great. Twenty years of groping to prove the things I'd done before were not accidents. Seminars and lectures to rows of fools who couldn't begin to understand my systems. Colleagues. Colleagues laughing behind my back at the boy wonder and becoming famous building on my work. Building on my work.

INCOMING MESSAGE:

It is important to treat others with respect.

The philosophical question also appears on the big screen in "Star Trek: The Motion Picture" (1979):

SPOCK: No, Captain, not for us... for V'Ger—I weep for V'Ger, as I would for a brother. As I was when I came aboard, so is V'Ger now, empty, incomplete—searching. Logic and knowledge are not enough.

McCOY: Spock, are you saying that you've found what you needed, but V'Ger hasn't?

DECKER: What would V'Ger need to fulfill itself?

SPOCK: Each of us, at some time in our life, turns to someone, a father, a brother, a god and asks 'Why am I here?' 'What was I meant to be?'. V'Ger hopes to touch its Creator to find its answers.

KIRK: 'Is this all that I am? Is there nothing more?'

Being Useful

Picard also understands the importance of having a purpose and being valued for one's contribution. When Captain Montgomery Scott is rescued in "Relics" (1992, TNG; 6:4), Picard enlists the assistance of his own chief of engineering Geordi La Forge to help Scotty feel useful.

PICARD: Mr. La Forge, I understand that before the Jenolan crashed, it had conducted an extensive survey of the Dyson sphere. Have we been able to access any of those records?

LA FORGE: We did try to download their memory core, but it was pretty heavily damaged in the crash. We actually haven't been able to get much out of it.

PICARD: Perhaps Captain Scott could be of use in accessing that material.

LA FORGE: It's possible. He does know those systems better than any of us. I'll have Lt. Bartel beam down with him.

PICARD: Mr. La Forge, I would like you to accompany Captain Scott.

LA FORGE: Me, sir?

PICARD: Yes. Look, this is not an order, it's a request and it's one which you must feel perfectly free to decline. You see, one of the most important things in a person's life is to feel useful. Now, Mr. Scott is a Starfleet officer and I would like him to feel useful again.

LA FORGE: I'll go with him, sir.

PICARD: Thank you.

INCOMING MESSAGE:

Being able to use the knowledge one has acquired
increases a person's quality of life.

Scotty initially has trouble fitting into this stardate, seventy-five years past the one he left. But when Scotty and La Forge must rescue the Enterprise, the crisis restores Scotty's sense of being a miracle worker. The experience causes him to delay his retirement and he sets off in a shuttlecraft loaned to him by Picard.

INCOMING MESSAGE:

Purpose and meaning of life are important to the quality of life.

One of the touching moments in "Star Trek: The Wrath of Khan" (1982) is when Bones gives Kirk a pair of glasses for his birthday. Then they argue, in typical fashion, about growing older.

MCCOY: What the hell do you want? This is not about age—and you know it. This is about you flying a goddamn computer console when you wanna be out there hopping galaxies.

KIRK: Spare me your notions of poetry, please. We all have our assigned duties.

MCCOY: Bull. You're hiding—hiding behind rules and regulations.

KIRK: Who am I hiding from?

MCCOY: From yourself, Admiral!

KIRK: Don't mince words, Bones. What do you really think?

MCCOY: Jim, I'm your doctor and I'm your friend. Get back your command. Get it back before you turn into part of this collection. Before you really do grow old.

INCOMING MESSAGE:

Pursuing enjoyable activities, at any age,
is part of a person's of quality of life.

Quality of life issues become increasingly important to adults as we approach retirement age. Some people never retire. Others look forward to increased time for activities that were put on the back burner when much of the day was spent working and raising families. People with disabilities who have never been employed will experience different quality of life concerns, such losing their primary caregivers. Those with recently acquired chronic medical conditions may become focused on finding a cure or treatment.

In "Too Short A Season" (1988, TNG; 1:15) Picard's assignment is to transport Admiral Jameson to Mordan Four to negotiate with Karnas. Admiral Mark Jameson is eighty-five years old and looks frail when he arrives on the Enterprise with Annie, his wife. Jameson has a medical condition, which limits his ability to walk, so he uses a wheelchair. That is, until he miraculously gets out of the wheelchair and takes the captain's chair on the bridge. Picard consults with Dr. Crusher about Jameson's health.

> CRUSHER: Captain, no one recovers from Iverson's Disease. There is no known cure, and there are no cases where it has gone into remission. I have never heard of any therapy that would produce results like that.
>
> PICARD: Then how do you account for it?
>
> CRUSHER: I can't. All I can tell you is that the Admiral has been confined [*sic*] to his support chair for the last four years by the effects of Iverson's. By all the medical facts we know, he should never have walked again.
>
> PICARD: I want you to look into it, Doctor. Thoroughly.
>
> CRUSHER: Yes, sir.

As I have previously pointed out, no one is "confined to" a wheelchair unless in the 24th century they use confinement beams rather than safety belts.

RED ALERT!
No rehabilitation counselor consulted
on the script for this episode.

After Jameson keels over in his quarters, Dr. Crusher is given the opportunity to solve the medical mystery of why Jameson seems to be aging backwards. The good doctor finds traces of an alien compound which she can't identify. Picard demands answers from the now baby-faced Admiral.

> JAMESON: There's a planet in the Cerebus system, Cerebus Two. They say the natives have a process that rejuvenates the body, gives you your youth back.

PICARD: Yes, I've heard of that story. It's a myth.

JAMESON: It's true, Picard. I'm living proof. Oh, it's dangerous. The mortality rate is high, and it's very painful. Aliens are seldom allowed to obtain the process, but I managed it. I negotiated a treaty for Cerebus Two some years ago, and they felt obligated to honor my request for the process.

PICARD: Obviously it works very rapidly, but how does it work?

JAMESON: The herb and drug combinations are self-administered slowly over a period of two years. Every response is different, depending on a being's DNA. I got enough for both of us, Annie, but I had to test it on myself first. I couldn't risk you. If I died, well, I was half a man, so what did it matter.

Jameson accurately depicts the mindset of someone willing to risk their life in hopes of finding a cure for their condition. In traditional Star Trek irony, Jameson's cure kills him.

It's not uncommon when people in their final years begin to contemplate death, they may seek to deal with unresolved issues in their lives. Just as Admiral Jameson tries to atone for violating the Prime Directive, the Cardassian file clerk Aamin Marritza attempts to right a wrong from his past in "Duet" (1993, DS9; 1:18) by pretending to be Gul Darhe'el, the labor camp commander known as the Butcher of Gallitep.

KIRA: The Butcher of Gallitep died six years ago. You're Aamin Marritza, his filing clerk.

MARRITZA: That's not true. I am alive. I'll always be alive. It's Marritza who's dead. Marritza, who was only good for cowering under his bunk and weeping like a woman. Who, every night, covered his ears because he couldn't bear to hear the screaming for mercy of the Bajorans.

[He breaks down in tears]

MARRITZA: I covered my ears every night. I couldn't bear to hear those horrible screams. You have no idea what it's like to be a coward, to see these horrors and do nothing. Marritza's dead. He deserves to be dead.

[Dialogue omitted]

KIRA: You didn't commit those crimes, and you couldn't stop them. You were only one man.

MARRITZA: No, don't you see? I have to be punished. We all have to be punished. Major, you have to go out and tell them I'm Gul Darhe'el. It's the only way.

KIRA: Why are you doing this?

MARRITZA: For Cardassia. Cardassia will only survive if it stands in front of Bajor and admits the truth. My trial will force Cardassia to acknowledge its guilt. And we're guilty, all of us. My death is necessary.

KIRA: What you're asking for is another murder. Enough good people have already died. I won't help kill another.

INCOMING MESSAGE:
When a person feels their life has lacked meaning,
they may try to find meaning in their death.

Marritza, like Jameson, believes that atoning for previous wrongs will give his life more meaning. While most people don't need to atone for having violated the Prime Directive or being a file clerk at a forced labor camp, many people at the end of their lives will seek to make up with estranged family and friends, or right perceived wrongs.

Finishing A Life's Work

In "Sarek" (1990, TNG; 3:23), the Enterprise has the honor of hosting the first meeting between the Federation and the mysterious aliens known as the Legarans. In spite of his two hundred and two years of age, Ambassador Sarek is the principal negotiator for this historic meeting which he's been working on for only ninety-three years. But Sarek has an age-related disorder that he isn't even aware of, which is causing havoc on the ship.

CRUSHER: There's a very rare condition that sometimes affects Vulcans over the age of two hundred. Bendii syndrome. Its early symptoms include sudden bursts of emotion, mostly irrational anger. Eventually, all emotional control is lost.

PICARD: I can imagine nothing that would be more offensive to a Vulcan. Their emotional detachment is the very core of their being. How would this affect others on board the ship?

TROI: Vulcans possess telepathic ability. Sarek may unintentionally be projecting intense emotions onto other people, at random.

The senior officers conclude that Sarek, with his Bendii syndrome, is the cause of the random emotional and violent outbreaks aboard the Enterprise. At the same time, they are faced with what to do about the Legaran diplomatic mission.

DATA: Sakkath has been able, until recently, to use his telepathic skills to reinforce Sarek's emotional control, thus protecting others from the effects of his deterioration.

RIKER: He hasn't been doing a very good job.

DATA: The strain of this mission on Sarek has made it impossible.

PICARD: It's ironic, isn't it? All this magnificent technology and we find ourselves still susceptible to the ravages of old age. The loss of dignity, the slow betrayal of our bodies by forces we cannot master. Do you still want to be one of us, Data?

DATA: Sir, it is conceivable, even for me, that time will eventually lead to irreparable circuit failure. But there is one thing I do not understand. Sarek is a logical, intelligent being. The effects of Bendii syndrome are apparent. Why would such a man choose to ignore them?

PICARD: Logic fails us sometimes, Data. I think this is one of those times. I can only guess that he does not see, or he does not wish to see, the truth. And he is being insulated against that truth by those who love him most.

INCOMING MESSAGE:

It's important to be honest with those who are impaired about the nature of their impairments.

The sentiments described by Captain Picard are pertinent to a discussion regarding quality of life. While advanced directives are generally created regarding prolonging life by artificial means, people should talk with their loved ones about the role of honesty as someone loses insight or emotional control. While someone may actually choose ignorance over truth, it should be a matter of choice.

Picard and Sarek mind meld in order to provide Sarek with the emotional control he needs to conclude the negotiations and sign the treaty with the Legarans. Unfortunately, the emotional strength given by Picard to Sarek has no equivalent in our current catalog of assistive technology even though Alzheimer's disease bears similarities to Bendii syndrome.

Chronic Pain

In "Star Trek V: The Final Frontier" (1989), the crew of the Enterprise-A is hijacked by Mr. Spock's long-lost half-brother, Sybok. The robed and bearded Vulcan guru is searching for God—much to the embarrassment of *Star Trek* fans everywhere. Sybok has a Vulcan-style superpower which reveals and heals a person's innermost psychic pain. At the same time, his mind melds subvert the will of the other person. Although Spock and Kirk are apparently immune, Sybok takes McCoy back to the death of McCoy's father.

MCCOY 'S FATHER: Leonard.

MCCOY: I'm here, Dad. I'm with you, Dad.

MCCOY 'S FATHER: The pain—stop the pain.

MCCOY: I've done everything I can do. You've got to hang on.

MCCOY 'S FATHER: I can't stand the pain—Help me.

MCCOY: All my knowledge and I can't save him.

SYBOK: You've done all you can. The support system will keep him alive.

MCCOY: You call this alive?

MCCOY 'S FATHER: Son—release me.

MCCOY: I can't do that, Dad—But how can I watch him suffer like this?

SYBOK: You're a doctor.

MCCOY: I'm his son!

[McCoy turns off the life-support.]

SYBOK: Why did you do it?

MCCOY: To preserve his dignity.

SYBOK: That wasn't the worst of it was it?

MCCOY: No.

SYBOK: Was it? Share it.

MCCOY: Not long after—they found a cure. A goddamn cure!

SYBOK: If you hadn't killed him, he might have lived.

MCCOY: No! I loved my father. I released him!

SYBOK: Then you did what you thought was right.

MCCOY: Yes! No!

INCOMING MESSAGE:

Prolonging suffering is not the same thing as being alive.

McCoy's psychological distress negatively impacts his quality of life—just as his father's chronic physical pain diminished McCoy Senior's quality of life. While physical pain can be abated to some degree by medications, the side effects from medication can be nearly as undesirable as the pain experience. Every person has their own pain threshold, and it is impossible for anyone to judge for another person how much pain is too much.

There may be times when a person might feel death is preferable to a life that isn't worth living. These feelings may be the result of depression, but they could also result from a realistic evaluation of the available options. The issue becomes whether a person should be allowed to end their own life and have medical assistance in doing so. These dilemmas are examined in several episodes on *Star Trek*.

The Final Frontier: Suicide and Death with Dignity

Cultural differences surrounding death and suicide have been explored in more episodes than I can cover in this chapter. There are multiple episode just dealing with the Klingons' sense of honorable death and *Sto-Vo-Kor*, the Klingon afterlife for the honored dead. In "Ethics" (1992, TNG; 5:16), Worf asks Riker to assist him with performing the *Hegh'bat* ceremony because Worf believes it's more honorable to die than to live as a Klingon with a disability. Later, on *Star Trek: Deep Space Nine* in "The Sons of Mogh" (1996, DS9; 4:14), it's Worf who is asked by his brother, Kurn, to perform a *Mauk-to'Vor* ritual so that Kurn can restore his honor in death and attain a place in *Sto-Vo-Kor*. In "Sleeping Dogs" (2002, ENT; 1:13) T'Pol provides new meaning to the expression *no good deed goes unpunished*.

T'POL: They don't want our help.

HOSHI: How do you know?

T'POL: They're Klingons. To die at their post assures them a path to the afterlife. If we rescue them, they'd be dishonored.

REED: Well, I for one don't intend to just fly off and let these people die, honorable deaths or not.

T'POL: Your compassion is admirable, but misguided. If they awake and find us on their ship, they'll kill us.

INCOMING MESSAGE:
When dealing with death,
it's important to consider the person's culture.

While it may be easy to scoff at the obsession Klingons have with honorable death, it's because that warrior culture is alien to many Humans. Indeed, respect for other cultures may be the most difficult for people to accept when the differences entail death and suicide.

Perhaps the best example of culture clashes surrounding death is seen in "Half a Life" (1991, TNG; 4:22). Lwaxana Troi falls in love with Timicin, a visiting scientist on board the Enterprise. Her sense of cultural sensitivity is overpowered by her libido and her ambassador-style respect for the customs of others is jettisoned when she learns that Timicin is about to commit suicide because he has reached the ripe old age of sixty years. She confronts Picard with her new knowledge.

[Lwaxana enters the Ready Room.]

LWAXANA: Are you aware these people you are so graciously helping are murderers?

PICARD: I beg your pardon?

LWAXANA: Well the next thing to it. When a person on this benighted little planet reaches the age of sixty, which Timicin is about to do, they're expected to simply kill themselves. Did you know that?

PICARD: Mr. Data?

DATA: The people of Kaelon Two are isolationists, almost to the point of being xenophobes. Regrettably, we know very little about their customs.

LWAXANA: Well, I know. Timicin himself just told me. He is supposed to go down there, to his loving friends, be wined, dined, honored for his achievements and then kill himself. It's a barbaric ritual. The Resolution, it's called. Obviously, you can't let him go, Jean-Luc.

PICARD: I'm afraid I have no choice.

LWAXANA: I don't think you've been listening to me. The man is supposed to kill himself. You don't just let that happen. You don't just turn your back. What's the matter with you!

PICARD: Lwaxana, I'm sorry, but whatever my personal feelings, I have no jurisdiction here. I simply cannot interfere.

LWAXANA: But you have to. In a situation like this, you absolutely have to interfere. You've got to go down there and talk to those people, Jean Luc. Open their eyes, educate them.

PICARD: The Prime Directive forbids us to interfere with the social order of any planet.

LWAXANA: Well, that's your Prime Directive, not mine! [Lwaxana leaves.]

PICARD: Computer, locate Counselor Troi.

INCOMING MESSAGE:
Sixty is not that old.

Later, Lwaxana discusses her frustration with her daughter, the ever-patient Counselor Troi.

LWAXANA: I don't know. I just can't accept that fate will allow me to meet him like this and then take him away. I mean, he's not ill. He hasn't had a tragic accident. He's just going to die, and for no good reason. Because his society has decided that he's too old, so they just dispose of him as though his life no longer had value or meaning. You can't possibly understand at your age, but at mine, sometimes you feel tired and afraid.

TROI: You're feeling very vulnerable. Very mortal, if I may say so. I know you, Mother, and believe me, you will never be one of those who dies before they die.

INCOMING MESSAGE:
Some people are afraid of death.
Suicide should not be an arbitrary decision.

Timicin tries to explain to Lwaxana how his culture arrived at the Resolution custom. It's an explanation for why some elderly people in our own time might consider suicide.

TIMICIN: I want to explain. I want very much for you to understand. Fifteen or twenty centuries ago, we had no Resolution. We had no such concern for our elders. As people aged, their health failed, they became invalids. Those whose families could no longer care for them were put away in deathwatch facilities, where they waited in loneliness for the end to come, sometimes for years. They had meant something, and they were forced to live beyond that, into a time of meaning nothing, of knowing they could now only be the beneficiaries of younger people's patience. We are no longer that cruel, Lwaxana.

LWAXANA: No, no, you're not cruel to them. You just kill them.

TIMICIN: The Resolution is a celebration of life. It allows us to end our lives with dignity.

LWAXANA: A celebration of life. It sounds very noble, very caring. What you're really saying is you got rid of the problem by getting rid of the people.

TIMICIN: It may sound that way, but it is a time of transition. One generation passing on the responsibilities of life to the next.

LWAXANA: What about the responsibility of caring of the elderly?

TIMICIN: That would place a dreadful burden on the children.

LWAXANA: We raise them, we care for them, we suffer for them. We keep them from harm their whole lives. Eventually, it's their turn to take care of us.

TIMICIN: No parent should expect to be paid back for the love they've given their children.

[Dialogue Omitted]

LWAXANA: You should have tried it while you were still alive. No reason to bother now. Why sixty? Why not sixty-two, or fifty-eight?

TIMICIN: A reasonable age had to be set.

LWAXANA: But it's not reasonable. Certainly not in your case. You're as vital and healthy a man as I've ever known.

TIMICIN: That is why I wish to say goodbye to my family and colleagues while I am this way, in complete command of my faculties, knowing they will always remember me as a strong and vigorous man.

LWAXANA: But it makes no sense. Some of your people could still be active at seventy or eighty, and others might be seriously ill at fifty. How cruel of you to make them wait so long to commit suicide.

TIMICIN: Setting a standard age for the Resolution makes it uniform for everybody. To ask individual families to decide when their elders are to die, that would be heartless.

LWAXANA: I agree. Why not let everybody die when they die?

TIMICIN: Lwaxana.

LWAXANA: You have a grandson, you said.

TIMICIN: Yes, almost seven.

LWAXANA: Well, wouldn't it be better for him to know his grandfather? Not some vague memory of someone who once loved him, but a real living person who does love him. Don't you really think that would be better?

TIMICIN: I attended the Resolution of my parents when it was their time. It was beautiful. Lwaxana, this is a custom I've known and accepted all my life.

RED ALERT!

Trying to talk a person out of their cultural beliefs is not respectful.

Burden to Others

In "Emanations" (1995, VOY; 1:8), Kim meets Hatil, an alien who is preparing to die. Hatil explains to Ensign Kim that he's going along with his family's wishes rather than continue to be a burden on them.

> KIM: Is that why you're here? Because you're not happy with your life?
> HATIL: Ever since the er, accident, life hasn't been easy. But I have to say, this is more my family's idea than it is mine.

KIM: Your family?

HATIL: I'm a burden to them right now. It takes a lot of their time and resources to care for me, and I can't give much back to them. So, there was a family meeting and it was agreed that I should move on to the Next Emanation. You look appalled.

KIM: It's not my place to judge your culture, but from my perspective, it's a little chilling to hear that.

HATIL: Even though the family did it out of love, and everyone was happy for me, and they said they'd see me when they got to the Next Emanation, I have to admit there is a little voice inside of me that is terrified of dying. And since I've been talking to you, that little voice has started to get louder.

INCOMING MESSAGE:
Families are often involved in quality of life decisions.

Mortality and Immortality

On *Star Trek* even death isn't a constant. There are several episodes that deal with immortality as well. But immortality isn't without its cost. When Kirk, Spock and McCoy meet the immortal Mr. Flint in "Requiem for Methuselah" (1969, TOS; 3:19), it's Flint's immortality that has condemned him to suffer unimaginable loneliness as the people in his life all die of old age.

FLINT: I am Brahms.

SPOCK: And da Vinci?

FLINT: Yes.

SPOCK: How many other names shall we call you?

FLINT: Solomon, Alexander, Lazarus, Methuselah, Merlin, Abramson. A hundred other names you do not know.

SPOCK: You were born?

FLINT: In that region of Earth later called Mesopotamia, in the year 3834 BC, as the millennia are reckoned. I was Akharin, a soldier, a bully and a fool. I fell in battle, pierced to the heart and did not die.

McCoy: Instant tissue regeneration coupled with some perfect form of biological renewal. You learned that you were immortal and—

Flint: —And to conceal it. To live some portion of a life, to pretend to age and then move on before my nature was suspected.

Spock: Your wealth and your intellect are the product of centuries of acquisition. You knew the greatest minds in history.

Flint: Galileo—Socrates—Moses—I have married a hundred times, Captain. Selected—loved—cherished. Caressed a smoothness, inhaled a brief fragrance. Then age—death—the taste of dust. Do you understand?

INCOMING MESSAGE:
Most people do not want to live forever.

When Data's head is recovered in an archaeological dig under San Francisco, Data receives the news as a positive event in "Time's Arrow: Part 1" (1992, TNG; 5:26). Data had already considered what his life would be like if he was never *turned off*, so to speak.

Data: I have often wondered about my own mortality as I have seen others around me age. Until now—it has been theoretically possible that I would live an unlimited period of time. And although some might find this attractive, to me it only reinforces the fact that I am artificial—It provides a sense of completion to my future. In a way, I am not that different from anyone else. I can now look forward to death—One might also conclude that it brings me one step closer to being human. I am mortal.

INCOMING MESSAGE:
Death isn't necessarily something everyone fears.

When quality of life is diminished, the discussion moves into aspects of death with dignity. Suicide, including physician-assisted suicide, is a difficult topic because of the legal, cultural, and religious implications. *Star Trek* episodes provide a vehicle to discuss these issues hypothetically, metaphorically, and nakedly.

In "Death Wish" (1996, VOY; 2:18) we learn that Vulcans practice ritual suicide under certain conditions.

> TUVOK: It is true that Vulcans who reach a certain infirmity with age, do practice ritual suicides...

To avoid the confusion that exists because everyone in the Q Continuum is called "Q" I will refer to the Q played by John de Lancie, as "Q." And I will refer to the Q seeking asylum as "Quinn;" the name he takes at the end of the episode.

The Voyager crew unintentionally helps Quinn escape from his prison and he asks for asylum on Voyager. Janeway decides to hold a hearing regarding the request for asylum, and Q calls himself as a witness. Q then is both standing and asking questions, while seated on the witness stand, because unlike the rest of us, Q can be in two places at the same time.

> WITNESS Q: No Q has ever tried to commit suicide. Immortality is one of the defining qualities of being a Q. By every measure of the Continuum, his remarks would have to be considered as mentally unbalanced.
>
> Q: Mentally unbalanced. And no civilized people in the universe, including the primitive Federation societies, would condone the suicide of a mentally unbalanced person.
>
> TUVOK: Tell me Q, can you offer any other evidence of mental instability on the part of my client?
>
> WITNESS Q: What more do I need? He wants to kill himself.
>
> TUVOK: In fact, until this issue arose, he was known in the Continuum as one of your great philosophers. Is that not true?
>
> WITNESS Q: Not anymore, it isn't.
>
> TUVOK: So, your entire basis for judging him mentally unbalanced is his wish to commit suicide. I submit that is a faulty premise. In many cultures, suicide is acceptable, and in and of itself cannot be used as evidence of mental illness.

INCOMING MESSAGE:
If a person is suffering,
suicide may be a logical choice.

Tuvok correctly states that allowing someone to commit suicide who is not competent due to their psychological condition would be morally wrong. In most places on Earth in the present day, if a person is suicidal due to depression, they can be involuntarily hospitalized until they're stabilized and no longer a threat to themselves. Keeping someone in prison for over three hundred years is, at best, overkill. (Pun intended.)

Soon the hearing takes an interesting turn. While Janeway knows that granting Quinn asylum may result in his suicide, the argument Tuvok provides is one for the case of assisted suicide. Foreshadowing with all the subtlety of a photon torpedo.

TUVOK: I would submit that the quality of life that my client will have to endure should be considered in this proceeding.

JANEWAY: I don't like those conditions any more than you do, Mr. Tuvok, and I wouldn't want to spend another day there if I were you, Q [Quinn], but I'm here to rule on a request for asylum, not to judge the penal system of the Q Continuum. And he does have a point. You were confined only to prevent you from doing harm to yourself. I've been doing a great deal of research, studying a variety of cultural attitudes on suicide, to help me frame the basis of a decision. Mr. Tuvok, are you familiar with the double effect principle on assisted suicide that dates back to the Bolian Middle Ages?

TUVOK: I believe it relates to the relief of suffering, does it not, Captain?

JANEWAY: It states, an action that has the principal effect of relieving suffering may be ethically justified even though the same action has the secondary effect of possibly causing death. This principle is the only thing I can find that could possibly convince me to decide in your favor, Q [Quinn]. And yet, as I look at you, you don't seem by our standards, aged, infirm, or in any pain. Can you show this hearing that you suffer in any manner other than that caused by the conditions of your incarceration? Any suffering that would justify a decision to grant you asylum?

Quinn takes Janeway, Tuvok and the prosecuting Q to the Continuum to show them the dreadful conditions that he has to endure in the name of immortality. It consists of a dusty road, a small building, and a few people who don't talk because they have already said all they need to say. They have no purpose. They are the epitome of boredom. Quinn attempts to explain the threat he poses to the Continuum in terms Janeway can understand.

QUINN: Not for my safety. For theirs. I was the greatest threat the Continuum had ever known. They feared me so much they had to lock me away for eternity. And when they did that, they were saying that the individual's rights will be protected only so long as they don't conflict with the state. Nothing is so dangerous to a society. My life's work is complete, but they force immortality on me, and when they do that they cheapen and denigrate my life and all life in the Continuum. All life. Captain, you're an explorer. What if you had nothing left to explore? Would you want to live forever under those circumstances? You want me to prove to you that I suffer in terms that you can equate with pain or disease. Look at us. When life has become futile, meaningless, unendurable, it must be allowed to end. Can't you see, Captain? For us, the disease is immortality.

INCOMING MESSAGE:
Being alive isn't the same thing as living.

In the end, Quinn is granted his asylum, and he commits suicide with an alien form of hemlock. I get it; he was a philosopher like Socrates. And who gave him the hemlock? Well, Q, of course. Q understands suicide. After all, when he was stripped of his Q powers and reduced to a mere mortal in "Déjà Q" (1990, TNG; 3:13), he selfishly left the Enterprise to surrender to an alien lifeform who was out for revenge and not concerned with who got hurt in the crossfire.

PICARD: Q, there is no dignity in this suicide.
Q [On viewscreen]: Yes, I suppose you're right. Death of a coward, then. So be it. But as a human, I would have died of boredom.

INCOMING MESSAGE:
Quality of life issues are important to discussions about end of life choices.

While Quinn may have suffered from immortality, the unnamed pilot in "Operation: Annihilate!" (1967, TOS; 1:30) was trying to relieve himself of intense pain when he committed suicide by flying his ship into the sun. The arguments are the same. For some people, death is preferable to pain and suffering, or a life without meaning.

Physician-Assisted Suicide

When Dr. Bashir and Lieutenant Dax answer a distress call from a planet in the Gamma Quadrant, they find a civilization ravaged by a plague in "The Quickening" (1996, DS9; 4:23). In his desire to practice frontier medicine, Bashir goes to the local hospital hoping to be the doctor-savior to the people on this planet. As one patient, Tamar, talks about his care at the hospital, Bashir quickly learns Trevean, the local doctor, assists in ending their suffering.

TAMAR: Yesterday, when I woke up, I saw that it had finally happened. I'd quickened. I always thought I'd be afraid but I wasn't, because I knew I could come here. Last night I slept in a bed for the first time in my life. I fell asleep listening to music. This morning I bathed in hot water, dressed in clean clothes. And now I'm here with my friends and family. Thank you, Trevean, for making this day everything I dreamed it could be.

[Tamar toasts the doctor with his goblet and drinks deeply.]

TREVEAN: You brought Norva here?

DAX: How is she?

TREVEAN: It was too late for her. If only she'd come sooner, I could have helped.

BASHIR: Then there is a treatment for the Blight?

TREVEAN: There is no cure. It's always fatal.

BASHIR: I'm sorry, I don't understand. I thought you said you could have helped her.

TREVEAN: Why are you here?

DAX: We received a distress call. We're here to help in any way we can.

BASHIR: I'm a doctor, and I have access to sophisticated diagnostic equipment.

TREVEAN: We had sophisticated equipment once. Do you think our world was always this way? Two centuries ago, we were no different from you. We built vast cities, travelled to neighboring worlds. We believed nothing was beyond our abilities. We even thought we could resist the Dominion. [Bashir and Dax exchange knowing looks.] I see you've heard of them. Then take care not to defy them or your people will pay the same price we did. The Jem'Hadar destroyed our world as an example to others. [To the off screen attendant.] Bring me Milani's child. More than anything, the Dominion wanted my people to bear the mark of their defiance. So—they brought us the Blight.

[The baby has the blue welts.] We're all born with it. We all die from it. When the Blight quickens, the lesions turn red. Death soon follows—some in childhood—most before they can have children of their own. Only a few live to be my age.

BASHIR: Trevean, if you tell us what you know about the Blight, we may be able to help.

TREVEAN: No. You should go. If the Jem'Hadar find you here—

DAX: We're willing to take that risk.

[Tamar has a seizure, and dishes go clattering to the floor. Bashir rushes to Trevean's side.]

TREVEAN: Don't.

BASHIR: Make some room. I'm a doctor. [People are pushing Bashir out of the way.]

ATTENDANT: Leave him alone. You don't understand.

BASHIR: Can't you see he's dying?

TREVEAN: Of course he's dying. He came here to die. People come to me when they quicken. I help them leave this world peacefully—surrounded by their families and friends.

BASHIR: What are you saying?

TREVEAN: The herbs I give them cause death within minutes.

DAX: You poison them?

TREVEAN: The Blight kills slowly. No one wants to suffer needlessly—not like that woman you brought me—

BASHIR: You killed her? [Words dripping with judgment.]

TREVEAN: I did what she asked.

BASHIR: I thought this was a hospital and that you were a healer.

TREVEAN: I am. I take away pain. [Voice is full of scorn.] Now you've disrupted Tamar's death. I'm going to have to ask you to leave.

Dr. Bashir's incredulousness at doctor-assisted suicide reflects the values of a Starfleet doctor who easily cures those around him, usually with nothing more than a hypospray. The involvement of a physician in ending a person's life may appear contrary to the Hippocratic Oath, but one of the reasons for the oath was to end physician-assisted suicide without patient consent. In the end, Bashir develops a treatment that prevents the plague from being passed on to the unborn children on the planet. Although he is unable to discover a cure for those already suffering, future generations will be born without the disease. Even in the future, medical advancements will take time.

In 1997, Oregon passed the Death with Dignity Act which allows terminally ill patients to end their lives by taking lethal medications prescribed by their doctor for that purpose. The public health department annually reports the number of prescriptions and deaths under the law. In every year since 1997, more prescriptions than deaths have been reported. "The three most frequently mentioned end-of-life concerns were loss of autonomy (93.0%), decreasing ability to participate in activities that made life enjoyable (88.7%), and loss of dignity (73.2%)." Three more states (Vermont, Montana, and Washington) have since passed similar laws.

Righting the Future

When I began writing this book, I started out on a mission to educate, amuse, and provide a rehabilitation counseling lens through which Star Trek could be viewed. A few times I may have magnified the viewscreen in order for you to see my angle. Most of the time, I only needed to sharpen your focus in a particular direction. Only you can decide if I was successful on this mission. Any alien possession was out of my control.

Star Trek has motivated countless people besides me. The creators of the cell phone and the iPad cite *Star Trek* as the inspiration for their inventions. And just as Star Trek inspired technological inventions, it can also provide a path to inclusion, acceptance, and the ability to see past individual differences to the humanity we all share.

In the future we see on *Star Trek*, disability is a non-issue. Geordi can see just fine with his VISOR, thank you.

There is a delicate balance that has yet to be achieved. We will still have people with disabilities in the future, even if we are able to eliminate some disabilities through genetic engineering. Random mutations in the genome or injuries which can occur at any age may create a disability. Through assistive technology we will be able to compensate for many of those limitations. The balance is that while seeking to reduce the incidence of disability, we should also concentrate on reducing the stigma and prejudice that people with disabilities experience.

Star Trek eloquently handled many difficult subjects in the seven hundred plus stories told. I've laughed and I have cried, hopefully at the right places. We all have our own lens through which we watch *Star Trek*, and I thank you for viewing it through my lens with me.

Star Trek is not necessarily *our* future. Instead, it is a vision of possible directions our current path may take us. It is up to each one of us to work towards promoting a civilization that values individual differences. In truth, we have a better chance of achieving inclusion and acceptance than in building transporters and warp drives. The future has yet to be written, and we are only limited by our imaginations.

Bibliography

Chapter 1

American Psychiatric Association. Commission on Psychotherapy by Psychiatrists. 2000. "Position statement on therapies focused on attempts to change sexual orientation (reparative or conversion therapies)." *The American Journal of Psychiatry,* 157:10, p. 1719. http://mpipp.org/American-Psychiatric-Assoc-position-statement.pdf

Americans with Disabilities Act of 1990, 42 U.S.C. § 12101 *et seq.* (West 1993).

Falvo, Donna. 2009. *Medical and Psychosocial Aspects of Chronic Illness and Disability.* 4th ed. Sudbury, Mass.: Jones and Bartlett Publishers.

Nichols, Nichelle. 1997. *Beyond Uhura: Star Trek and Other Memories.* New York, NY: G. P. Punam's Sons.

Oliver, Mike. July 23, 1990. "The Individual and Social Models of Disability." leeds.ac.uk. http://disability-studies.leeds.ac.uk/files/library/Oliver-in-soc-dis.pdf

Siegel, Lee. May 29, 1985. "Homosexual Scientists' Group Blasts AIDS Research Priorities." http://www.apnewsarchive.com/1985/Homosexual-Scientists-Group-Blasts-AIDS-Research-Priorities/id-8f06beae0a29025c796c0e26988b1849

World Health Organization. 2002. *Towards a Common Language for Functioning, Disability and Health: ICF* (2002). http://www.who.int/classifications/icf/training/icfbeginnersguide.pdf

Chapter 2

Barad, Judith. 2000. *The Ethics of Star Trek.* New York: HarperCollins.

MedLine Plus. 2011 Phenylketonuria. http://www.nlm.nih.gov/medlineplus/ency/article/001166.htm

Shapiro, Joseph P. 1993. *No Pity: People with Disabilities Forging a New Civil Rights Movement*. New York: Times Books.

Tyson, Peter. 2001. "The Hippocratic oath today." *NOVA Online.* http://www/pbs.org/wgbh/nova/body/hippocratic-oath-today.html

Chapter 3

Abraham L Halpern, John H Halpern, and Sean B Doherty. 2008. "Enhanced Interrogation of Detainees: Do Psychologists and Psychiatrists Participate?" *Philosophy, Ethics, and Humanities in Medicine.* http://www.ncbi.nlm.nih.gov/pmc/articles/PMC2561033/

Beauchamp, Tom L., and James F. Childress. 2008. *Principles of biomedical ethics*. 6th ed. New York: Oxford University Press.

CBS. February 11, 2009 "A Genetically Screened Baby Saved the Life of His Sister." http://www.cbsnews.com/2100-204_162-326728.html

Robinson, Walter M. and Unruh, Brandon T. 2008. "The Hepatitis Experiment at the Willowbrook School" in *The Oxford Textbook of Clinical Research Ethics*. (Ezkiel Emanuel el al., eds.) 80-85. http://science.jburroughs.org/mbahe/BioEthics/Articles/WilliowbrookRobinson2008.pdf

Chapter 4

Center for Genetics and Society. 2013. "About Inheritable Genetic Modification". http://www.geneticsandsociety.org/section.php?id=108

Disabled World - Disability News and Information. n.d. http://www.disabled-world.com/artman/publish/epilepsy-famous.shtml#ixzz2PTIVt2D7

Gould, S. J. 1981. *The Mismeasure of Man.* New York: W. W. Norton & Company.

Lombardo, Paul. n.d. "Eugenic Sterilization Laws" http://www.eugenicsarchive.org/html/eugenics/essay8text.html

McCaffery, Larry and Williamson, Jack. July, 1991. "An Interview with Jack Williamson." *Science Fiction Studies,* 18:2, pp. 230-252.

Mostert, Mark P. 2002. "Useless Eaters: Disability as Genocidal Marker in Nazi Germany." *The Journal of Special Education,* 36:3, pp 155-168.

Tachibana M, Amato P, Sparman M, Woodward J, Sanchis DM, Ma H, Gutierrez NM, Tippner-Hedges R, Kang E, Lee HS, Ramsey C, Masterson K, Battaglia D, Lee D, Wu D, Jensen J, Patton P, Gokhale S, Stouffer R, Mitalipov S. 2013. "Towards Germline Gene Therapy of Inherited Mitochondrial Diseases. *Nature.* 1;493(7434): pp. 627-31. doi: 10.1038/nature11647.

Genetic Information Nondiscrimination Act (Pub.L. 110–233, 122 Stat. 881, enacted May 21, 2008, GINA)

Scott, Cameron. January 6, 2014. "Gene Therapy Turns Several Leukemia Patients Cancer Free. Will It Work for Other Cancers, Too?" http://singularityhub.com/2014/01/06/gene-therapy-delivers-dramatic-success-in-treating-leukemia-will-it-work-for-other-cancers-too/

Scott, Cameron. December 13, 2013. "Evidence Mounts for Gene Therapy as Treatment for Heart Failure." http://singularityhub.com/2013/12/13/evidence-mounts-for-gene-therapy-as-treatment-for-heart-failure/

Chapter 5

Adel El-Hadidy, Mohamed. 2012. "Schizophrenia With and Without Homicide: A Clinical Comparative Study. *The Journal of Forensic Psychiatry and Psychology.* 23:1, pp. 95-107.

National Academy of Sciences. 2002. *The Polygraph and Lie Detection.* Washington, DC: National Academy Press.

Rissmiller, David J. and Rissmiller, Joshua H. June 1, 2006. "Evolution of the Antipsychiatry Movement Into Mental Health Consumerism." *Psychiatric Services* 57, pp.863-866. http://www.mindfreedom.org/campaign/media/mf/apa-history-debate/apa-essay-on-movement

World Health Organization. 1992. *The ICD-10 Classification of Mental and Behavioural Disorders.*

Chapter 6

Belluck, Pamela. February 11, 2013. "Promising Depression Therapy." *The New York Times.* http://well.blogs.nytimes.com/2013/02/11/promising-depression-therapy/?_r=0

Jones, Edgar and Wessely, Simon. 2005. "The Origins of British Military Psychiatry Before the First World War." *War & Society*, 19:2, pp. 91-108.

Siegel-Itzkovich, Judy. January 8, 2014. "Hebrew University Researchers Find Mechanism Underlying Depression. *The Jerusalem Post.*

Chapter 7

Ewing, J. A. 1984. "Detecting Alcoholism: The CAGE Questionnaire" *JAMA*, 252, 1905-1907.

Goodman A. November 1990. "Addiction: Definition and Implications". *British Journal of Addiction*. 85:11, 1403–1408. doi:10.1111/j.1360-0443.1990.tb01620.x. 7

Chapter 8

Barrie, Allison (2013, March 21). World's only bionic eyes keep getting better. Fox News.com
http://www.foxnews.com/science/2013/03/21/worlds-only-bionic-eyes-keep-getting-better/

Barrett, Claire. May 19, 2013. "One Day It Will Be Possible to Print a Human Liver. *Dezeen Magazine*. http://www.dezeen.com/2013/05/19/3d-printing-organs-medicine-print-shift/

Freitas, Robert A. Jr. 2010. "The Future of Nanomedicine." *The Futurists*. http://www.wfs.org/Dec09-Jan10/freitas.htm

Hansen, Shaikat. June 11, 2012. "Cochlear Implants and the Deaf Culture: A Transhumanist Perspective." http://hplusmagazine.com/2012/06/11/cochlear-implants-and-the-deaf-culture-a-transhumanist-perspective/

Heiney, Anna. November 3, 2005. "A Second Set of Eyes." NASA
http://www.nasa.gov/vision/earth/technologies/jordy.html

Jack, David, Boian, Rares, Merians, Alma S., Tremaine, Marilyn, Burdea, Grigore C. Adamovich, ,Sergei V., Recce, Michael and Poizner, Howard. 2001. "Virtual Reality-Enhanced Stroke Rehabilitation." *IEEE Transactions On Neural Systems and Rehabilitation Engineering*, 9:3.
http://shrp.umdnj.edu/dept/PT/rivers/publications/2001_ieee_tnsre.pdf

National Institutes of Health March, 2011. Cochlear Implants. NIH Publication No. 11-4798 http://www.nidcd.nih.gov/health/hearing/pages/coch.aspx

Paddock, Catherine January 7, 2013. "Blind Mice Have Sight Restored." *Medical News Today*. http://www.medicalnewstoday.com/articles/254639.php

Pascolini, Donatella. 2010. "Global Estimates of Visual Impairment – 2010." *World Health Organization* http://www.who.int/blindness/VI_BJO_text.pdf

Parsons, S. & Cobb, S. 2011. "State-of-the-Art of Virtual Reality Technologies for Children on the Autism Spectrum. *European Journal of Special Needs Education*, 26:3, 355-366

Trimble, Bjo, *Star Trek Concordance: The A to Z Guide to the Classical Original Television Series and Films* (New York: Balantine Books, 1995).

Chapter 9

Falvo, Donna. 2009. *Medical and Psychosocial Aspects of Chronic Illness and Disability*. 4th ed. Sudbury, Mass.: Jones and Bartlett Publishers.

Liveh, Hanoch, 2001. "Psychosocial Adaptation to Chronic Illness and Disability." *Rehabilitation Counseling Bulletin*. 44:3, pp. 151-160.

Reeve, Christopher. 1999. *Still Me*. New York, NY: Ballantine Books

Chapter 10

AAC Funding Help. 2012. SDG funding fast facts. http://www.aacfundinghelp.com/fast_facts.html

Gluck, Robert. July, 2013. "Leonard Nimoy, from Star Trek to Jewish-themed Photography, Has Lived Long and Prospered" The Jewish Chronicle. http://thejewishchronicle.net/view/full_story/23225237/article-Leonard-Nimoy--from-Star-Trek-to-Jewish-themed-photography--has-lived-long-and-prospered?instance=news_special_coverage_right_column#ixzz2fJGgJUQ6

Chapter 11

Wu, Stephen S. and Goodman, Marc. Winter 2012. "Science and Technology Law: Neural Implants and Their Legal Implications" The SciTech Lawyer, 8:3, p. 14.

Carey, Benedict. September 14, 2012. "Brain Implant Improves Thinking in Monkeys, First Such Demonstration in Primates." The New York Times (online edition). http://www.nytimes.com/2012/09/14/health/research/brain-implant-improves-thinking-in-monkeys.html?_r=0

Dane, Erik, Rockmann, Kevin, W. and Pratt, Michael, G. 2012. "When Should I Trust My Gut? Linking Domain Expertise to Intuitive Decision-Making Effectiveness." Organizational Behavior and Human Decision Processes, 119:2, pp. 187-194.

Harper, Benard, and Latto, Richard. June 2001. "Cyclopean Vision, Size Estimation, and Presence in Orthostereoscopic Images." Presence: Teleoperators and Virtual Environments, 10:3, pp. 312-330.

Shepherd, Terry L. 2007. "Infinite diversity in infinite combinations: Portraits of individuals with disabilities in Star Trek." TEACHING Exceptional Children Plus, 3:6 Article 1.

Chapter 12

Falvo, Donna. 2009. Medical and Psychosocial Aspects of Chronic Illness and Disability. 4th ed. Sudbury, Mass.: Jones and Bartlett Publishers.

Liveh, Hanoch, 2001. "Psychosocial Adaptation to Chronic Illness and Disability." *Rehabilitation Counseling Bulletin.* 44:3, pp. 151-160.

Oregon.gov 2013. "Oregon's Death with Dignity Act 2013". http://public.health.oregon.gov/ProviderPartnerResources/EvaluationResearch/Deathwit hDignityAct/Documents/year16.pdf

Acknowledgements

First and foremost, I want to thank my editor, friend, and fellow Star Trek fan, Susan Frager. Her editing skills made this book readable. Her encouragement got it done. I should also thank her four-legged children, Sophie and Spencer, for begrudgingly giving up their mom for hours on the weekends as Susan found my mistakes. Bones for the cute beagles. And yes, Susan, I know "cute beagles" is redundant.

Special thanks to James Kent, PhD, director of the University of California-Santa Cruz and Genome Browser Project and research scientist in the Department of Bimolecular Engineering. In less time than it takes to listen to a Klingon opera he reviewed and commented on Chapter 4, ensuring that I was accurate in my discussion of genetic engineering.

While writing this book, I participated in several critique groups which provided feedback on where I wasn't clear in my explanations, lost the connection to disability, when jokes fell flat, where I had too much or too little dialogue, and even if my verbs were out of agreement. I am grateful to these authors and soon-to-be authors, who reached outside their own genre, and helped improve my book with their feedback.

Linda Stirling, founder of SW WA/OR Write To Publish, author of several books including "Confessions of a Sunday School Psychic" and some of her wisdom can be found on her website www.thepublishingauthority.com. From this meetup: Karla Von Huben, author of several books including "The Youngest Elf and Other Stories." Harsh Arora, author of "Undesired Duty." Rajiv Arya, Amanda Cherry, Kris Jongkindt, Susan O'Toole, Phyllis Peabody, Anna Marie Smith, Adam Stewart, Rick Thomas, Josh Wheelan, and Noelani Yuen.

Three cheers for Leila Rose Foreman, one for writing "The Shatterworld Triology Opines," one for her interview about her cochlear implant, and one for serving as one of my beta readers.

Elizabyth (Burtis) Harrington, co-founder of the Portland, Oregon chapter of the Coffee House Writers Group, author of several books including "Demonology: Book of Gabriel" graphic artist extraordinaire who designed my book cover. Her husband Mark Harrington, co-founder of the local chapter and fellow *Star Trek* fan who shared his marriage proposal at "The Best Meetup Ever." I still get tears in my eyes when I think of it. Vargus Pike, author of "April Song," and "October Song", fellow *Star Trek* fan, and my "poetry crack dealer." (I am totally hooked on his work.) His support of my work and his friendship are highly appreciated. Arwen Spicer, author of several books including "The Hour Before Morning". And the rest of the gang who come together on Saturdays for a read-out-loud critique meeting.

Richard Pope of Peoples Ink, in Portland, Oregon; and critiques from those who worked on my various pieces, thank you.

I also want to thank these professionals who were my beta readers for some of the chapters.

Rene Thompson, Independent Living Specialist, Center for Accessible Living – Northern Kentucky office. Sandi Parker-Allen, Retired Rehabilitation Counselor, Policy Analyst Consultant, and fellow Saluki. I never knew what a Star Trek fan she was until I began writing this book. Lois Benjamin, Retired Rehabilitation Counselor. Aleshia Clark, Substance Abuse Counselor. Chad Pettingill, Speech Language Pathology graduate student, and fellow member of Star Trek Fans of the Northwest (Meetup). Leslie Manning, autism blogger, author, and advocate.

Mike Phillips, Jan Bear, and members of the Book Marketing Meetup sponsored by the Neo Com Group.

About the Author

Ilana Lehmann is like no one you have met before. A high school drop-out who went on to earn a Ph.D. She was born and raised in San Diego, CA and has lived at over 50 addresses across the United States. A former member of the Air Force Reserves and AFROTC student at San Diego State University, she chose to have a family rather than pursue her childhood dream to become an aerospace engineer, test pilot, and astronaut. Among her various careers, she has worked as a waitress, retail clerk, receptionist, psychotherapist, case manager, and rehabilitation counselor, before she decided to become a professor. She has a bachelor's degree in psychology and a master's degree in guidance and counseling with an emphasis on community mental health. While getting a divorce, she attended Southern Illinois University and earned her doctorate in Rehabilitation Counseling Education. She is a Certified Rehabilitation Counselor, and previously was a National Board Certified Counselor. In 2009, she won an outstanding research award from the American Rehabilitation Counseling Association for her publication on the unintended consequences of the Family and Medical Leave Act. Currently, she teaches research methods at Capella University through their online program. She is writing more books and promises to continue to write until she is no longer educational or entertaining. Dr. Lehmann is bossed around by her cat, Hobbes, and her corgi named Susie Derkins.

I would love to hear from you. Keep up with the latest information about this and other books as well as personal appearances.

Please visit my website: www.ilanalehmann.com.

Follow me on Twitter: http://twitter.com/rehabprof

Friend me on Facebook: https://www.facebook.com/ilana.s.lehmann

Like my Facebook Author page: www.facebook.com/StarTrekandDisability

Subscribe to my blog: http://www.ilanalehmann.com/to-boldly-blog.html

Favorite me at Smashwords: https://www.smashwords.com/profile/view/IlanaLehmann

www.ingramcontent.com/pod-product-compliance
Lightning Source LLC
Chambersburg PA
CBHW080244030426

42334CB00023BA/2692